D0929124

AMOS

12.75

HIS TIMES & HIS PREACHING

AMOS

The Eighth~Century Prophet

JOHN H. HAYES

Abingdon Press
Nashville

17267

18   1535

AMOS
THE EIGHTH-CENTURY PROPHET: HIS TIMES AND HIS PREACHING

Copyright © 1988 by John H. Hayes

Manufactured by the Parthenon Press at
Nashville, Tennessee, United States of America

Contents

Abbreviations

AA	*Acta Antiqua*
ABR	*Australian Biblical Review*
AEL	*Ancient Egyptian Literature*, by M. Lichtheim (3 vols.; Berkeley: University of California Press, 1973-1980)
ANEP	*The Ancient Near East in Pictures Relating to the Old Testament*, by J. B. Pritchard (Princeton: Princeton University Press, 1954)
ANET	*Ancient Near Eastern Texts Relating to the Old Testament*, ed. J. B. Pritchard (Princeton: Princeton University Press, 1969)
AOAT	Alter Orient und Altes Testament
ARAB	*Ancient Records of Assyria and Babylonia*, by D. D. Luckenbill (2 vols.; Chicago University of Chicago Press, 1926-27)
ARI	*Assyrian Royal Inscriptions*, by A. K. Grayson (2 vols.; Wiesbaden: Otto Harassowitz, 1972-76)
ARW	*Archiv für Religionswissenchaft*
ATA	*Alttestamentliche Abhandlungen*
AUSS	*Andrews University Seminary Studies*
BA	*Biblical Archaeologist*
BAH	Bibliothèque archéologique et historique
BAR	*Biblical Archaeologist Reader*
BARev	*Biblical Archaeology Review*
BASOR	*Bulletin of the American Schools of Oriental Research*
BBB	Bonner biblische Beiträge
BDB	*A Hebrew and English Lexicon of the Old Testament*, by F. Brown, S. R. Driver, and C. A. Briggs (London: Oxford University Press, 1907)
BEvTh	Beiträge zur evangelischen Theologie
BHS	*Biblia hebraica stuttgartensia*
Bib	*Biblica*
BibOr	Biblica et Orientalia
BN	*Biblische Notizen*
BRev	*Biblical Review*
BT	*Bible Translator*
BTAVO	Beihefte Tübinger Atlas des Vorderen Orients

BTB	*Biblical Theology Bulletin*
BZ	*Biblische Zeitschrift*
BZAW	Beihefte zur Zeitschrift für die alttestamentliche Wissenschaft
CAD	*The Assyrian Dictionary of the Oriental Institute*
CAH	*Cambridge Ancient History (revised edition)*
CBQ	*Catholic Biblical Quarterly*
CBOTS	Coniectanea biblica Old Testament Series
CurTM	*Currents in Theology and Mission*
DJD	Discoveries in the Judaean Desert
EB	*Estudio bíblicos*
EHST	Europäische Hochschulschriften. Theologie
ET	*Expository Times*
EvTh	*Evangelische Theologie*
GNB	Good News Bible
HAR	*Hebrew Annual Review*
HDR	Harvard Dissertations in Religion
HS	*Hebrew Studies*
HTR	*Harvard Theological Review*
HUCA	*Hebrew Union College Annual*
Int	*Interpretation*
IDB	*Interpreter's Dictionary of the Bible*
IEJ	*Israel Exploration Journal*
JANESCU	*Journal of the Ancient Near Eastern Society of Columbia University*
JAOS	*Journal of the American Oriental Society*
JB	Jerusalem Bible
JBL	*Journal of Biblical Literature*
JCS	*Journal of Cuneiform Studies*
JETS	*Journal of the Evangelical Theological Society*
JNES	*Journal of Near Eastern Studies*
JNSL	*Journal of Northwest Semitic Languages*
JSOT	*Journal for the Study of the Old Testament*
JSOTSS	Journal for the Study of the Old Testament Supplement Series
JSS	*Journal of Semitic Studies*
KAI	*Kanaanäische und Aramäische Inschriften*, ed. H. Donner and W. Röllig (Wiesbaden: Otto Harrassowitz, 1962)
KJV	King James Version
MGWJ	*Monatsschrift für Geschichte und Wissenschaft des Judentums*

NAB	New American Bible
NEB	New English Bible
NJPSV	New Jewish Publication Society Version
NKZ	*Neue kirchliche Zeitschrift*
OTE	*Old Testament Essays*
OTS	*Oudtestamentische Studiën*
OTWSA	*Die Outestamentiese Werkgemeenskap in Suid-Afrika*
PEQ	*Palestine Exploration Quarterly*
PJB	*Palästina-Jahrbuch*
PWCJS	*Proceedings of the World Congress of Jewish Studies*
RB	*Revue Biblique*
RE	*Review and Expositor*
RelBib	*Religion och Bibel*
ResQ	*Restoration Quarterly*
RLA	*Reallexikon der Assyriologie*
SBLDS	Society of Biblical Literature Dissertation Series
SBLSP	*Society of Biblical Literature Seminar Papers*
SDB	*Supplements Dictionaire de la Bible*
SEÅ	*Svensk exegetisk årsbok*
SH	*Scripta Hierosolymitana*
SJLA	Studies in Judaism in Late Antiquity
SOTSMS	Society for Old Testament Study Monograph Series
SR	*Studies in Religion/Sciences religieuses*
SVT	Supplements to Vetus Testamentum
TBT	*The Bible Today*
TDOT	*Theological Dictionary of the Old Testament*
THBA	*A Translator's Handbook on the Book of Amos*, by J. de Waard and W. A. Smalley (New York: United Bible Societies, 1979)
TLZ	*Theologische Literaturzeitung*
TQ	*Theologische Quartalschrift*
TR	*Theologische Rundschau*
TRE	*Theologische Realenzyklopädie*
TTZ	*Trierer theologische Zeitschrift*
TZ	*Theologische Zeitschrift*
UF	*Ugaritische Forschungen*
VT	*Vetus Testamentum*
WBC	Word Biblical Commentary
WD	*Wort und Dienst*

WHJP   *World History of the Jewish People*
WMANT   Wissenschaftliche Monographien zum Alten
              und Neuen Testament
WO   *Welt des Orients*
ZAW   *Zeitschrift für alttestamentliche Wissenschaft*
ZDMG   *Zeitschrift der deutschen morgenländischen
              Gesellschaft*
ZDPV   *Zeitschrift des deutschen Palästina-Vereins*
ZTK   *Zeitschrift für Theologie und Kirche*

General Bibliography
(noted in the text by last name with an asterisk)

Amsler, S., "Amos," in E. Jacob et al. *Osée, Joël, Abdias, Jonas*
          (Commentaire de l'Ancien Testament 11a;
          Neuchâtel: Delachaux & Niestlé, 1965)157-291
Auld, A. G., *Amos* (Old Testament Guides; Sheffield: JSOT
          Press, 1986)
Bic, M., *Das Buch Amos* (Berlin: Evangelische-Verlagsanstalt,
          1969)
Coote, R., *Amos Among the Prophets: Composition and Theo-
          logy* (Philadelphia: Fortress Press, 1981)
Cripps, R. S., *A Critical and Exegetical Commentary on the Book
          of Amos* (2d ed., London: SPCK, 1955)
Driver, S. R., *The Books of Joel and Amos* (Cambridge Bible for
          Schools and Colleges; Cambridge: Cambridge
          University Press, 1898; 2d ed., 1915)
Edghill, E. A. and G. A. Cooke, *The Book of Amos* (2d ed.;
          Westminster Commentaries; London: Methuen
          1926)
Fosbroke, H. E. W., "The Book of Amos: Introduction and
          Exegesis," *Interpeter's Bible* 6(Nashville: Abingdon
          Press, 1956)761-853
Gordis, R., "Studies in the Book of Amos," *Proceedings of the
          American Academy for Jewish Research*
          46-47(1979-80)201-64
Hammershaimb, E., *The Book of Amos: A Commentary* (Oxford:
          Basil Blackwell, 1970)
Harper, W. R., *A Critical and Exegetical Commentary on Amos
          and Hosea* (International Critical Commentary;

Edinburgh: T. and T. Clark, 1905)

Kapelrud, A. S., *Central Ideas in Amos* (Oslo: Aschehoug & Co., 1956)

King, P. J., *Amos, Hosea, Micah - An Archaeological Commentary* (Philadelphia: Westminister Press, 1988)

Koch, K. et al., *Amos. Untersucht mit den Methoden einer strukturalen Formgeschichte* (3 vols.; AOAT 30; Kevelaer/Neukirchen-Vluyn: Butzon & Bercker/Neukirchener Verlag, 1976)

Maag, V., *Text, Wortschatz und Begriffswelt des Buches Amos* (Leiden: E. J. Brill, 1951)

Markert, L., *Stuktur und Bezeichnung des Scheltworts. Eine gattungskritische Studie anhand des Amosbuches* (BZAW 140; Berlin: Walter de Gruyter, 1977)

Marti, K., *Das Dodekapropheten erklärt* (Kurzer Hand-Commentar zum Alten Testament 13; Tübingen: J. C. B. Mohr [Paul Siebeck], 1904)

Martin-Achard, R., *Amos: l'homme, le message, l'influence* (Geneva: Labor et Fides, 1984)

Mays, J. L., *Amos: A Commentary* (Old Testament Library; London/Philadelphia: SCM Press/Westminster Press, 1969)

Neher, A., *Amos. Contribution à l'étude du prophetisme* (Paris: J. Vrin, 1950)

Nowack, W., *Die kleinen Propheten* (Handkommentar zum Alten Testament III/4; Göttingen: Vandenhoeck & Ruprecht, 1922)

Osty, E., *Amos, Osee* (La sainte Bible; Paris: Cerf, 1952)

Reventlow, H. G., *Das Amt des Propheten bei Amos* (Forschungen zur Religion und Literatur des Alten und Neuen Testaments 80; Göttingen: Vandenhoeck & Ruprecht, 1962)

Robinson, T. H. and F. Horst, *Die Zwölf Kleinen Propheten* (Handbuch zum Alten Testament 1/14; Tübingen: J. C. B. Mohr [Paul Siebeck], 1938)

Routtenberg, H., *Amos of Tekoa: A Study in Interpretation* (New York: Vantage Press, 1971)

Rudolph, W., *Joel-Amos-Obadja-Jona* (Kommentar zum Alten Testament 13/2; Gütersloh: Gerd Mohn, 1971)

Sellin, E., *Das Zwölfprophetenbuch* (Kommentar zum Alten Testament 12/1; Leipzig: A. Deitchert, 1922)

Smith, G. A., *The Book of the Twelve Prophets* (2 vols.;

                    Expositor's Bible; London: Hodder and Stoughton,
                    1896-98)
Smith, G. V., *The Book of Amos* (Grand Rapids: Zondervan,
                    1988)
Snaith, N. H., *The Book of Amos* (2 vols.; London: Epworth
                    Press, 1945-46)
Soggin, J. A., *The Prophet Amos: A Translation and Commentary*
                    (London: SCM Press, 1987)
Vollmer, J., *Geschichtliche Rückblicke und Motive in der
                    Prophetie des Amos, Hosea, und Jesaja* (BZAW
                    119; Berlin: Walter de Gruyter, 1971)
Watts, J. D. W., *Vision and Prophecy in Amos* (Grand Rapids:
                    Wm. B. Eerdmans, 1958)
Weiser, A., *Die Prophetie des Amos* (BZAW 53; Giessen: Alfred
                    Töpelmann, 1929)
Weiser, A. and K. Elliger, *Das Buch der zwölf Kleinen Propheten*
                    (Das Alte Testament Deutsch 24-25; Göttingen:
                    Vandenhoeck & Ruprecht, 1949)
Wellhausen, J., *Die kleinen Propheten übersetzt und erklärt*
                    (Berlin: Georg Reimer, 1892)
Willi-Plein, I., *Vorformen der Schriftexegese innerhalb des
                    Alten Testaments. Untersuchungen zum literarischen
                    Werden des Amos, Hosea und Micha* (BZAW 123;
                    Berlin: Walter de Gruyter, 1971)
Wolff, H. W., *Joel and Amos* (Hermeneia; Philadelphia:
                    Fortress Press, 1977)
Würthwein, E., "Amos-Studien," *ZAW* 62(1950)10-52 = his *Wort
                    und Existenz* (Göttingen: Vandenhoeck &
                    Ruprecht, 1970)68-110

Preface

During the past century of research on Amos, scholars have repeatedly defended a number of conclusions about the book and activity of the prophet, some of which have reached the level of presupposed axioms from which any interpretation must begin. The following are the most widely held and reiterated. (1) Amos was the earliest of the so-called classical prophets to appear in Israel. (2) The prophet addressed a kingdom ruled by Jeroboam II that was economically prosperous, politically secure, and militarily strong. (3) Amos delivered a large number of short addresses, most of them only two or three verses long. (4) The primary concerns of the prophet were issues of social justice, especially inequities in the Israelite judicial system. (5) For Amos, the essence of religion was ethical behavior and he criticized his contemporaries for excessive emphasis on ritual and the worship of more than one god. (6) Amos proclaimed a totally pessimistic view of the people's future. (7) The prophet saw Assyria as the great enemy of Israel that would serve as the instrument of God's judgment in the nation's destruction. (8) The book of Amos is the product of a long editorial process during which the material was shaped, reinterpreted, and augmented in various stages of redaction. None of these conclusions can withstand close scrutiny; all should be discarded as interpretive assumptions.

The present volume is a companion to J. H. Hayes and S. A. Irvine, *Isaiah: The Eighth-century Prophet - His Times and His Preaching* (Nashville: Abingdon Press, 1987) and will be followed by works on Micah and Hosea. The chronology utilized in the book is based on J. H. Hayes and P. K. Hooker, *A New Chronology for the Kings of Israel and Judah and Its Implications for Biblical History and Literature* (Atlanta: John Knox Press, 1988).

The bibliography on Amos is enormous. Only a selection of the material has been noted in the following pages. A complete bibliography is available in A. van der Wal, *Amos - A Classified Bibliography* (3rd ed.; Amsterdam: Free University Press, 1986).

I am indebted to Julie Galambush, Margaret Reeves, and Gregory Broussard, graduate students at Emory University, for assistance in preparing the manuscript and to Dorcas Doward for typing and preparing the copy. My colleague, Jane McAuliffe, provided assistance on Arabic and Persian matters.

Most diacritical marks have been omitted in the transliteration of Semitic words to facilitate typesetting. The author's translation of the text is provided in italics at the beginning of each rhetorical unit.

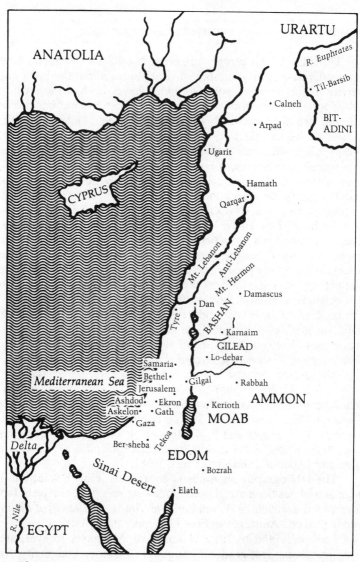

The Eastern Mediterranean Seaboard in the Eighth-century B.C.E.

I
THE HISTORICAL BACKGROUND
OF AMOS'S PREACHING

R. D. **Barnett**, "Urartu," *CAH* 3/1(1982)314-71; J. **Briend**, "Jéroboam II, sauveur d'Israël," *Melanges bibliques et orientaux en l'honneur de M. Henri Cazelles* (ed. A. Caquot and M. Delcor; AOAT 212; Kevelaer/Neukirchen-Vluyn: Butzon & Bercker/Neukirchener Verlag, 1981)41-49; S. **Cohen**, "The Political Background of the Words of Amos," *HUCA* 36(1965)153-60; H. J. **Cook**, "Pekah," *VT* 14(1964)121-35; M. **Elat**, "The Campaigns of Shalmaneser III against Aram and Israel," *IEJ* 25(1975)25-35; J. **García** Trapiello, "Situación histórica del profeta Amós," *EB* 26(1967)249-74; A. K. **Grayson**, "Assyria: Ashur-dan II to Ashur-Nirari V (934-745 B.C.)," *CAH* 3/1(1982)238-81; **Grayson**, "Studies in Neo-Assyrian History: The Ninth Century," *BO* 33(1976)134-45; W. W. **Hallo**, "From Qarqar to Carchemish: Assyria and Israel in the Light of New Discoveries," *BA* 23(1960)34-61 = *BAR* 2(1964)152-88; M. **Haran**, "The Rise and Decline of the Empire of Jeroboam ben Joash," *VT* 17(1967)266-97; **Haran**, "Observations on the Historical Background of Amos 1:2 - 2:6," *IEJ* 18(1968)201-7; J. D. **Hawkins**, "The Neo-Hittite States in Syria and Anatolia," *CAH* 3/1(1982)374-441; A. **Lemaire** and J.-M. **Durand**, *Les Inscriptions Araméennes de Sfiré et l'Assyrie de Shamshi-ilu* (Genéve/Paris: Droz, 1984); B. **Mazar**, "The Aramean Empire and Its Relations with Israel," *BA* 25(1962)98-120 = *BAR* 2(1964)127-51; J. M. **Miller**, "The Elisha Cycle and the Accounts of the Omride Wars," *JBL* 85(1966)441-54; **Miller**, "The Rest of the Acts of Jehoahaz (I Kings 20; 22:1-38)," *ZAW* 80(1968)337-42; J. **Morgenstern**, *Amos Studies* (Cincinnati: Hebrew Union College, 1941); L. M. **Muntingh**, "Political and International Relations of Israel's Neighbouring Peoples according to the Oracles of Amos," *OTWSA* 8/9(1964-65)134-42; N. **Na'aman**, "Looking for KTK," *WO* 9(1978)220-39; **Na'aman**, "Historical and Chronological Notes on the Kingdoms of Israel and Judah in the Eighth Century B.C.," *VT* 36(1986)71-92; W. T. **Pitard**, *Ancient Damascus: A Historical Study of the Syrian City-State from Earliest Times Until its Fall to the Assyrians in 732 B.C.E.* (Winona Lake, IN: Eisenbrauns, 1987); W. H. **Shea**, "Adad-nirari III and Jehoash of Israel," *JCS* 30(1978)101-13; C. C. **Smith**, "Jehu and the Black Obelisk of Shalmaneser III," *Scripture in History & Theology: Essays in Honor of J. Coert Rylaarsdam* (ed. A. L. Merrill and T. W. Overholt; Pittsburgh: Pickwick Press, 1977)71-105; H. **Tadmor**, "Azriyau of Yaudi," *SH* 8(1961)232-71; **Tadmor**, "The Historical Inscriptions of Adad-nirari III," *Iraq* 35(1973)141-50; **Tadmor**, "Assyria and the West: The Ninth Century and Its Aftermath," *Unity and Diversity: Essays in the History, Literature and Religion of the Ancient Near East* (ed. H. Goedicke and J. J. M. Roberts; Baltimore: Johns Hopkins University, 1975)36-48.

Amos's brief prophetic mission to Israel took place during the northern state's declining years. By Amos's time Israel's days of glory were past. The state was surrounded by hostile kingdoms, was hard pressed to retain control of territory in Galilee and Transjordan, and was torn internally by differences over international and domestic politics. King Jeroboam II, who had earlier enjoyed economic success and political stability, now reigned over a rapidly deteriorating situation. A survey of the history of Israel during the years of the Jehu dynasty, of which Jeroboam was the last significant ruler, is necessary in order to understand the historical and sociological conditions of Amos's day. The discussion that follows will focus on strategic issues rather than survey the history in its entirety.

1. ISRAEL'S PRO-ASSYRIAN STANCE

Jeroboam II was a member of the royal house of Jehu. Five members of this family ruled over Israel - Jehu, Jehoahaz, Jehoash, Jeroboam II, and Zechariah. The dynasty's rule began when Jehu, with Assyrian assistance, acquired the throne. He rose to power under the following circumstances. In the ninth century, Assyria had again become a dominant power in the ancient world after a long period of weakness. Two kings, Ashur-nasir-pal II (883-859) and Shalmaneser III (858-824), campaigned widely outside Assyria proper in order to gain control of trade routes and commerce (see Grayson, 1982, 253-69; Tadmor, 1975). Their campaigns to the west precipitated the formation of an anti-Assyrian coalition in that region. In his sixth, tenth, eleventh, and fourteenth years, Shalmaneser fought this western coalition (*ANET* 278-81; *ARAB* I §§ 563, 568, 571, 610-11, 646-47, 651-54, 658-59) and although he consistently claims to have defeated his foes, it is clear that his "triumphs" were far from complete victories (see Elat).

In his sixth year, begun in the spring of 853, Shalmaneser fought this group for the first time. At this battle, fought at Qarqar in northern Syria, the anti-Assyrian forces included troops from kingdoms as far north as western Asia Minor and from as far south as Egypt. The three dominant figures in the coalition were Irhuleni of Hamath who contributed 700 chariots, 700 horsemen, and 10,000 foot soldiers, Hadadezer of Damascus who contributed 1,200 chariots, 1,200 horsemen, and 20,000 foot soldiers, and Ahab of Israel who contributed 2,000 chariots and 10,000 foot soldiers (*ANET* 278-79; *ARAB* I § 611). The Israelite forces, led by Ahab of the Omride dynasty, probably included troops from Judah, Moab, and Edom, states subordinate to Israel at the time.

In his fourteenth year (845-844), Shalmaneser fought the anti-Assyrian coalition for the fourth and last time (*ANET* 280; *ARAB* I §§ 658-59). In his accounts of this final engagement, as in those describing the second and third wars, Hadadezer, king of Damascus, is depicted as a primary leader in the coalition. Hadadezer died either during this fourth engagement or shortly thereafter and was replaced by Hazael, a usurper. For some unknown reason, the coalition dissolved following Hazael's coup. The new Syrian king soon attacked Israel, and presumably other states in the neighborhood. Jehoram, ruling Israel at the time, was wounded in battle at Ramoth-gilead, protecting Israelite holdings against Hazael (2 Kings 8:25-28). Jehoram returned from the battlefield to recuperate, leaving the army under the command of Jehu (2 Kings 8:29; 9:14-15).

While Jehu was defending Ramoth-gilead against Syria, the Assyrians again campaigned in the west, in Shalmaneser's eighteenth year (841-840), but were opposed by Hazael alone (*ANET* 280; *ARAB* I § 672). The Assyrian army was unable to capture Damascus, Hazael's capital, but did inflict heavy damage in the environs of the city and in the northern Transjordan. Before departing Syria-Palestine, Shalmaneser received homage from Jehu, and bestowed his blessing upon him as the new king of Israel. Jehu then seized the throne in Samaria killing Kings Jehoram and Ahaziah and many Israelite and Judean leaders (2 Kings 9:21-10:14).

On the Black Obelisk, an inscription commemorating his first thirty-one years of rule, Shalmaneser reports that two rulers, Sua of Gilzan and Jehu of Bit-Omri, presented him not only with special tribute gifts but also with a "staff *(ḫutartu)* of the king's hand" (*ANET* 281; *ARAB* I §§ 589-90). Although no other references to such a staff appear in Assyrian royal inscriptions it apparently symbolized placing the kingdoms under the protection and custody of the Assyrian monarch (see Elat, 33-34; Smith, 96-98). At any rate, the Jehu dynasty, thoughout its reign, never adopted an anti-Assyrian posture. Assyrian inscriptions never refer to any anti-Assyrian action by Israel prior to Pekah's takeover of Samaria in 734.

Three aspects of this alliance between Israel and Assyria are of particular significance. (1) When Assyria was strong and exerting pressure in the west, Israel was a beneficiary of such a policy; when Assyria was weak and uninvolved in western affairs, Israel was weak. (2) The tendency to form anti-Assyrian coalitions was endemic to the west. Such coalitions, intent on protecting regional commercial interests, could only view Israel as a non-supporter of regional concerns; thus, when the coalitions were strong, Israel suffered. (3) Amos's ministry occurred at a time when Jeroboam II was continuing to adhere to a pro-Assyrian policy even though Assyria was weak, western regionalism strong, and anti-Assyrianism rampant.

2. ISRAEL AS A VASSAL TO DAMASCUS

Throughout the ninth and eighth centuries, the strongest inland states in the eastern Mediterranean seaboard were the Aramean kingdoms of Arpad, Hamath, and Damascus. These states were often leaders in the formation of anti-Assyrian coalitions in the west. Arpad, farther to the north and closer to Assyria, generally felt the brunt of Assyrian power first. Hamath, located along the middle Orontes River, was the major power in central Syria. Damascus was the southernmost major Aramean power. These states could submit to Assyria when political and economic expediency demanded, and when the price was not considered too high. Generally, however, their posture was anti-Assyrian (see below on 6:2).

Damascus was Israel's nearest Aramean neighbor and the power with which the nation had to deal most directly (see Pitard). Hazael, who probably secured the throne of Damascus in the early spring of 844, inaugurated a policy based on domination of the small kingdoms in southern Syria-Palestine. This represented a radical break from Hadadezer's policy of cooperation with the coalition states. Hazael's usurpation of the throne may itself have led to the temporary collapse of the western coalition. If so, his policy of hostility toward neighboring states would have been a reaction to their withdrawal of voluntary cooperation. The neighboring states may have become unwilling to pay the price of constant military preparedness. On the other hand, Hazael may have felt that only a strongly united western force was capable of halting the advance of Assyrian power. To insure the strength of his own kingdom and the cooperation of the southern Syro-Palestinian states he moved to acquire direct control over them.

At any rate, Hazael attacked Israel shortly after becoming king, perhaps to regain Damascus-claimed territory in Transjordan which the Omrides had brought under Israelite control. The Israelites and Judeans were fighting Hazael at Ramoth-gilead when Jehoram was wounded and Jehu subsequently moved to seize the throne (2 Kings 8:28-29; 9:14b-15a). Jehu's submission to the Assyrians would only have intensified Hazael's antagonism against Israel.

Within a few years after becoming king, Hazael had reduced Israel and the other kingdoms in southern Syria-Palestine to vassal status (see Pitard, 145-60). The following developments were part of this process.

(1) Hazael defended his kingdom against Shalmaneser's attacks in 841-840 and 838-837. The 841-840 Assyrian campaign, after which Jehu took over the Israelite throne, was apparently more successful than the 838-837 campaign (*ANET* 280; *ARAB* I §§ 672, 578). In the latter campaign, cities controlled by Hazael but not the capital itself seem to have come under Assyrian attack (Pitard, 148-50). This would imply that between 841-840 and 838-837, Hazael had enlarged his territory and increased his military power. For three decades after 838-837, the Assyrians conducted no campaigns into central and southern Syria and exerted little pressure on the region.

(2) Under Jehu (839-822), all of Transjordan was quickly lost to Hazael (2 Kings 10:32-33). The Syrian king probably took control of the port of Elath on the Red Sea during this period of expansion in Transjordan (note that Rezin later "recovered" Elath for Syria; 2 Kings 16:6).

(3) Jehu's successor, Jehoahaz (821-805), inherited a state in which Israelite territory west of the Jordan was controlled by Damascus, and Israel was reduced to a vassal state (2 Kings 13:3, 7, 22).

(4) Portions if not all of Philistia and Judah as well were forced into submission if not vassalage to Damascus (2 Kings 12:17-18). Thus, under Hazael, probably all the southern Syro-Palestinian states, except for Phoenicia, were dominated by Damascus.

(5) The Zakkur stela (*ANET* 655), set up by the king of Hamath and Lu'ash in northern Syria, reports on a military assault against him by several kings from northern Syria and western Asia Minor (see Pitard, 170-74). At the head of these forces was Bar-hadad (the biblical Ben-hadad), son of Hazael. This text demonstrates that Damascus wielded influence throughout the length of the eastern Mediterranean seaboard. Zakkur had probably usurped the throne and adopted a pro-Assyrian policy early in the reign of Adad-nirari III (810-783). The coalition headed by Ben-hadad sought unsuccessfully to topple him from power.

3. THE RESURGENCE OF ASSYRIA AND ISRAEL

Second Kings 13:5 notes that after Jehoahaz had petitioned Yahweh over the oppression of the Syrians "Yahweh gave Israel a savior so that they escaped from the hand of the Syrians; and the people dwelt in their tents as formerly." The savior of Israel was Assyria, now ruled by a fairly aggressive and successful king, Adad-nirari III (see Grayson, 1982, 271-76). Assyrian pressure in the west must have been felt early in Adad-nirari's reign; by his fifth year (806-805), Assyrian forces had attacked the west in strength, probably under the command of the Assyrian *turtanu* Shamshi-ilu. In reality, it was probably Shamshi-ilu rather than the Assyrian king himself who early in Adad-nirari III's reign proved to be Jehoahaz's "savior" (see below on 1:3).

As a result of Assyrian pressure in the west, Jehoahaz and Jehoash of Israel were able to regain some Israelite independence and occasionally take the offensive against Damascus. Although the exact course of events is of little consequence for the present discussion the following scenario probably occurred (see Miller; Pitard, 114-25). Late in his reign, Jehoahaz

defeated Hazael's forces in the vicinity of Samaria and later at
Aphek in the Jezreel Valley. (1 Kings 20 seems to describe
these victories. Although the present accounts identify the
kings of Israel and Syria as Ahab and Ben-hadad respectively,
these stories probably originally concerned Jehoahaz and
Hazael.) Jehoahaz was subsequently defeated in battle in
Transjordan by Hazael. (1 Kings 22:1-36 describes this battle
but in the present form of the story, Ahab and Jehoshaphat are
identified as the Israelite and Judean kings rather than
Jehoahaz of Israel and Jehoash of Judah [note the reference to
Jehoash as the northern king's son in 1 Kings 22:26].)

The Assyrians campaigned in the west in Adad-nirari's
fifth through eighth years (806-805 through 803-802) and again
in his thirteenth year (797-796). On one of these campaigns,
probably in 806-805 or 805-804, the Assyrians forced the submission of Damascus and received tribute from Mari', a ruler
in Damascus (*ANET* 281-82; *Iraq* 35[1973]143; *ARAB* I §§ 739-
40). This Mari' was probably Ben-hadad, son of Hazael. Describing Assyria's western conquests, Adad-nirari claimed to
have received the submission of rulers "from the banks of the
Euphrates, Amurru-country in its full extent, Tyre, Sidon,
Israel, Edom, Philistia, as far as the shore of the Great Sea of
the Setting Sun: I made them all submit to my feet, imposing
upon them tribute" (*ANET* 281).

Assyria's renewed presence in the west allowed Jehoash of
Israel (804-788) to recover territory previously taken by
Damascus although not without occasional setbacks. (See 2
Kings 6:24 - 7:20, which describes a siege of Samaria, probably
during Jehoash's reign. The siege may have been lifted when
Assyrian forces moved into the Lebanese region of Mansuate in
797-796.) Second Kings 13:25*b* (see 13:14-19) notes that
Jehoash defeated Ben-hadad on three occasions. (Apparently
Hazael and Jehoahaz had died relatively close in time, the for-
mer about 807-806 and the latter in 805-804.) Presumably
Jehoash reconquered portions of Transjordan.

Under Jeroboam II, Israel and Judah enjoyed a period of
relative peace and prosperity. Unfortunately only two biblical
verses describe Jeroboam's success and no non-biblical texts
mention him. Second Kings 14:25 reports that "he restored the
border (or "territory") of Israel from the entrance of Hamath to
the Sea of the Arabah." The "entrance of Hamath," an expression parallel to the "entrance of the desert" (see 1 Chron. 5:9) or

the "entrance of Egypt" (2 Chron. 26:8) simply refers to the southern border of the kingdom of Hamath, or the southern entry into the valley leading north to Hamath, probably the southern entrance to the Beqaa Valley (see Num. 13:21; Judg. 3:3; 1 Chron. 13:5). The Sea of the Arabah must refer to the Dead Sea; thus the statement "from the entrance of Hamath to the Sea of the Arabah" denotes the territory from southern Lebanon to the area west of the Jordan at the northern end of the Dead Sea. First Chron. 5:11-22, however, provides some specifics about Transjordanian territory ruled by Jeroboam in conjunction with Jotham of Judah. Part of this territory, the land of Sharon (1 Chron. 5:16), is mentioned in line thirteen of the Mesha Inscription (*ANET* 320; *KAI* #181) and appears to have been in the central plateau north of the Wadi Arnon. Jeroboam thus may have ruled over much of Transjordan, perhaps as far south as the Wadi Arnon, the traditional northern border of Moab. Both 2 Kings 14:25 and 1 Chron. 5:22 indicate that Jeroboam's conquests were carried out with prophetic and divine sanction.

In summarizing Jeroboam's reign, 2 Kings 14:28 notes the might with which he fought and that "he restored Damascus and Hamath to Judah in Israel." This text is obviously fragmentary and is best understood as an allusion to Jeroboam's regaining Israelite and Judean territory held or claimed by Damascus and Hamath. Israel's expansion to the north involved encroachment on Hamath-claimed territory and expansion to the east and northeast involved encroachment on Damascus-claimed territory. One could hypothesize that Damascus and Hamath probably controlled the Red Sea port of Elath during the first part of Jeroboam's reign; thus 2 Kings 14:28 once referred to how Jeroboam restored control of Elath to Judah from Damascus and Hamath (see 2 Kings 14:22). At any rate, Jeroboam II expanded Israelite territory at the expense of these two powers.

Throughout much of the reign of Jeroboam II, both Israel and Judah enjoyed a period of prosperity. The fact that Elath was again under Israelite/Judean control meant income and goods from foreign commerce again contributed to the national economy. The old commercial connection with Phoenicia which had benefitted Israel during the days of David and Solomon and again during the Omride period was probably renewed. A wealthy upper class as well as the expansion of royal land holdings were probably characteristic of the time. The Israelite upper class condemned by Amos was an upper class that had become accustomed to the life of a prosperous economy.

4. JUDAH AS A VASSAL TO ISRAEL

Judah was subordinate to Israel for most of the century and a half between Omri and Pekah (879-734). The exceptions were the years of Jehoram's reign (851-840) when a Judean king temporarily ruled over both Israel and Judah and the years of Jehu and Jehoahaz when Israel was itself a vassal to Damascus.

Israel's dominance over Judah began during the reign of Omri and was sealed by intermarriage between the two ruling dynasties: "Jehoshaphat also made peace with the king of Israel" (1 Kings 22:44). This Israelite dominance continued under Ahab; at the battle of Qarqar his forces probably included troops from Judah, Moab, and Edom. No Assyrian inscription refers to Judah prior to the time of Ahaz and Tiglath-pileser and the Syro-Ephraimitic siege of Jerusalem in 734. In noting the powers in the west that offered him submission, Adad-nirari III mentions Aram, Tyre, Sidon, Israel, Edom, and Philistia, or Amurru-country in its full extent (*ANET* 281; *ARAB* I § 739). Such a list probably represented conditions at the time early in the reigns of Ben-hadad of Damascus and Jehoash of Israel. Moab's absence from the list is probably due to Damascus's subjugation of the Transjordan (2 Kings 10:32-33). Judah is absent because the Davidic kingdom was considered part of Israel. Israel's dominance over Judah was so complete that the prophet Micah could refer to the "kings" of Israel (Mic. 1:14), apparently Jotham of Judah and Jeroboam II of Israel, and Isaiah could speak of Israel and Judah as the "two houses of Israel" (Isa. 8:14).

When the Judean nationalist, Amaziah, attempted to assert his authority over against Jehoash of Israel, he was defeated by the Israelite king (2 Kings 14:8-12). Amaziah was taken captive to Samaria by Jehoash after the latter had looted the temple and royal treasuries in Jerusalem and torn down part of the city's walls (2 Kings 14:13-14). After Amaziah had been held hostage in Samaria for some years, the Judeans placed Azariah (Uzziah) on the Jerusalem throne (2 Kings

14:21). Uzziah and Jotham, his successor, both seem to have
followed a policy of complete submission to Jeroboam II. The
"booth of David" (Amos 9:11) at the time of Amos's ministry
was indeed delapidated and in need of restoration (see Ps.
89:38-51).

5. THE TEMPORARY DECLINE OF ASSYRIA

The Assyrian successors to Adad-nirari, contemporaries
of Jeroboam II, were Shalmaneser IV (782-773), Ashur-dan III
(772-755), and Ashur-nirari V (754-745). Under these kings,
for whom we possess practically no inscriptional material, three
significant changes occurred (see Grayson, 1982, 276-79).

(1) Urartu, a kingdom located around Lake Van north of
Assyria, became a major opponent of Assyria during this period
(see Barnett, 333-56). Under Kings Argishti I (about 786-764)
and Sarduri II (about 763-734), Urartu applied pincer pressure
on Assyria from both the northwest and northeast, dominating
many of the trade routes leading into Mesopotamia. In addition, these Urartian rulers took an active role in stimulating
and organizing anti-Assyrian sentiment in the eastern Mediterranean seaboard. Shalmaneser IV campaigned against Urartu
during six of his ten years, but apparently without overwhelm-
ing success.

(2) Powerful figures in the Assyrian administration, even
under Adad-nirari III, tended to function almost as independent rulers, thus dissipating the power of the Assyrian monarch.
One of the most powerful of these second level administrators
or governors was Shamshi-ilu, the chief Assyrian authority in
the west (see Lemaire-Durand; Hawkins, 399-405). Already
under Adad-nirari III, Shamshi-ilu had negotiated the settlement of a boundary dispute between Arpad and Hamath. It
was most probably he who put pressure on the anti-Assyrian
coalition headed by Damascus. In the eponym or year lists of
the Assyrian kings, in which the years were named after important administrators in the empire, Shamshi-ilu is listed first
after the accession of all three new Assyrian kings (for the
years 780, 770, and 752). Thus his career spanned the reigns of
four Assyrian kings. He is probably referred to in Amos 1:5
(see the commentary below). Shamshi-ilu set up inscriptions of
his own describing himself in royal terminology. The Assyrian
eponym lists notes that a campaign was conducted against

Damascus in 773-772. Recently discovered inscriptions from Pazarcik and Antakya in Turkey reveal that it was actually Shamshi-ilu who conducted this campaign against the city, ruled at the time by King Hadianu.

(3) With the passage of years, central authority gradually eroded in the Assyrian homeland itself. The eponym lists report campaigns for every year of Shalmaneser IV, the last of his reign against Damascus (in 773-772; but led by Shamshi-ilu). Under Ashur-dan II campaigns became sporadic. Domestic revolts and rebellion raged in Assyrian cities between 763 and 760. The eponym list for 759-758 notes that peace was finally established in the land. Urartian pressure on Assyrian trade and the resulting shortage of goods and raw materials appear to have precipitated these widespread revolts.

During Ashur-dan's reign, however, campaigns were conducted against Hatarika (biblical Hadrach) in northern Syria in 772-771, 766-765, and 756-755, although again these campaigns were probably carried out by Shamshi-ilu rather than the Assyrian monarch himself. The west, especially northern Syria, now under the influence of Urartu, was a primary trouble spot throughout Ashur-dan's reign. Under Ashur-nirari V the Assyrians conducted few significant campaigns. During five of his ten years, Ashur-nariri and the Assyrian army stayed in the land. In his last year, revolt raged again in Assyria itself, this time in the capital city of Calah. During Ashur-nirari's first year (754-753), however, an Assyrian campaign was conducted against Arpad, again probably led by Shamshi-ilu. Copies exist of a treaty document or loyalty oath between Ashur-nirari V and Mati'ilu, king of Arpad, probably concluded at this time (*ANET* 532-33; *ARAB* I §§ 750-60).

The period of Assyria's severely declining influence in the west no doubt began in the years 765 and following when internal revolt tore at the heart of the empire. The decline reached its nadir under Ashur-nirari V. By the time Tiglath-pileser III moved west in 743, Assyrian authority in the eastern Mediterranean seaboard was at its lowest ebb. Powers in northern Syria were strongly organized under the influence of Urartu. Tiglath-pileser notes that even Mati'ilu of Arpad had allied with the Urartian king. In maintaining its pro-Assyrian policy, Israel thus seemed to be adhering to a losing cause. During this period of Assyrian weakness, Jeroboam's kingdom began to suffer from external and internal troubles.

6. JEROBOAM'S EXTERNAL AND INTERNAL TROUBLES

In Jeroboam's final years, Israel and Judah were under enormous pressure from neighboring states and a rival king vied for the loyalty of Israelite subjects. Several factors indicate the nature of Israel's troubles.

(1) Assyria's weakness and Urartu's intervention in the west meant that Israel and Judah as pro-Assyrian powers became isolated in the region. In the time of Tiglath-pileser, Assyrian inscriptions indicate that the leaders of anti-Assyrian sentiment in the west were Damascus, Philistia, and Phoenicia. The same situation probably also prevailed earlier. Their actions against Israel are reflected in the book of Amos indicating that their anti-Assyrian and anti-Israelite sentiments were already evident before the rise of Tiglath-pileser.

(2) Rezin had apparently assumed the kingship in Damascus before the end of Jeroboam's reign, possibly as early as the 760s. As later actions demonstrate, Rezin's goal was to reestablish a "greater Syria" under Damascus's leadership in imitation of Hazael's earlier rule. Like Hazael, Rezin gained control of the seaport of Elath. The context of 2 Kings 16:6 which notes that Rezin "recovered" Elath would suggest that this occurred at the time of the Syro-Ephraimitic siege of Jerusalem but such action seems hardly possible at that time. The siege of Jerusalem, late in 734 or early in 733, was interrupted by Tiglath-pileser's invasion, after which Rezin had no occasion to take Elath.

(3) The prophet Isaiah offers a review of Israelite history (Isa. 9:8-10:4) in which he alludes to an earthquake (see Amos 1:1; Zech. 14:5) and Syrian-Philistine attacks on Israel (9:8-12a) before commenting on the assassination of Jeroboam's son Zechariah by Shallum (9:13-17a). This would indicate Syrian and Philistine attacks against Israel before the death of Jeroboam. In Isa. 9:11, the coalition headed by Rezin is mentioned as a source of Israel's troubles. Similarly, "the former ruler who brought into contempt (that is, "lost control of") the land of Zebulun and the land of Naphtali" in Isa. 9:1 is an allusion to Jeroboam II.

(4) The prophet Hosea, a slightly older contemporary of Amos, appears to expect a battle in the Valley of Jezreel (Hos. 1:4-5) where the house of Jehu, represented by Jeroboam II,

would be defeated. Such a prediction would indicate that forces hostile to Israel, apparently Syria, had already moved into Galilee and were prepared to wrest the Jezreel Valley from Israelite control. Hos. 1:5 and Isa. 9:1 probably reflect the same circumstances, namely, Syrian control over the main highway joining Damascus and the Mediterranean coast which cut through the tribal regions of Zebulun and Naphtali, passing through the Jezreel Valley and down the maritime coast.

(5) A few years before his death in Nisan 747 and shortly before the prophet Amos appeared on the scene, Jeroboam II was confronted with a rival king, Pekah, the son of Remaliah (see Cook). Pekah, who was killed by Hoshea in 731, claimed a reign of twenty years (2 Kings 15:27) which means he began to rule in 751-750. Pekah is always depicted in the biblical tradition as a close associate of Rezin (see, for example, 2 Kings 16:5; Isa. 7:1-9). As an anti-Assyrian, Pekah was probably set up and supported by Rezin as a rival to Jeroboam II.

According to 2 Kings 15:37, Rezin and Pekah were already attacking and harassing Judah before the death of the Judean king, Jotham (759-744). Since Jotham and Jeroboam II had ruled jointly over parts of Transjordan (1 Chron. 5:17), this conquest of Judean territory by Pekah and Rezin probably began in Transjordan.

The prophet Amos thus addressed a situation of great political and economic decline in Israel. Numerous references in the book point to such circumstances. The attacks against Israelite territory noted in chapter 1 describe recent and contemporary circumstances, not conditions from the previous century or decades. The land was surrounded by an adversary (3:11) and in recent battles the people had suffered severe defeats (4:10). What was left of the house of Joseph was only a remnant of its former state (5:15; 6:6). Jacob is described as "so small" (7:2, 5). The upper class which Amos condemns was accustomed to prosperity and economic indulgence, but under the circumstances it was forced to live not off the fat but the lean of the land. The state's recent victories at Lo-debar and Karnaim (6:13) were probably counteroffensives against Damascus; the prophet recognized them as temporary successes only, not a trend in the state's struggles with foreign encroachment.

II
INTERPRETING THE PROPHET
AND THE BOOK

R. Bach, "Gottesrecht und weltliches Recht in der Verkündigung des Propheten Amos," *Festschrift für Günther Dehn* (ed. W. Schneemelcher; Neukirchen Kreis Moers: Verlag der Buchhandlungen des Erziehungsvereins, 1957) 23-34; J. Barr, *The Semantics of Biblical Language* (London: Oxford University Press, 1961); J. F. Craghan, "The Prophet Amos in Recent Literature," *BTB* 2(1972)242-61; J. L. Crenshaw, "The Influence of the Wise on Amos," *ZAW* 79(1967)42-51; G. H. Davies, "Amos - The Prophet of Re-Union," *ET* 92(1980-81)196-200; S. R. Driver, *An Introduction to the Literature of the Old Testament* (Edinburgh: T. and T. Clark, 1891) 293-300; B. Duhm, *Die Theologie der Propheten als Grundlage für die innere Entwicklungsgeschichte der israelitischen Religion* (Bonn: Adolph Marcus, 1875); H. Gressmann, "Die literarische Analyse Deuterojesajas," *ZAW* 34(1914)254-97; H. Gunkel, "The Israelite Prophecy from the Time of Amos," *Twentieth Century Theology in the Making* (ed. J. Pelikan; New York/London: Harper & Row/William Collins Sons, 1969)48-75; A. R. Johnson, *The Cultic Prophet in Ancient Israel* (Cardiff: Univerity of Wales Press, 1944); P. H. Kelley, "Contemporary Study of Amos and Prophetism," *RE* 63(1966)375-85; L. Koehler, "Amos-Forschungen von 1917 bis 1932," *TR* 4(1932)195-213; A. Kuenen, *The Prophets and Prophecy in Israel: An Historical and Critical Enquiry* (London: Longmans, Green, and Co., 1877); L. Markert, "Amos/Amosbuch," *TRE* 2(1978)471-87; J. L. Mays, "Words About the Words of Amos: Recent Study of the Book of Amos," *Int* 13(1959)259-72; L. Monloubou, "Prophètes d'Israël: Amos," *SDB* 8(1969)706-24; S. Mowinckel, *Prophecy and Tradition: The Prophetic Books in the Light of the Study of the Growth and History of the Tradition* (Oslo: Jacob Dybwad, 1946); J. Muilenburg, "The 'Office' of the Prophet in Ancient Israel," *The Bible in Modern Research* (ed. J. P. Hyatt; Nashville: Abingdon Press, 1965)74-97; E. W. Nicholson, *God and His People: Covenant and Theology in the Old Testament* (Oxford: Oxford University Press, 1986); R. A. Oden, Jr., *The Bible Without Theology: The Theological Tradition and Alternatives to It* (San Francisco: Harper & Row,

1987); C. **Peifer**, "Amos the Prophet: The Man and His Book," *TBT* 19(1981)295-300; J. J. M. **Roberts**, "Recent Trends in the Study of Amos," *ResQ* 13(1970)1-16; G. **Synder**, "The Law and Covenant in Amos," *ResQ* 25(1982)158-66; C. **Stuhlmueller**, "Amos, Desert-Trained Prophet," *TBT* 4(1963)224-30; S. **Terrien**, "Amos and Wisdom," *Israel's Prophetic Heritage: Essays in Honor of James Muilenburg* (ed. B. W. Anderson and W. Harrelson; New York: Harper & Brothers, 1962)108-15; A. **van der Wal**, "The Structure of Amos," *JSOT* 26(1983)107-13; J. **Wellhausen**, *Prolegomena to the History of Israel* (Edinburgh: A. & C. Black, 1885); C. **Westermann**, *Basic Forms of Prophetic Speech* (Philadelphia/London: Westminister Press/Lutterworth Press, 1967); H. W. **Wolff**, *Amos the Prophet: The Man and His Background* (Philadelphia: Fortress Press, 1973); A. S. **van der Woude**, "Three Classical Prophets: Amos, Hosea and Micah," *Israel's Prophetic Tradition: Essays in Honour of Peter Ackroyd* (ed. R. Coggins et al.; Cambridge: Cambridge University Press, 1982)34-43; W. **Zimmerli**, *The Law and the Prophets: A Study of the Meaning of the Old Testament* (Oxford/New York: B. H. Blackwell's/Harper & Row, 1965/67).

Three major phases may be distinguished in the modern history of the interpretation of Israelite prophecy in general and Amos in particular. In each of these phases, certain scholars played important roles and a cluster of interrelated issues became the primary focus of academic research thereby dominating the discussion, but without completely suppressing other matters.

The modern phase of prophetic research was inaugurated in the 1870s and was in some regards a by-product of the triumph of the literary analysis and criticism of the Pentateuch. The division of the Pentateuch into various sources and the dating of the most legally oriented and pervasive of these, the deuteronomic and the priestly, to the seventh century and later allowed the eighth-century prophets to emerge from their shadows and become topics of research in their own right. The first scholars to examine the prophets in this new light were Abraham Kuenen, Bernard Duhm, and Julius Wellhausen.

Three issues became the primary concerns of scholarship on the prophets. First, the individual personality and experience

of the prophet were highly emphasized. Older research treated
the prophets as expounders of the law and channels of revelation about the future. But if the legal portions of the Old
Testament were post-prophetic and even the consequence of
prophetic preaching (see Wellhausen, 484-88), way was open to
understand the prophets in terms of their individuality and
creativity. Duhm began his general discussion of the prophets
with the question: "Why do we begin our investigation of
prophetic religion with a discussion of the person of the
prophet?" (p. 73). Since he anchored prophetic religion in the
person of the prophet this constituted the logical starting point.
The individual personality, the human contexts from which they
derived, and the historical contexts in which they functioned
thus became indispensable elements in understanding the
prophets. "The representative men are always single, resting on
nothing outside themselves" (Wellhausen, 398). In a classic
statement, Wellhausen summed up this focus.

> The element in which the prophets live is the
> storm of the world's history, which sweeps away
> human institutions; in which the rubbish of past gen-
> erations with the houses built on it begins to shake,
> and that foundation alone remains firm, which needs
> no support but itself. When the earth trembles and
> seems to be passing away, then they triumph because
> Jehovah alone is exalted. They do not preach on set
> texts; they speak out of the spirit which judges all
> things and itself is judged of no man. Where do they
> ever lean on any other authority than the truth of
> what they say; where do they rest on any other foun-
> dation than their own certainty? It belongs to the
> notion of prophecy, of true revelation, that Jehovah,
> overlooking all the media of ordinances and institu-
> tions, communicates Himself to the *individual*, the
> called one, in whom that mysterious and irreducible
> rapport in which the deity stands with man clothes
> itself with energy. Apart from the prophet, *in
> abstracto*, there is no revelation; it lives in his divine-
> human ego. This gives rise to a synthesis of apparent
> contradictions: the subjective in the highest sense,
> which is exalted above all ordinances, is the truly
> objective, the divine. (p. 398)

In light of this new perspective, Amos came to be understood as an outsider, one seasoned by poverty and austerity, whose message reverberates with the plain and harsh words of the world of his origins.

> The men of Tekoa looked out upon a desolate and haggard world. South, west, and north the view is barred by a range of limestone hills, on one of which directly north the grey towers of Jerusalem are hardly to be discerned from the grey mountain lines. Eastward the prospect is still more desolate, but open; the land slopes for nearly eighteen miles to a depth of four thousand feet. . . .This is the *Wilderness* or *Pastureland of Tekoa* (2 Chron. 20:20), across which by night the wild beasts howl, and by day the blackened sites of deserted camps, with the loose cairns that mark the nomads' graves, reveal a human life almost as vagabond and nameless as that of the beasts. Beyond the rolling land is Jeshimon, or Devastation - a chaos of hills, none of whose ragged crests are tossed as high as the shelf of Tekoa, while their flanks shudder down some further thousands of feet, by crumbling precipices and corries choked with debris, to the coast of the Dead Sea. The northern half of this is visible, bright blue against the red wall of Moab, and the level top of the wall, broken only by the valley of the Arnon, constitutes the horizon. Except for the blue water - which shines in its gap between the torn hills like a bit of sky through rifted clouds - it is a dreary world. Yet the sun breaks over it, perhaps the more gloriously; mists, rising from the sea simmering in its great vat, drape the nakedness of the desert noon; and through the dry desert night the planets ride with a majesty they cannot assume in our troubled atmospheres. It is also a very empty and silent world, yet every stir of life upon it excites, therefore, the greater vigilance, and man's faculties, relieved from the rush and confusion of events, form the instinct of marking, and reflecting upon, every single phenomenon. And it is a very wild world. Across it, the towers of Jerusalem give the only signal of the spirit, the one token that man has a history.

Upon this wilderness, where life is full of poverty,
and danger - where nature starves the imagination,
but excites the faculties of perception and curiosity;
with the mountain tops and the sunrise in his face,
and with Jerusalem so near-Amos did the work
which made him a man, heard the voice of God calling him to be a prophet, and gathered those symbols
and figures in which his prophet's message still
reaches us with so fresh and so austere an air.
(*Smith, pp. 72-74, revised edition, 1929)

This romantic understanding of the prophet struck a
sympathetic cord in both popular and academic circles (for a
modern restatement of the position, see Stuhlmueller).

A second interest of this phase of scholarship was the religion advocated by the prophet. Since the prophets were
understood as condemning the society of their day and as
proclaiming the downfall of the nation, this religious aspect had
two foci, namely, the wrongs in the religion and behavior of
their contemporaries and the alternatives to these proposed by
the prophets. The prophets were interpreted as protesting
against religious practices that were communally oriented,
ritually focused, ethically hollow, and infused with polytheistic
and heathen elements and against social behavior that was
wealth oriented, legally corrupt, judicially unfair, and insensitive
to the poor. What the prophets proposed as an alternative was
individual and ethical idealism (see Duhm, 109-26, for a treatment of Amos). About Amos, Wellhausen wrote:

Neither Jehovah nor His prophet recognizes two
moral standards; right is everywhere right, wrong
always wrong, even though committed against
Israel's worst enemies (ii.1). What Jehovah demands
is righteousness,- nothing more and nothing less;
what He hates is injustice. Sin or offence to the
Deity is a thing of pure moral character; with such
emphasis this doctrine had never before been heard.
Morality is that for the sake of which all things exist;
it is the alone essential thing in the world. (p. 472)

As God of the righteousness which is the law of the
whole universe, Jehovah could be Israel's God only

in so far as in Israel the right was recognized and followed. The ethical element destroyed the national
character of the old religion. It still addressed itself,
to be sure, more to the nation and to society at large
than to the individual; it insisted less upon a pure
heart than upon righteous institutions; but nevertheless the first step toward universalism had been
accomplished, towards at once the general diffusion
and the individualisation of religion. Thus, although
the prophets were far from originating a new conception of God, they none the less were the founders of
what has been called "ethical monotheism". (p. 474)

A third important issue raised during this phase of
prophetic research concerned the integrity of the prophetic
books and consequently the authenticity of the material
attributed to the prophet. Duhm challenged the authenticity of
2:4-5; 4:13; 5:8-9; and 9:5-6 and Wellhausen added 1:9-12;
3:14b; 5:26; 6:2; 8:6, 8, 11-12; and 9:8-15 to that list (see Driver,
318). By the time George Adam Smith published the revised
edition of his commentary in 1929, the number of challenged
passages had grown to include much of the book: (1) references
to Judah in 2:4-5; 3:1b; 6:1; 9:11-12, (2) the hymnic texts in 4:13;
5:8-9; 9:5-6, (3) the optimistic ending in 9:8-15, (4) texts judged
later on the basis of historical, linguistic, or theological considerations in 1:2, 6-12; 3:7, 14b; 5:26; 6:2, 14; 8:11-14, and (5)
various expansions and glosses in 2:10, 12, 14-15; 3:1, 3; 4:7-8,
10; 5:6, 13, 16, 22; 6:9-11a; 8:6, 8, 13, and so on (see *Smith,
1929 edition, p. 57).

As a rule, scholars working along the lines laid down by
Kuenen, Duhm, and Wellhausen still considered Amos to have
written a version of his speeches to which had been added the
biographical narrative in 7:10-17, the superscription in 1:1, and
various supplements noted above. The following is characteristic:

In view of the well planned disposition of his
prophecies, it is responsible to suppose that, after he
had his prophetic ministration at Bethel, he returned
to his native home, and there at leisure, arranged his
prophecies in a written form. (*Driver, 1898, 97)

A second phase in modern research on the prophets is associated with the names of Hermann Gunkel, Hugo Gressmann, and Sigmund Mowinckel. These scholars belonged to the broad movement known as the *religionsgeschichtliche Schule* (the history of religions school) which was concerned with elucidating the religion and literature of the Old Testament in light of the religious literature and practices in the world at large but with particular focus on the ancient near eastern and hellenistic cultures. In a narrower sense, they were concerned with analyzing prophetism and prophetic literature from the perspectives of *Gattungsgeschichte* or form criticism.

The history of religions school criticized Wellhausen and the literary critics for not being sufficiently historical in their research (see Oden, 28-35). By this, Gunkel and others meant that the scholar must delve behind the literary stage of the material to discover and elucidate both its antecedents and its pre-written forms.

According to Gunkel, the following factors must be taken into consideration in studying the prophetic books.

(1) The prophets were speakers and not writers. They were the recipients of revelation, generally received in a state of ecstasy, which was then transmitted to their audience in the form of the spoken word.

(2) The prophets primarily saw themselves as messengers transmitting the revelations which they had received but occasionally supplementing these with their own words in order to clarify or provide reasons for the divine words.

(3) Prophetic speech, although utilizing genres borrowed from many areas of Israelite life, was characterized by a number of features. Prophetic addresses were short, future oriented, poetic, metrical, often mysterious, and dominated by certain syntactical constructions such as introductory and concluding formulas. (These conclusions were partially reached through analysis of the prophetic narratives in the Old Testament and through comparative materials from other cultures, primarily the sayings of Greek oracles.) Most prophetic sayings were considered to be composed of two main elements: a prediction about coming events and the rationale or motivation for the prediction (see Mowinckel, 46).

(4) Prophetic addresses were both delivered and transmitted orally. Sayings of the prophets were remembered and circulated as isolated units.

(5) The creation of prophetic literature in written form was a later development and was carried out by persons other than the prophets themselves.

(6) Study and exegesis of prophetic addresses or oracles must begin by dividing the prophetic literature into its original units of oral presentation, that is, by dividing the material into its smallest, isolated units.

This approach's conclusions about the origin and development of the prophetic material have been summarized by Mowinckel.

> The result with which we shall have to rest satisfied, is that the relatively brief, in itself, complete and concluded, independent separate saying ("oracle") is the original and real form of prophet "speech", his message, and that this is also largely the case with the historically known prophets, "the scripture prophets" as they are generally, and misleadingly, termed. - These separate sayings have been transmitted by oral tradition in the prophet circles, partly unchanged, partly adapted to and revived in the new situations of new times; they have been living a *life* in tradition and have been serving a religous purpose within the circle; the tradition has not been static. - In the course of the history of the tradition there have arisen greater "tradition complexes" and collections out of these separate sayings, which again in their turn have been joined together to final collections of tradition. The latter may also have been handed on by word of mouth. Finally, however, they have been recorded; they have become "books". This written fixing may have started earlier, with the separate minor complexes, and the oral tradition may have continued side by side with the written one. (p. 60)

On the basis of introductory and concluding formulas, Mowinckel argued that the book of Amos can be divided into "28 - 30 lesser, independent units, which neither presuppose nor demand each other - actually there are still more" (p. 48).

The third phase in modern prophetic research is associated primarily with the German scholar Albrecht Alt and his students. This group was influenced not only by Gunkel but also by the sociological theories of Max Weber and the neo-orthodox theology of Karl Barth. Weber had argued in 1917-19 that in its origin ancient Israel was a confederated group of tribes (an amphictyony) bound to one another and to Yahweh through covenant agreement and covenant law. The prophets, according to Weber, based their teaching and preaching on the old covenant law tradition of the tribal confederacy (see Nicholson, 37-44). Barth's theology of the word of God which stressed the transcendental character of the word which encounters humans in direct confrontation provided a model for understanding the biblical prophets.

The reconstruction of the history of Israel by Martin Noth and the interpretation of Israelite religion and theology by Gerhard von Rad placed the concepts of a divine-human covenant, the traditions of Israel's sacred history, and the role of covenant law at the center of biblical interpretation. All of these were assumed to be related closely to the cult and liturgies of ancient Israel. Related to all of these were the questions of the institutional life of ancient Israel and the history and development of traditions within this larger institutional life. In one respect, prophetic interpretation had come full circle; the prophets were again understood as individuals dependent on and interpreters of earlier sacred and legal traditions rather than as creative individuals whose influence changed and shaped the life and religion of ancient Israel (for this development, see Zimmerli, especially pp. 31-75).

It became customary to speak of the "office" of prophet and even to argue for a succession of prophetic figures who filled this office as guardian of the covenant law (see Muilenburg). Scholars considered some of the prophets as cultic functionaries, locating their office within the cultic life of ancient Israel, a position already advocated by Mowinckel (see Johnson). Würthwein argued that Amos's career should be divided into two phases. In the first, Amos functioned as a cultic prophet whose task was to aid in securing peace and salvation for Israel. The oracles on the nations in 1:3 - 2:6 belong to this phase of his career. The visions manifest the prophet's transition from cultic prophet of peace to a non-cultic prophet of judgment. Even the genre of Amos's judgment speeches and the practice of judgment proclamation were borrowed from the cult (on Würthwein, see Roberts).

Reventlow sought to associate the whole of Amos's preaching with the cult, arguing that he functioned in the context of an annual covenant renewal festival in which curses against foreign nations, judgments against Israel, intercession, and proclamation of the future all had their place.

Most other scholars have been more skeptical about Amos's connection with the cult and have seen him as dependent on only certain aspects of the cultic life of the times. Bach, for example, argued that Amos's condemnation of Israel was based on his use of the apodictic laws proclaimed in the cult as the will of Yahweh for the people.

Others have sought to associate the prophet with other institutions and traditions. Terrien and Wolff, for example, relate Amos to non-cultic wisdom circles. The ethical outlook, moral principles, and cultic criticisms of Amos as well as his forms of speech and terminology are understood as characteristic of folk or clan wisdom (for a critique, see Crenshaw).

On one problem, issues from all three phrases of modern research tend to come together. This is the question of the authenticity and integrity of the material in the book. Matters surrounding the text's authenticity, the oral nature of its origin, and the problems of its transmission and history are now focused in what is called the *Redaktionsgeschichte* or redactional/compositional history of the text.

The most elaborate theories of the formation and composition of the book are those proposed by *Wolff and *Coote, the latter offering a modified version of the former (see Craghan, 243-46, on Wolff). According to Wolff, six stages can be detected in the formation of the book (see *Wolff, 106-13). (1) The first stage or layer is comprised of the "words of Amos" now found in chapters 3-6. (2) A second layer consists of the vision reports in chapters 7-9 and the speeches against the nations in chapters 1-2 (but excluding the Tyre, Edom, and Judah sections). Both of these layers may be traced back to Amos, but not necessarily in written form. (3) A third layer of material derives from a circle of Amos's disciples or from an "old school of Amos" which functioned for two or three decades after the prophet's ministry. To this group belong such texts and additions as the Amos narrative (7:10-17), 5:13-15; 6:2, and references to Beer-sheba and Joseph. (4) A fourth extensive redaction was carried out during the reign of Josiah in the second half of the seventh century. After Josiah destroyed the temple at Bethel (see 2 Kings 23:15-20), the material in Amos mentioning Bethel and "altar" was augmented, probably for liturgical use, since the hymnic material in 4:13; 5:8-9; 9:5-6 was added at the same time. (5) In deuteronomistic circles in the south during the exile, additional material was added to make clear that Amos's preaching was directed against Jerusalem and Judah. In addition, the oracles on Edom and Tyre were added to reflect present historical realities. (6) A final stage of redaction consists of the post-exilic addition of 9:11-15 to emphasize that Yahweh's judgment of death was not God's last word.

The treatment of Amos in the present volume is based on a number of positions with regard to the book and its contents which differ considerably from positions reflected in the history of scholarship. At this point, these can only be noted without much detail. The exposition of the book itself constitutes the supporting evidence.

(1) The book of Amos must be understood in terms of a close reading of the text in light of the historical events as reconstructed from all available sources. The prophets addressed specific historical situations and conditions; they did not address religious, moral, or political issues in general. The historical horizons within which Amos worked involved the rapidly declining reign of the pro-Assyrian king Jeroboam II, whose kingdom was surrounded by the hostile powers of a regional anti-Assyrian coalition, and was threatened from within by both Israelite and Judean anti-Assyrian factions. Amos's preaching at Bethel probably lasted only a single day at the least and a few days at the most. It took place just prior to the fall festival beginning the year 750-749, which witnessed the coronation of Pekah as a rival king to Jeroboam II.

(2) There is nothing especially creative in Amos's preaching. While there is no evidence that the prophet drew upon any specific collection of Old Testament laws, it is clear he was acquainted with what might be called Israelite customary law and morality as well as international customary law. There is no evidence in the book that the relationship between Yahweh and Israel was understood in terms of covenant theology at the time. Amos's distinctiveness probably lies in his proclamation of a rapidly approaching disaster that would serve as the judgment of God on the social strife and oppressive rule that characterized the period. His critique of the religion of his day was part of his critique of cultural and political conditions at large.

He certainly offered the people no such alternative as a religionless morality or universal ethical monotheism.

(3) Too little is known about Amos's background to speculate on how this influenced his preaching. His language and thought are probably more reflective of the culture at large than of a particular segment such as the cult or wisdom circles.

(4) There is nothing in the book that would indicate the Israelites were officially practicing any form of religion other than Yahwism. Since Amos refers only to religious practices at major national sanctuaries, nothing else comes into the purview of the book.

(5) The material in the book is best understood in terms of large rhetorical units rather than in terms of a multiplicity of small isolated units. To treat the book as a collection of several dozen small units (as in the commentaries by *Wolff and *Mays) is to involve form-critical concerns in the same fallacies that beset the old etymologizing word study approach to Scripture (see Barr, especially pp. 107-60). The latter approach isolated the individual word as the bearer of meaning, and assumed that the original, "root" meaning of the word was always and everywhere retained. Similarly much modern form-critical work divides the material into its smallest sense unit or genre, and then postulates an original intention and meaning for each genre, that is everywhere retained.

(6) How the book of Amos came into being remains unknown. It is easier to assume either that Amos wrote his own words, whether before or after delivering them or, more likely, that they were written down by someone in the audience, than it is to believe in the existence of a circle of disciples or an old school of Amos, for which there is no evidence whatever. Additions and glosses to the text are minimal. Texts often treated as extraneous, as glosses, or additions are shown in the exegesis to be integral elements of the prophet's preaching.

(7) Amos never unequivocally proclaimed the total destruction and end of the people.

III
AMOS'S PREACHING AND THE AMOS NARRATIVE

1. THE SUPERSCRIPTION (1:1)

M. **Bic**, "Der Prophet Amos - ein Haepatoskopos," *VT* 1(1951)293-96; K. **Budde**, "Die Überschrift des Buches Amos und des Propheten Heimat," *Semitic Studies in Memory of Rev. Dr. Alexander Kohut* (ed. G. A. Kohut; Berlin: S. Calvary & Co., 1897)106-10; P.C. **Craigie**, "Amos the *noqed* in the Light of Ugaritic," *SR* 11(1982)29-33; D. N. **Freedman**, "Headings in the Books of the Eighth-Century Prophets," *AUSS* 25(1987)9-26; H. F. **Fuhs**, "Amos 1, 1. Erwägungen zur Tradition und Redaktion des Amosbuches," *Bausteine biblischer Theologie: Festgabe für G. Johannes Botterweck* (ed. H. J. Fabry; BBB 50; Köln/Bonn: Peter Hanstein, 1977)271-89; H. **Heicksen**, "Tekoa: Historical and Cultural Profile," *JETS* 13(1970)81-89; C. D. **Isbell**, "A Note on Amos 1.1," *JNES* 36(1977)213-14; S. **Klein**, "Drei Ortsnamen in Galilaea. 3. *tekoa* in Galilaea," *MGWJ* 67(1922)270-73; A. **Murtonen**, "The Prophet Amos - a Hepatoscoper?," *VT* 2(1952)170-71; F. E. **Peiser**, *shenatayim lipne hara'ash*: Eine philologische Studie," *ZAW* 36(1916)218-24; S. N. **Rosenbaum**, "A Northern Amos Revisited: Two Philological Suggestions," *HS* 18(1977)132-48; M. **San-Nicolo**, "Materialien zur Viehwirtschaft in den neubabylonischen Tempeln. I," *Orientalia* 17(1948)273-93; H. **Schmidt**, "Die Herkunft des Propheten Amos," *Karl Budde zum siebzigsten Geburtstag* (ed. Karl Marti; BZAW 34; Giessen: A. Töpelmann, 1920)158-71; W. H. **Schmidt**, "Die deuteronomistische Redaktion des Amosbuches. Zu den theologischen Unterschieden zwischen dem Prophetenwort und seinem Sammler," *ZAW* 77(1965)168-93; S. **Segert**, "Zur Bedeutung des Wortes *noqed*," *Hebräische Wortforschung: Festschrift zum 80. Geburtstag von Walter Baumgartner* (ed. B. Hartmann; Leiden: E. J. Brill, 1967)279-83; J. A. **Soggin**, "Das Erdbeben von Amos 1, 1 und die Chronologie der Könige Ussia und Jotham von Juda," *ZAW* 82(1970)117-21; S. **Speier**, "Bemerkungen zu Amos," *VT* 3(1953)305-10; J. J. **Stamm**, "Der Name des Propheten Amos und sein sprachlicher Hintergrund," *Prophecy: Essays Presented to Georg Fohrer on His Sixty-fifth Birthday, 6 September 1980*

(ed. J. A. Emerton; Berlin: Walter de Gruyter, 1980)137-42; H.
J. **Stoebe**, "Der Prophet Amos und sein bürgerlicher Beruf,"
WD 5(1957)160-81; W. **Sütterlin**, "Thekoa. Eine geographisch-
archäologische Skizze," *PJB* 17(1921)31-46; G. M. **Tucker**,
"Prophetic Superscriptions and the Growth of a Canon," *Canon
and Authority: Essays in Old Testament Religion and Theology*
(ed. G. W. Coats and B. O. Long; Philadelphia: Fortress Press,
1977)56-70; B. **Uffenheimer**, "The Consecration of Isaiah in
Rabbinic Exegesis," *SH* 22(1971)233-46; S. **Wagner**,
"Überlegungen zur Beziehung des Propheten Amos zum
Südreich," *TLZ* 96(1971)654-70; T. J. **Wright**, "Did Amos
Inspect Livers?," *ABR* 23(1975)3-11; Y. **Yadin** et al., *Hazor II:
An Account of the Second Season of Excavations, 1956*
(Jerusalem: Hebrew University/Magnes Press, 1960)24-26, 36-
37.

1:1 *The words of Amos, who was among the shepherds from
Tekoa, which he saw concerning Israel in the days of Uzziah, king
of Judah, and in the days of Jeroboam, son of Joash, king of
Israel, two years before the earthquake.*

The superscription to the book of Amos, like those for the
other prophetical books, was not written by the prophet. It is
biographical rather than autobiographical. As the heading to
the book, the superscription serves to identify the content and
source of the writing and thus belongs to the editorial and reading stage rather than the oral presentation stage of the
material. The superscription alerts the reader as to what is
contained in the document that follows. In this way, the superscription functions like the title and sub-title of a book.

The practice of providing written materials with identifica-
tory headings is illustrated by an inscription set up by a Syrian
king early in the eighth century, almost contemporary with
Amos. It contains the following superscription: "A stele set up
by Zakkur, king of Hamath and Lu'ash, for Ilu-wer [his god]"
(see *ANET* 655). Such a superscription indicates that public
writings in their original form could provide the reader with
information about the authors and the material's contents.

Three types of information are presented the reader in
1:1.

(1) First of all, the document's contents are identified.
"The words of Amos . . . which he saw concerning Israel." The

opening expression, "the words of Amos," is modified by the second relative clause, "which he saw concerning Israel." The term translated "saw" is the verb *ḥazah*. Like *ra'ah* it could have the meaning "to see, perceive." With regard to revelation and the future, the verb could thus refer to the reception of revelations or perceptions about the future. The noun, *ḥazon*, was used to designate not only the experience of revelation or perception but also the vision or message perceived and proclaimed (see Isa. 1:1; 21:2; 29:11). The term *ḥazah* thus appears not only to have described the act of reception/perception but also the act of making known what had been seen (see Isa. 2:1; Mic. 1:1). Thus the terms *ḥozeh* or *rô'eh*, "seer," could be used of one who perceived and also made known a message attributed to divine origin. Thus it is possible to translate either "the words of Amos . . . which he saw" or "which he proclaimed concerning Israel." The latter sense may be implied in this context, that is, in the superscription to the written record of a message already proclaimed.

Somewhat surprisingly, the content of the book is said to be "words of Amos." Other prophetic books which begin with reference to the "word" attribute this to Yahweh (Ezek. 1:3; Hos. 1:1; Joel 1:1; Jonah 1:1; Micah 1:1; Zeph. 1:1; Hag. 1:1; Zech. 1:1) and use the singular. Jer. 1:1 is an exception and like Amos 1:1 provides vocational data about the prophet. Rabbinic tradition declared that "there were three prophets to whom, because it consisted of words of reproach, their prophecy was attributed personally (Eccl. 1:1; Amos 1:1; Jer. 1:1)" rather than to God (*Eccl. Rabbah* I.1 § 2).

The prophet's name, *'amos*, is unique to the biblical traditions although a similar form, *'amasiah*, with a theophoric ending, appears in 2 Chron. 17:16. Names based on the root *'ms* ("to press, load, carry") appear in Akkadian, Phoenician, and Punic (see Stamm). Rabbinic tradition understood the prophet's name to mean "stammerer" or "heavy (*'amus*) of tongue" (*Eccl. Rabbah* I. 1 § 2), an interpretation with which Jerome was apparently familiar (*imperitus sermone, sed non scientia*).

(2) In addition to the identification of the document's contents, the superscription provides also information about Amos, the source of the words contained in the document. The relative clause, "who was among the *noqedim* from Tekoa," may be read as stressing the prophet's geographical roots ("Amos from

Tekoa") or his normal vocational and social status ("Amos who was among the *noqedim*") or both. One would assume that the geographical statement "from Tekoa" was originally intended to be read as a modifying description of Amos rather than of the *noqedim* although the latter interpretation is also possible.

Some uncertainty surrounds both the geographical and vocational information. The medieval Jewish scholar, David Kimchi, like some modern interpreters (see Klein, Rosenbaum, H. Schmidt, and Speier), associated Amos's hometown with a Galilean Tekoa mentioned in the Talmud. This would mean that the prophet was a northerner and thus a native Israelite. Two arguments have been offered for such an interpretation. (a) Amos's work with sycomore trees, mentioned in 7:14, is best understood in terms of some locale other than the Judean Tekoa to which sycomores are not native. (b) The charge of conspiracy leveled against Amos (7:10) presumably would have made more sense if he were a subject of King Jeroboam II; his activity could be viewed as the effort of a native northerner to overthrow the reigning monarch.

In all likelihood, Amos was from the southern village of Tekoa (modern *Taqu'a*), about ten miles south of Jerusalem, as tradition has long asserted. Located on a ridge overlooking the Dead Sea basin and the Judean wilderness (2 Chron. 20:20), Tekoa served as an observation post for the region (see Jer. 6:1) and was apparently occupied throughout Judean history. One of David's "mighty men" was from Tekoa (2 Sam. 23:26) and the village supplied laborers for the refortification of Jerusalem at the time of Nehemiah (Neh. 3:5, 27).

Two texts indicate that Tekoa was not as isolated from the mainstream of Judean life as its size and location might suggest. According to 2 Sam. 14:1-24, a wise woman from Tekoa was brought to Jerusalem by David's military commander, Joab, to convince the king to permit his disfavored son Absalom to return to the court. In 2 Chron. 11:5-12, Tekoa appears as one of the cities fortified by King Rehoboam to defend his reign and kingdom. (For additional remarks on Tekoa, see below on 7:14-15.)

The Hebrew noun, *noqed*, translated above as "shepherd" (or "sheep breeder" in some modern translations), is used to speak about Amos. The more common expression for shepherd is *rô'eh*. The exact meaning of the term *noqed* is difficult to determine since it occurs in the Bible only in Amos 1:1

and 2 Kings 3:4. In the latter text, King Mesha of Moab, as a vassal to the Israelite king, is said to have paid to Israel as tribute "a hundred thousand lambs, and the wool of a hundred thousand rams." What a prophet from Tekoa and a king from Moab shared in common is not immediately obvious.

Forms of the root *nqd* occur in biblical Hebrew meaning something like "speckled, spotted" (Gen. 30:22; Jos. 9:5; I Kings 14:3), but this may be a homonym. The root *nqd* was used in Akkadian, Arabic, and Syriac for sheep and shepherd (see *Harper, 8; *Kapelrud, 5-7; Segert; and San-Nicolo). The term *nqd* also appears in about a dozen texts (mostly lists) from Ras Shamra, the site of the ruins of the fourteenth-century coastal city of Ugarit in northern Syria (see Craigie). One text refers to a person who was both the "chief of the *noqedim*" (*rb nqdm*; see *ANET* 141) and "chief of the priests" (*rb khnm*). In other texts *nqdm* appear along with other vocational groupings including priests, singers, gate-keepers, and votaries. In administrative texts, *nqdm* are mentioned as both tax payers and as recipients of land grants. Such texts would indicate that the *nqdm* at Ugarit were a vocational group or guild associated with the temple and temple service and/or the palace and royal service. It has been argued that in the Neo-Babylonian period, three classes of officials were associated with temple herds in Babylonia: the *rabi-bûli* was a general overseer, the *naqidu* was a second level official, and the *rê'u* was the actual shepherd (San-Nicolo, 284-85). The organization of temple and royal economics and support personnel in Israel and Judah is too little known to ascertain whether organized herding staffs existed or not. One could speculate that *noqedim* were in the service of the temple or palace and that Amos was one of these, namely, a member of a dependent group in charge of flocks in the area of Tekoa or a member of a shepherding band recruited from Tekoa. This could lead to the presumption that Amos as a *noqed* was a type of official associated with temple/court service. One highly speculative view conceives of a *noqed* as a special diviner of some sort, perhaps a hepatos-coper or liver-reading expert (so Bic who bases his reading on the Akkadian verb *naqadu* meaning "to probe," in the sense of liver augury).

Some ancient translations indicate unclarity and uncertainty about the meaning of the term *noqedim*. Some translators simply transliterated the word, considering it a place name. The Aramaic Targum understood the term as specifying "an owner of flocks."

On the basis of 1:1, the least that can be said about Amos's vocational background and social status is that he was occupationally involved with the raising of sheep, either as a shepherd or, more likely, as a sheep breeder. Whether his occupation was also related to temple service and religious activity remains unknown but is certainly a possibility. If a *noqed* was associated with sheep raising in some capacity and was also in a dependent relationship to the court and/or the temple establishment, then Amos and Mesha may have shared the same official designation if a quite different social status.

(3) The third type of information conveyed in the superscription is chronological and contextual, serving to place both the prophet and his words within a historical context. Three pieces of information are provided, all temporal in character: "in the days of Uzziah, king of Judah," "in the days of Jeroboam ben-Joash, king of Israel," and "two years before the earthquake." Unfortunately no information is provided about either the particular conditions under which Amos arrived at his words or the circumstances under which he proclaimed them (see below on 7:10-17).

Of the three temporal references, two are general and one is specific. "The days of Uzziah, king of Judah" are difficult to pin down since biblical references to Uzziah (or Azariah as he is called in most texts) seem to imply a reign of fifty-two years, which is impossible to fit into a chronological scheme which takes into account other biblical data. For example, 2 Kings 15:27 says Pekah became king of Israel in Samaria in Uzziah's fifty-second year, yet texts such as Isa. 7:1, 7 and the inscriptions of Tiglath-pileser suggest that Ahaz was king in Jerusalem during the reign of Pekah in Samaria. This allows no time for the sixteen-year reign of Uzziah's son Jotham (2 Kings 15:33). The best solution to the problems of chronology for Uzziah seems to be one which operates on two assumptions. First, that Uzziah reigned for a time but had to abdicate the throne because of an illness which rendered him unclean and therefore unable to participate in cultic services (see 2 Kings 15:5). Second, the total years attributed to Uzziah as "king" include all the years from when he became king until his death. Using these considerations and taking into account other biblical data, one can calculate the actual years of his reign as 785-760 and the fifty-two years assigned him, beginning with the first year of his reign, as 785-734. He was succeeded in 759 by his son Jotham who reigned sixteen years or until 744 (2 Kings 15:33). If Amos's short ministry occurred about 750-749, then Jotham was actually the Judean king at the time. Why, then, does the superscription refer only to Uzziah? Perhaps because he was a revered ruler with great popular appeal, Uzziah's years were used to date materials even after he ceased to be reigning monarch (see 2 Kings 15:8, 13, 17, 23, 27; Isa. 6:1). Second Chron. 26:22 even claims that the prophet Isaiah wrote an account of the reign of Uzziah. During the reign of his son Jotham and the early years of the rule of his grandson Ahaz, Uzziah must have remained a dominant figure in Jerusalem life. Even in death, his remains were given special attention. An ossuary used for secondary burials survives with the words: "Here were brought the bones of Uzziah, king of Judah. Not to be opened."

Jeroboam son of Joash (or Jehoash) ruled for forty-one years, from 788 until 748 according to our chronology. If we only had the statements that Amos preached during the days of Uzziah and Jeroboam, it would be impossible to date Amos's career accurately. Fortunately two other bits of evidence allow us to pinpoint his career more closely.

First, as we shall argue below in discussing 1:5b, Amos makes reference to Pekah, a rival claimant to the throne in Samaria. Pekah was killed by Hoshea in 731, a date established on the basis of biblical and Assyrian inscriptional evidence (2 Kings 15:30a). Since Pekah was assigned twenty years of rule (2 Kings 15:27), he must have begun his rival reign sometime in 751-750. Amos would thus have prophesied after this year.

Second, in Isa. 9:8-10:4, the prophet provides a historical review of Israel's recent past, dividing the time into phases. In 9:8-12a Isaiah describes the effects of an earthquake on Samaria, the oppression under Rezin, and the encroachment of Syria and the Philistines on Israelite territory. In 9:13-17a he alludes to the murders of Zechariah, the son of Jeroboam II, and of Shallum, his assassin (see 2 Kings 15:8-14). Isa. 9:18-21a describes the subsequent civil war between the supporters and opponents of Menahem, perhaps some of the latter being supporters of Pekah (2 Kings 15:16). This sequence of events indicates that the earthquake mentioned in Amos 1:1 (see Zech. 14:5) occurred before the death of Jeroboam II, although per-

haps in his final year. Jeroboam II died, according to our cal-
culation, in the fifth month of his forty-first year, Nisan (March-
April) of 747. This date is computed on a Marheshvan to Marheshvan year with the king's regnal year being calculated from
the autumn festival which climaxed on the fifteenth of the
month (see 1 Kings 12:32-33). If Amos preached for a short
time two years before the earthquake, then his career can be
dated to the year 750-749. If one reads the reference to the
earthquake as "during two years before the earthquake" (so
RSV margin), this would refer to the period of about 750-748.
As we shall see, however, Amos's preaching is best understood
as occurring in conjunction with the fall festival in Marheshvan
750.

The earthquake which ravaged the countryside during
Uzziah's lifetime must have been an extraordinary event. In a
region where earthquakes are common, this one was especially
memorable (see Zech. 14:4-5). It provided the occasion and
imagery for some of Isaiah's preaching (see Isa. 1:2-20; 2:6-22)
and has left evidence of destruction at such sites as Samaria
and Hazor (see Yadin).

In his *Antiquities*, Josephus reports the following about the
effects of the quake: "before the city [Jerusalem] at a place
called Eroge (= En-rogel?) half of the western hill was broken
off and rolled four stades till it stopped at the eastern hill and
obstructed the roads and the royal gardens" (IX 225). Josephus
associated the earthquake with the outbreak of Uzziah's
leprosy (*Ant* IX 222-27; see 2 Kings 15:5), as did later rabbinic
tradition which also connected the earthquake with Isaiah's
temple vision (Isaiah 6; see Uffenheimer). The quake probably
produced the depression separating Mount Scopus and the
Mount of Olives (see Soggin).

This ravaging earthquake may have been viewed as fulfillment of some of the words of Amos (see 2:13; 9:1). This would
explain the inclusion of the editorial note "two years before the
earthquake" in the superscription to his speeches.

2. A SPEECH AGAINST THE
NATIONS (1:2-2:16)

S. **Amsler,** "Amos et les droits de l'homme (Etude d'Am 1 et
2)," *De la Tôrah au Messie* (ed. M. Carrez et al.; Paris: Desclée,
1981)181-86; J. **Barton,** *Amos's Oracles against the Nations: A
Study of Amos 1:3-2:5* (SOTSMS 6; Cambridge: Cambridge
University Press, 1980); A. **Bentzen,** "The Ritual Background of
Amos i.2-ii.16," *OTS* 8(1950)85-99; A. **Carlson,** "Prophetin
Amos och Davidsriket," *RelBib* 25(1966)57-78; D. L.
Christensen, "The Prosodic Structure of Amos 1-2," *HTR*
67(1974)427-36; **Christensen,** *Transformations of the War
Oracle in Old Testament Prophecy: Studies in the Oracles
Against the Nations* (HDR 3; Missoula: Scholars Press, 1975);
B. **Duhm,** "Anmerkungen zu den Zwölf Propheten. I. Buch
Amos," *ZAW* 31(1911)1-18; F. C. **Fensham,** "Common Trends
in Curses of the Near Eastern Treaties and *kudurru*-
Inscriptions Compared with Maledictions of Amos and Isaiah,"
ZAW 75(1963)155-75; V. **Fritz,** "Die Fremdvölkersprüche des
Amos," *VT* 37(1987)26-38; H. S. **Gehman,** "Natural Law and the
Old Testament," *Biblical Studies in Memory of H. C. Alleman*
(ed. J. M. Myers et al.; Locust Valley, NY: J. J. Augustin,
1960)109-22; H. **Gese,** "Komposition bei Amos," *SVT*
32(1981)74-95; R. **Gordis,** "The Heptad as an Element of Biblical and Rabbinic Style," *JBL* 62(1943)17-26 = his *Poets,
Prophets and Sages: Essays in Biblical Interpretation* (Blooming-
ton: Indiana University Press, 1971)95-103; M. **Haran,** "Observations on the Historical Background of Amos 1:2-2:6," *IEJ*
18(1968)201-12; **Haran,** "The Graded Numerical Sequence and
the Phenomenon of 'Automatism' in Biblical Poetry," *SVT*
22(1972)238-67; J. **Hehn,** "Zur Bedeutung der Siebenzahl," *Karl
Marti zum siebzigsten Geburtstage* (ed. K. Budde; BZAW41;
Giessen: Alfred Töpelmann, 1925)128-36; D. R. **Hillers,** *Treaty-
Curses and the Old Testament Prophets* (BibOr 16; Rome:
Pontifical Biblical Institute, 1964); J. **Limburg,** "Sevenfold
Structures in the Book of Amos," *JBL* 106(1987)217-22; K.
Marti, "Zur Komposition von Amos 1:3-2:3," *Abhandlungen zur
semitischen Religionskunde und Sprachwissenschaft* (ed. W.
Frankenberg and F. Küchler; BZAW 33; Giessen: Alfred
Töpelmann, 1918)323-30; J. **Mauchline,** "Implicit Signs of a

Persistent Belief in the Davidic Empire," *VT* 20(1970)287-303; L. M. **Muntingh**, "Political and International Relations of Israel's Neighboring Peoples According to the Oracles of Amos," *OTWSA* 7-8(1964-65)134-43; S. M. **Paul**, "Amos 1:3 - 2:3: A Concatenous Literary Pattern," *JBL* 90(1971)397-403; **Paul**, "A Literary Reinvestigation of the Authenticity of the Oracles Against the Nations of Amos," *De la Tôrah au Messie* (ed. M. Carrez et al.; Paris: Desclée, 1981)189-204; D. L. **Petersen**, "The Oracles Against the Nations: A Form-Critical Analysis," *SBLSP* (1975)1.39-61; G. **Pfeifer**, "Denkformenanalyse als exegetische Methode, erläutert an Amos 1:2-2:16," *ZAW* 88(1976)56-71; M. H. **Pope**, "Seven, Seventh, Seventy," *IDB* 4.294-95; W. M. W. **Roth**, "The Numerical Sequence X/X+1 in the Old Testament," *VT* 12(1962) 300-311; **Roth**, *Numerical Sayings in the Old Testament: A Form-Critical Study* (SVT 13; Leiden: E. J. Brill, 1965); W. **Rudolph**, "Die angefochtenen Völkersprüche in Amos 1 und 2, " *Schalom. Studien zu Glaube und Geschichte Israels, A. Jepsen zum 70. Geburtstag dargebracht* (ed. K. H. Bernhardt; AT 1/46; Stuttgart: Calwer, 1971)45-49; W. H. **Schmidt**, "Die deuteronomistische Redaktion des Amosbuches. Zu den theologischen Unterschieden zwischen dem Prophetenwort und seinem Sammler," *ZAW* 77(1965)168-93; S. **Segert**, "A Controlling Device for Copying Stereotype Passages (Amos i 3-ii 8, vi 1-6)," *VT* 34(1984)481-82; J. M. **Ward**, *Amos and Isaiah: Prophets of the Word of God* (Nashville: Abingdon Press, 1969)92-112; M. **Weiss**, "The Pattern of Numerical Sequence in Amos 1-2: A Re-examination," *JBL* 86(1967)416-23; **Weiss**, "The Pattern of the 'Execration Texts' in the Prophetic Literature," *IEJ* 19(1969)150-57.

The speech material in Amos begins with a long section containing charges against and pronouncements of destruction upon eight Syro-Palestinian states - Damascus, Gaza, Tyre, Edom, Ammon, Moab, Judah, and Israel. The individual "oracles on the nations" in this material are developed with a repetitive regularity. After an attributive formula designating the following declaration as a divine word (*ko 'amar YHWH* "thus says [or "has said"] Yahweh"), the individual subunits are introduced with a formulaic expression, "For three transgressions of . . . and for four, I will not recall it, because. . . ." The only variation in this opening formula is the name of the people being denounced.

Two other components are characteristic of these nation oracles. (1) Following the "because," the wrongdoings of each of the individual peoples are stated. (2) The statement of the offense or wrongdoing is followed by a pronouncement of coming punishment or disaster.

Within this general structure, the nation oracles manifest considerable diversity. Four of the initial seven oracles - those concerning Damascus (1:3-5), Gaza (1:6-8), Ammon (1:13-15), and Moab (2:1-3) - contain very brief statements of the offenses (see 1:3b, 6b, 13b; 2:1b) followed by somewhat lengthier pronouncements of coming disaster (1:4-5, 7-8, 14-15; 2:2-3). All four oracles also contain concluding attributive formulas (*'amar* [*'adonay*] *YHWH*) "says [the Lord] Yahweh") at the end (1:5, 8, 15; 2:3). The other three oracles - those concerning Tyre (1:9-10), Edom (1:11-12), and Judah (2:4-5) - contain statements of the offenses (1:9b, 11b; 2:4b) lengthier than the pronouncements of coming disaster (1:10, 12; 2:5). None of these latter three oracles contains a final attributive formula.

The Israel section (2:6-16) differs from all seven preceding oracles, possessing both a lengthy statement of offenses (2:6b-12) and a lengthy pronouncement of coming disasters (2:13-16) as well as two attributive formulas ("says Yahweh" or "declares Yahweh" *ne'um YHWH*).

Within the two non-Israelite sub-groups, a number of stylistic variations appear (see Ward; Paul, 1981, 198-200). Within the Damascus - Gaza - Ammon - Moab set, the following differences are noteworthy.

(1) In the designations of those being denounced, one is a capital city (Damascus), another is a leading city (Gaza), the third is a population at large (the sons of Ammon), and the fourth is a nation as a whole (Moab).

(2) In the pronouncements of disaster, three first-person verbs occur in the Damascus oracle ("I will send, I will break, I will cut off") and in the Gaza oracle ("I will send, I will cut off, I will turn") but only one in the Ammon oracle ("I will set fire to") and two in the Moab oracle ("I will send, I will cut off").

(3) Five different terms ("send, break, cut off, turn, set fire to") are used in the first-person verbal forms; no two oracles share the same combination of verbs. Although all four oracles associate Yahweh's action with fire, three oracles have Yahweh declare "I will send fire on" (first person hiphil of *shlk*) while one has "I will set fire to" (first person hiphil of *yṣt*). The

latter case is the Ammon oracle which has only one first-person verbal form.

(4) In three of the four oracles (Gaza, Ammon, Moab), the reason for the wrongdoing is expressed by a result clause introduced by the particle *le* or *lema'an* (1:6b, 13b; 2:1b). The purpose of Damascus's action, however, is not given.

(5) The statement of the wrongdoing uses plural forms in three cases ("Damascus - they threshed"; "Gaza - they exiled"; "Ammon - they ripped open"). The remaining oracle, however, uses the singular ("Moab - it burned").

Thus in spite of the overall pattern of these four oracles, internal stylistic variations are introduced so that no two oracles have identical formulations. The variations extend beyond the content and nature of the individual accusations.

Similarly, structural variations appear in the sub-group of three oracles (Tyre, Edom, and Judah) in which the description of the wrongdoing is longer than the description of coming disaster.

(1) The condemnation of Tyre (1:9b) is spelled out in two statements, that of Edom in four (1:11b), while the Judean oracle (2:4b) specifies three.

(2) The object of the coming attack is different in all three cases: "the wall of Tyre and . . . its fortresses," "Teman and . . . the fortresses of Bozrah," and "Judah and . . . the fortresses of Jerusalem."

(3) Both plural and singular forms occur in the statements of the wrongdoing: "Tyre . . . because they," "Edom . . . because it," and "Judah . . . because they."

The following summarizes the structural features of the oracles on the nations. (1) A common framing pattern is characteristic of all the sub-units. (2) Within this structuring framework, two sub-categories can be detected: one group contains an expanded description of the coming disaster, thus highlighting the punishment, and the other an expanded description of the wrongdoing, thus highlighting the crimes. (3) The units alternate between the two types. Two of the former (Damascus and Gaza) are followed by two of the latter (Tyre and Edom) and the pattern is then repeated (Ammon-Moab and Judah). (4) Variations in terminology and mode of expression occur within both categories. (5) The Israel section (2:6-16) contains an elaboration of both the descriptions of the wrongdoings and of the coming disasters.

A number of issues are involved in the interpretation of these oracles on the nations in Amos. These include (1) questions of the unity and authenticity of the individual sub-units on the various nations, (2) the historical events underlying the atrocities and wrongdoings condemned, (3) the relationship of 1:2 to the material in 1:3-2:16, (4) the presuppositions underlying the condemnation of non-Israelite nations by an Israelite prophet, and (5) the rhetorical function and intention of the material. These will now be discussed in turn.

(1) The authenticity of specific oracles in 1:3-2:5 are questioned several grounds. These may be sub-divided into (a) syntactic-stylistic, (b) historical, and (c) structural.

(a) The proclamations on Tyre (1:9-10), Edom (1:11-12), and Judah (2:4-5) have frequently been considered secondary on the basis of syntax and style. As we noted above, the sub-units in 1:3-2:5 fall into two groups. The pattern reflected in the oracles on Damascus (1:3-5), Gaza (1:6-8), Ammon (1:13-15), and Moab (2:1-3) is often taken as the standard for declaring secondary the remaining oracles. These four addresses contain five elements (see *Wolff, 135-39):

(i)   an introductory formula ("thus says Yahweh") which ascribes the subsequent proclamation to the divine;

(ii)   a formulaic statement ("for three transgressions and for four, I will not recall it") which proclaims the inevitability of disaster;

(iii)   a statement of a specific wrongdoing intro duced by the preposition ʿal plus an infinitive construct with pronominal suffix;

(iv)   the proclamation of the coming disaster presented in the form of three two-part lines with an identical (or almost identical) opening statement about "fire" and a concluding declarative sentence giving the consequences of divine action; and

(v)   a concluding formula ("says Yahweh" or "says the Lord Yahweh").

In the Tyre, Edom, and Judah sections, only (i) and (ii) reappear verbatim. Otherwise the following variations are noted (*Wolff, 139-41):

    (iii)   the 'al plus infinitive clause is expanded by the use of one or more finite verbs;

    (iv)   the description of coming disaster employs only the formulaic expression about "fire" common to all the other pronouncements and contains no declarative sentence stating the consequences of divine punishment; and

    (v)   a concluding formula is consistently lacking.

In addition to these syntactic-stylistic "deviations" in the Tyre, Edom, and Judah sections from an original standard form, scholars challenging the authenticity of these passages point to their more generalized character, the similarity between the accusation against Tyre and that against Gaza, the parallels between the accusation against Edom and those against Damascus and Ammon, and the theological rather than political charges levelled against Judah.

(b) Historical arguments have been used to challenge the authenticity of not only the Tyre, Edom, and Judah denunciations but also that against Gaza (and the Philistines).

The arguments for seeing the Tyre section as a later addition are threefold. First, Tyre is associated with slave trade only in 1:9 and in a clearly later text (Ezek. 27:13) and a presumably later text (Joel 3:4-8). Second, it is generally presumed that biblical oracles against Tyre (see Jer. 27:3; 47:4; 25:22; Ezek. 26:1-28:19; Joel 3:4-8; and even Isaiah 23) all date from a time after Nebuchadrezzar and the rise of Babylonia (see *Wolff, 158). Third, the expression "to remember a covenant" appears only in texts considered late in origin (Gen. 9:15-16; Exod. 2:24; 6:5; Lev. 26:42, 45; see Ezek. 16:60).

The Edom oracle is declared secondary because Edomite-Judean hostility supposedly reached its apogee in the exilic and post-exilic periods, that is, after the fall of Jerusalem in 586. Most anti-Edomite statements come from the literature of this period (see Jer. 49:7-22; Ezek. 25:12-14; 35; Obad. 1:10-14; Mal. 1:4; Ps. 137:7; Lam. 4:21-22).

Doubts have been raised about the Judah oracle because the theological formulations used to condemn Judah are traditionally assigned to a later period, namely, the time after Josiah's reformation more than a century after Amos. The rather insipid charges leveled against Judah, their formulation as sins against God, and their failure to specify crimes against other human communities are seen as evidence of the deuteronomic piety of a redactor.

A redactional origin for the Gaza oracle has been argued on historical grounds but less frequently so than for the oracles on Tyre, Edom, and Judah. The fact that all the Philistine cities except Gath are mentioned is viewed as reflecting historical circumstances following the capture of Gath by the Assyrian king Sargon in 711 (Duhm; Marti). The passage on Gaza and the Philistine cities would thus have been composed after 711.

(c) According to some scholars, structural considerations indicate that some of the nation oracles should be treated as secondary additions. Omitting these oracles would restore the original form of the prophet's preaching. Among these considerations is the argument that seven nations would be more appropriate than eight since seven is a formulaic number indicating totality and completeness. *Würthwein has argued that Amos delivered these scathing criticisms of neighboring powers while he was a professional cult prophet. As an official member of the cult, the prophet's task would have consisted in condemning other states, not his own people. Therefore the Israel oracle in 2:6-16 was not part of the original cycle of nation speeches but was delivered later, when Amos became a critic of his own fellow citizens.

*Marti has argued that the original structure of the cycle is to be found by deleting the Gaza, Tyre, and Edom speeches. Once these are omitted the cycle follows a natural geographical progression, from Damascus south to Ammon and Moab, and then to Judah-Israel. In addition, the length of the remaining oracles on non-Israelites parallels the length of the Israel speech.

Gese has proposed that Amos frequently employed a five-fold structure (2+2+1) in his speeches as well as in the vision reports and elsewhere (see *Auld, 46-47). On this basis, he argues that only the Damascus, Gaza, Ammon, Moab, and Israel speeches are genuine. Damascus and Gaza are paired as Israel's archetypal enemies (see Isa. 9:12) and are condemned for war atrocities. Ammon and Moab are linked geographically and genealogically and are condemned for breaking sacral law. These two pairs were originally followed by the Israel oracle, giving a 2+2+1 structure to the overall speech.

None of these arguments against the genuineness of any of the nation oracles seems well founded. The entire section appears to be a well-structured, artistic unit with sufficient framing to provide repetition and regularity, allowing the hearer/reader to anticipate, and yet with sufficiently varied structural blocks to stimulate interest and appeal to the intellect (so, most recently, *Rudolph; *Gordis; Paul). As will be noted in the subsequent discussion of the individual units, there are no compelling reasons for dating any of the oracles later than the time of Amos.

(2) The prophet's denunciations of wrongdoings by the nations obviously allude to particular historical events. The allusions, however, are not sufficiently precise to make identifications of these events absolutely certain. Thus proposals regarding the historical referents have varied from such indefinite suggestions as "traditional examples of inhuman conduct" or "the most recent memorable atrocities" to suggestions of specific historical contexts. Among the historical contexts proposed are periods a century or more before Amos's day (for example, the days of the breakup of the Solomonic state or the time of the Omride dynasty) or the more recent era of Syrian dominance of Israel during the reigns of Jehu and his immediate descendants Jehoahaz and Jehoash (see Barton, 25-35). The reign of Jeroboam II or Amos's own day is also proposed (see *Wolff, 148-51).

As we shall note in the discussion of particular nation oracles, the historical events alluded to are best understood as contemporary with the prophet and reflective of international political and military realities in which pro-Assyrian Israel found itself under assault from Syro-Palestinian members of an anti-Assyrian regional coalition.

(3) Amos 1:2 is considered by the vast majority of scholars to be a late addition to the book, perhaps based on or a modification of Joel 3:16 and Jer. 25:30. Even those who consider the verse authentic to Amos (most recently *Snaith; *Maag; *Gordis) display uncertainty about the verse's role. Whether original or redactional, the verse's function can be interpreted in various ways. (a) It may be viewed as a continuation of 1:1 and thus as a part of the superscription. In this case, it would comprise what later editors thought was a synopsis or characterization of the prophet's preaching. (b) The verse may be seen as an independent unit representing, in the form of a

motto or overture, the central thrust of the prophet's proclamation. (c) The verse may be understood as providing an introduction to the book as a whole before the addition of the superscription. (d) The verse may be viewed as the introduction to
the speeches against the nations, the opening of the unit 1:2-
2:16. As we shall see below, the latter position is to be
preferred.

(4) The basis on which Amos, an Israelite prophet, pronounced judgments on non-Israelite nations is not made clear
in the text. A number of possible rationales have been proposed (see Barton, 39-45).

(a) One approach sees the denunciations of foreign
nations as the expression of Israelite nationalism. Speeches
against and curses of one's enemies, particularly in times of
warfare, were a feature of ancient culture (see Petersen). For
example, a letter from eighteenth-century Mari addressed by a
state official to the court of King Zimri-Lim reports on the
delivery of an oracle denouncing Babylonia during conflicts
between the Mari king and Hammurabi.

> Speak to my lord [Zimri-Lim]: Thus Mukannishum
> your   servant. I offered a sacrifice to Dagan for the
> life of my lord, and then the *aplum* of Dagan of Tut-
> tul arose and spoke as follows: "O Babylon! How
> must you constantly be treated? I am going to gather
> you into a net. . . .I will deliver into the power of
> Zimri-Lim the houses of the seven confederates [of
> Hammurabi] and all their possessions". (*ANET* 625i)

Here the oracle, addressed to Babylon in the second person of
direct speech, functions as an oracle of salvation to Zimri-Lim.
If Amos's speeches were such nationalistic addresses, they
would serve a similar function. This is the view of *Würthwein
who understood Amos's early career as that of a cultic prophet
of salvation to Israel (see also *Weiser, 112).

Neither nationalist sentiments nor desire for revenge,
however, sufficiently explains the prophet's depiction and
denunciation of the nations' atrocities. The prophet does not
highlight Israel as the victim of these atrocities even where this
seems clearly the case. At the same time, Moab is condemned
for an act committed against Edom. In addition, in a statement
based strictly on nationalistic interests, one would expect that

the announced punishment would result in or contribute to Israel's well-being and salvation. Such a connection, however, is never made by Amos.

(b) Bentzen argued that the practice, known from Egyptian execration texts, of ritually execrating traditional enemies of the state, lies behind Amos's denunciations. In the Egyptian ritual, inscribed vessels and figurines representing such enemies were ritually smashed to symbolize the destruction of hostile parties and powers (see *Wolff, 144-47). If dependent on such practices, Amos would thus have been utilizing a standard pattern in his address, probably delivered at the new year celebration as part of the autumn Feast of Tabernacles. There are some broad parallels between Amos 1:2-2:16 and the Egyptian execration texts. Among these are the apparent use of a geographical scheme in the denunciations (though the scheme is not identical in the two sets of texts), the pronouncements of destruction on others, and the condemnation of internal powers and persons as well as foreigners. The absence of Amos's geographical scheme elsewhere in the Hebrew scriptures and the severity of his denunciation of Israel would suggest that the prophet was not simply using either a typical cult form employed in Israel or one borrowed from other cultures (see Weiss, 1969). This is not to deny that denunciations against national enemies were employed in Israel; they probably were (see Christensen, 1975) and Amos's audience would probably have been familiar with the practice. Such pronouncements against one's enemies and the nationalistic orientation on which they were based, however, do not provide an adequate basis for understanding Amos's preaching in 1:2-2:16.

(c) Another attempt to understand the rationale of Amos's denunciation of foreign states argues that at one time all of these states were actually or idealistically considered part of Israel's and Yahweh's special domain and thus owed Yahweh vassal obligations (see Barré; Carlson; Christensen, 1975, 55-72; Mauchline). As such, all of the states including Israel were related and obligated to Yahweh on the basis of covenant agreements. What the nations were guilty of was lack of fidelity to Yahweh's covenant will which would have included standards for relationships between the states.

The weaknesses in such an argument are serious. First, there is no substantial evidence that Israel, even during the age of David and Solomon, ruled over all the states enumerated in

Amos 1:3-2:5, in spite of such claims as Gen. 15:18; 1 Kings
4:21, 24. Second, Amos's preaching makes no reference to any
covenant agreement between Yahweh and Israel much less
between Yahweh and other nations. Third, when Amos does
refer to a covenant and covenant obligations, he does so with
reference to a covenant between nations, not between a nation
and Yahweh (1:9).

(d) According to some scholars, Amos's condemnation
of other nations was based on his creative extension of the
demands of Yahweh placed on Israelites to include other
peoples (see, for example, *Wolff, 106; *Mays, 27; Fensham).
Nineteenth-century commentators spoke of the prophets, and
Amos in particular, as the creators of ethical monotheism. The
prophets understood God in universal categories and saw the
divine will and demands as applicable to and the basis for judgment of all nations. As creator of the world and/or controller
of human history, Israel's God could thus make demands on all
people and judge and punish any disobedience. Such ideas
were considered part of the prophets' contributions to Israelite
thought.

The difficulties with this view are twofold. First, Amos
does not appear to advocate a new form of either theology or
ethics. He does not argue a case for the culpability of the
nations; he presupposes it. Second, the atrocities of the nations
are not described as infringements of Yahweh's laws or of an
ethical system imposed by Yahweh. The nations appear to be
judged guilty of overstepping the norms of behavior assumed to
be applicable to all people, not especially those demanded by
Yahweh.

(e) A final approach to understanding the prophet's
rationale for condemning the behavior of foreign states points
to what has been called "international customary law" (see
Barton, 43-45, 51-61). This view assumes that out of international diplomatic and political-military relationships there had
developed something approaching an accepted standard of
norms or at least an understanding of what constituted infringements of normal, customary behavior. Such an understanding
should not be seen as reflecting a theory of "natural law"
embodying a set of idealistic commitments such as devotion to
"the sacredness of human personality" (so Gehman, 113).
Instead, such norms would have embodied conventions ham-
mered out in response to the pragmatics of routine life.

In international relations, treaties stipulated the response to behavior expected from the signatories, and assigned to the gods of the nations involved the responsibility of punishing the infringements of such stipulations. An example of such a treaty, between Barga'yah king of *KTK* and Matti'el king of Arpad, can be seen in the Sefire inscriptions (*ANET* 659-61; see further below on 1:3-5). The gods in the text are not considered the source of the treaty stipulations; they are depicted as the guarantors of the obligations and the avengers of infringements.

Customary standards of morality no doubt involved not only patterns of behavior explicitly articulated with official sanction and documentation but also patterns of everyday behavior. For example, desecration of tombs and of the dead was widely condemned in the ancient world. The abhorrence of such a practice was probably assumed, having resulted from a long history of burying and respecting the dead.

Amos's preaching against the nations is best understood in light of such customary law. This, of course, does not mean that the nations surrounding Israel would all have agreed on any tabulation of such laws. Amos himself, however, apparently both assumed such ethics and presumed that his audience shared his viewpoint. In addition, Yahweh was understood as the guardian of such morality and avenger of the guilt for its infringement.

(5) A final issue concerning Amos's speech on the nations involves rhetorical intention. If the prophet viewed his primary task as proclamation to Israel and if the material on Israel in 2:6-16 represents the climax of 1:2-2:16, as seems to be the case, why did the prophet begin his proclamation with denunciations of foreign nations? A number of answers have been proposed for this question.

(a) Amos was merely following Israelite prophetic custom. One of the prophets' tasks in Israel is assumed to have been condemnation of hostile foreign powers. That is, they functioned in the interest of Israelite nationalism. In denouncing other states for their wrongdoing and in pronouncing destruction upon enemy powers, the prophets functioned in the cult to help insure salvation for their own people (*Würthwein, 35-40). Such a function may have been performed in the context of an annual new year celebration (so Bentzen) or as part of an annual covenant renewal ceremony (so *Reventlow 56-

75) or both. In such an interpretation, even the content of
Amos's words may have been traditional material; thus the
statements about wrongdoings and the nations condemned
could be understood as traditional sayings against traditional
enemies. Amos was fundamentally performing an inherited
role.

With two of these considerations, one can agree. First,
the prophets did deliver speeches about and addressed to (at
least theoretically in the latter case) foreign nations. Virtually
all the prophetical books contain examples of such speeches.
Second, all the nations denounced by Amos were probably
hostile to Israel at the time of his preaching.

To argue that Amos was merely performing a traditional
role, utilizing traditional material, however, goes far beyond the
evidence, and to see him functioning to support purely nationalistic interests ignores the central thrust of 1:2-2:16, and even
more so the remainder of the book.

(b) If the first approach understands Amos too narrowly
as the inheritor and imitator of traditional customs and as a
purveyor of traditional speech, the opposite extreme is also to
be found. For years, Amos and other prophets were
understood as radical innovators who sought to shift Israelite
thought away from a foundation anchored in cultic and national
interests to an idealistic ethical monotheism, individualistic in
mode, universal in scope, and moral in application. The oracles
on foreign nations gave expression to this new outlook. By
preaching an ethical monotheism applicable to all people,
Amos was also attempting to disabuse Israel of any belief in its
own particularity and distinctiveness as a consequence of divine
election and protection.

As we noted earlier, even in the ethical basis of his condemnations, Amos seems to presuppose rather than to advocate. His preaching apparently assumed the existence of international conventions and of God as the judge and avenger of
infringements, rather than propounding an ethical system with
God as the lawgiver.

(c) Some have seen Amos's denunciations of foreign
states as primarily an audience-attracting ploy. By denouncing
other countries, Amos was sure to gain an audience both interested in his subject mater, since it involved matters of national
welfare, and sympathetic to him, since he was advocating
Israel's cause against the world. Once he had theatrically

entrapped his audience, he could move to attack the real object of his scorn, namely, his own folk.

While Amos may have begun his prophetic preaching with the judgment and condemnation of foreigners as an audience enlisting gimmick, this feature probably served a deeper and more significant rhetorical function.

(d) Finally and most likely, a number of issues were probably involved in Amos's rhetorical strategy in 1:2-2:16. First, the denunciations of the foreign nations were genuine statements of judgment with their own integrity. The crimes should be considered recent events known to the prophet and his audience. The atrocities condemned would have been sufficiently contrary to customary law that the prophet's references would have convinced his audience of the nations' guilt. Second, the declaration that Yahweh was to execute judgment against these guilty parties would have helped establish, if not the belief, at least the hope, that Yahweh would function as judge in matters of wrongdoing. In this case, since the nations were enemies of Israel, the audience would have been prone to accept the scenario of Yahweh as judge. Third, his strategy was then to move to the more controversial issue, namely, Yahweh's present condemnation and present and future judgment against Israel. If Amos had satisfactorily convinced his audience that known moral laws hold other nations accountable and infringements bring divine reprisal, then the same condition would pertain to Israel as well. If, in speaking on the other nations, Amos could convince his Israelite audience that Yahweh was in charge, had condemned their atrocities, and would bring punishment upon them, then he was in a better position to convince his hearers that Yahweh had also judged and would bring judgment on Israel.

As we shall see, Amos was a skillful and persuasive rhetorician, concerned with what classical rhetoricians would have called invention (the planning of a discourse and the arguments to be employed), arrangement (the composition of the parts into a convincing whole), and style (the use of words and figures as well as the construction of sentences).

A. The Introduction (1:2)

A. **Bertholet**, "Zu Amos 1, 2," *Theologische Festschrift für G. Nathanael Bonwetsch* (Leipzig: A. Deichert, 1918)1-12; K.

Budde, "Amos 1, 2," *ZAW* 30(1910)37-41; J. L. **Crenshaw**, "Amos and the Theophanic Tradition," *ZAW* 80(1968)203-15; H. **Gottlieb**, "Amos und Jerusalem," *VT* 17(1967)430-63; J. **Jeremias**, *Theophanie. Die Geschichte einer alttestamentlichen Gattung* (WMANT 10; Neukirchen-Vluyn: Neukirchener Verlag, 1965); C. van **Leeuwen**, "Amos 1:2, Epigraphe du livre entier ou introduction aux oracles des chapitres 1-2?," *Verkenningen in een Stromgebied. Proeven van oudtestamentisch Onderzoek. Festschrift M. A. Beek* (ed. M. Boertien; Amsterdam: Theologisch Institut van de Universiteit van Amsterdam, 1974)93-101; T. N. D. **Mettinger**, *The Dethronement of Sabaoth: Studies in the Shem and Kabod Theologies* (CBOTS 18; Lund: CWK Gleerup, 1982); S. **Wagner**, "Überlegungen zur Frage nach den Beziehungen des Propheten Amos zum Südreich," *TLZ* 96(1971)653-70; M. **Weiss**, "Methodologisches über die Behandlung der Metapher dargelegt an Amos 1,2," *TZ* 23(1967)1-25.

1:2   *Yahweh from Zion shall roar,*
          and from Jerusalem give forth his voice;
       and the oases of the shepherds shall dry up,
       and the height of the woodlands shall wither.

This opening verse contains a double couplet. The first two lines describe the action of Yahweh and the second two depict the consequences of that action. Whether the action of the two imperfect verbs in the first two lines and the two consecutive perfects in the second two lines should be understood and translated as present or future has been a matter of debate. The Aramaic Targum read the actions as future while Greek translators generally understood the actions as present or past. One could perhaps understand the text in emphactic conditional terms: "When Yahweh roars . . . , when he gives forth his voice . . . , then . . ." (*Mays, 20-21; *Soggin, 28). Modern translations tend to read a present sense (see RSV, NEB) or a combination of present and future:

         The Lord roars from Zion,
         Shouts aloud from Jerusalem;
         And the pastures of the shepherds shall languish,
         And the summit of Carmel shall wither (NJPSV).

A future reading of the verbs not only respects the grammatical form of the expressions but also best reflects the context since the subsequent descriptions in 1:3-2:16 depict future divine action, the events consequent upon divine judgment are still to come.

The first of the couplets speaks of the actions of Yahweh in metaphorical images. Yahweh will roar like a lion, and send forth his voice like thunder. The imagery and form of expression here bear only remote similarity to the descriptions of divine theophanies in the Hebrew Bible (see Jeremias; Crenshaw), such as Psalm 50, and need not be explained by appeal to theophanic texts (see Bentzen and *Wolff, 121-22). In texts employing theophanic imagery, God "comes" from some locale (see Deut. 33:2; Judg. 5:4-5; Ps. 50:3; 68:7; Mic. 1:3; Hab. 3:3) to intervene on behalf of or, less frequently, to judge the people. In this verse, Yahweh is simply located in Zion/Jerusalem from which the divine roar emanates; no theophany is mentioned.

The verb sh'g ("to roar") with God as subject only occurs elsewhere in Job 37:4; Jer. 25:30; Hos. 11:10; and Joel 3:16. In Job 37:4, the roaring is associated with storm phenomena, lightning and thunder. In Hos. 11:10, God roars as part of the rallying process for returning exiles to their homeland. Joel 3:16 (4:16 in Hebrew) and Amos 1:2 contain almost identical wording: "(And) Yahweh from Zion will roar, and from Jerusalem give forth his voice." This has led some to conclude that the verse was added to the book of Amos by a Judean redactor perhaps dependent on the Joel text (see *Wolff, 121). Similar terminology is found in Jer. 25:30: "Yahweh from on high will roar, and from his holy habitation will give forth his voice." The Jeremiah passage, however, apparently reflects deuteronomic/deuteronomistic theology which spoke of Yahweh dwelling in the heavens rather than in the Jerusalem temple (see Mettinger, 31).

The prophet designates Jerusalem as the place from which Yahweh roars. Stressing Yahweh's association with Jerusalem before a northern, Israelite audience, Amos might seem a poor rhetorician. Would his foreign accent and theological assumptions not have alienated his hearers? Although Amos's rhetoric does appear to have been risky, several factors should be noted. First, Amos was from Judah, where Jerusalem/Zion was the dominant and royal city, home to the Solomonic temple. His audience would hardly have expected him to allude to some place with which he had no ties. Second, Israel and Judah at the time were more like two parts of one state than two competing political powers. Third, Yahweh was, after all, the national deity. Although it was Yahweh of Jerusalem to whom Amos referred, it was nonetheless Yahweh (see 1 Sam. 1:3 and 2 Sam. 15:7 which speak of "Yahweh Sebaoth in Shiloh" and "Yahweh in Hebron"). Fourth, the fact that Amos moved quickly to condemn non-Israelite nations could have tempered any immediate hostile reaction he may have produced.

The second couplet in v. 2*b* describes the effect of Yahweh's roar. Although the general tenor of the parallel statements is clear (namely, Yahweh's roaring will have widespread repercussions), the specifics are somewhat uncertain. In Hebrew, the couplet is structured on an AB - AB (verb-subject verb-subject) pattern.

The two verbs were apparently to be heard as synonymous and the subjects as contrasting. The first verb *'bl* is normally used in biblical texts to speak about mourning or actions associated with mourning (see *TDOT* I 44-48). It occasionally occurs, however, as parallel to *ybsh*, as in this verse (see Jer. 12:4; 23:10). The verb *ybsh* clearly means "to wither, dry up." (An Akkadian verb *abalu* also meant "dry up.") The use of *'bl* in certain contexts with reference to the land and soil (Isa. 24:4; 33:9; Hos. 4:3; Joel 1:10) or other items (Jer. 14:2; Isa. 3:26; 24:7) indicates that the verbal idea of mourning could be applied metaphorically to speak of a condition of abnormality with regard to nature and natural products. To refer to such an abnormal condition as mourning with regard to the plant world would thus have indicated the idea of withering or drying up.

The two subjects in the couplet are "the *ne'oth* of the shepherds" and "the height of the woodlands." The Targum interpreted these references as "the residences of the kings shall be desolate and their fortified cities shall be destroyed." Greek translators took *ne'oth* to mean "pastures" and this has been followed in most modern translations. Such a reading assumes that the term is based on the root *nwh* which occurs rather frequently in the Old Testament and parallels the Akkadian term *nawun* meaning "pasturage, encampments." In addition, it assumes that aleph and waw were interchangeable in the stem. The number of occurrences in the Old Testament where *ne'oth* appears spelled with the aleph could suggest that the root of the term was *n'h* rather that *nwh* (see Pss. 23:2; 65:13; 74:20; 83:12; Jer. 9:10; 23:10; 25:37; Lam. 2:2; Joel 1:19, 20; 2:22). *n'h* or *n'wh* has the general meaning of being lovely, well suited, or seemly. In its biblical usage, the plural form *ne'oth* is conditioned in several places by the addition of "(the) wilderness" (Jer. 9:10; 23:10; Joel 1:19, 20; 2:22). The term is used in contrast or parallel with "mountains/hills" (Jer. 9:10; Ps. 65:13), "the land" (Jer. 23:10), "trees" (Joel 1:19; 2:22), "strongholds" (Lam. 2:2), "dark places of the land" (Ps. 74:20), "brooks of water" (Joel 1:20), "still waters" (Ps. 23:2), and "pasture" (Jer. 25:37). Perhaps the expression referred not to pastures in general but to the comely places of the terrain, the gathering places for animals, the lowland where shade and water were found. Thus, the translation "oases" seems more appropriate than "pastures."

The "oases" stand as a polar opposite to the "height of the woodlands" (*r'sh hkrml* literally, "the head of the Carmel"). Carmel is to be understood not as denoting the Mt. Carmel range but rather in its more general meaning of forest, fruitful upperland, or horticultural terrain. This usage is fairly common in biblical texts (see, for example, Isa. 10:18; 16:10; 2 Kings 19:23). In Amos 9:3, *r'sh hkrml* contrasts with the depth of the sea. Amos is thus naming two topographically contrasting points: the depressed area around water holes and the fruitful upland orchard land to express a sense of totality.

Amos's depiction of Yahweh roaring like a lion from Zion and everything low and high wilting before the sound, was probably intended to produce an emotional effect on the audience as well as to state a thesis to be explicated in the examples that follow. Yahweh will roar and everything in the region will quail before the awesome reverberation. Attempts to discern a veiled meaning, such as a reference to the royal fortifications (so the Targum), to the nations ("the shepherds") and the Israelite king ("the head of Carmel"; so *Kapelrud, 19), to a coming drought or earthquake (see Weiss), or to a theological point such as "everything comes only by hearing; nothing is seen" (*Soggin, 30), are gratuitous.

The integral relationship between 1:2 and 1:3-2:16 and the verse's introductory role are demonstrated by two factors. First, in 1:2 the prophet sets the stage, creates the emotion, and introduces the deity and the divine action which will be explicated in first-person address in the verses that follow. Second, the "it" which Yahweh will not recall in 1:3-2:16 is his "voice" which will blast forth from Zion with withering force. That 1:2 envisions Yahweh roaring over the entire area constitutes a further basis for seeing all the subsequent sections as integral to Amos's preaching. Since Yahweh's roar affects the entire region, no major power could fail to be mentioned.

B. Against Damascus (1:3-5)

A. **Alt**, "Hosea 5, 8 - 6,6. Ein Krieg und seine Folgen in prophetischer Beleuchtung," *NKZ* 30(1919)537-68 = his *Kleine Schriften zur Geschichte des Volkes Israels* (Munich: C. H. Beck, 1953)2. 163-87; P. M. **Arnold**, *Gibeah in Israel's History and Tradition* (dissertation, Emory University, 1986); M. L. **Barré**, "The Meaning of *l' 'shybnw* in Amos 1:3-2:6," *JBL* 105(1986)611-31; J. **Begrich**, "Der syrisch-emphraimitische Krieg und seine weltpolitischen Zusammenhänge," *ZDMG* 83(1929)213-37 = his *Gesammelte Studien zum Alten Testament* (TB 21; Munich: Chr. Kaiser, 1964)99-120; M. **Cogan**, "Tyre and Tiglath-pileser III: Chronological Notes," *JCS* 25(1973)96-99; H. J. **Cook**, "Pekah," *VT* 14(1964)121-35; J. A. **Fitzmyer**, *The Aramaic Inscriptions of Sefîre* (BibOr 19; Rome: Pontifical Biblical Institute, 1967); S. **Gevirtz**, *Patterns in the Early Poetry of Israel* (Chicago: University of Chicago Press, 1963)15-30; C. R. **Gordis**, "Some Hitherto Unrecognized Meanings of the Verb *shub*," *JBL* 52(1933)153-62 = his *The Word and the Book: Studies in Biblical Language and Literature* (New York: Ktav Publishing Company, 1976)218-27; H. **Gordon**, "The Authenticity of the Phoenician Text from Parahyba," *Orientalia* 37(1968)75-80; N. K. **Gottwald**, *The Tribes of Yahweh: A Sociology of the Religion of Liberated Israel, 1250-1050 B.C.E.* (Maryknoll: Orbis Books, 1979)512-34; J. T. **Greene**, *The Old Testament Prophet as Messenger in the Light of Ancient Near Eastern Messengers and Messages* (dissertation, Boston University, 1980); H. G. **Grether**, "Some Problems of Equivalence in Amos 1:3," *BT* 22(1971)116-17; H. **Gunkel**, "IIB. The Israelite Prophecy from the Time of Amos," *Twentieth Century Theology in the Making; Volume I: Themes of Biblical Theology* (ed. J. Pelikan; London/New York: William Collins

Sons/Harper & Row, 1969)48-75; T. R. **Hobbs**, *2 Kings* (WBC 13; Waco: Word Books, 1985); P. **Höffken**, "Eine Bemerkung zum 'Haus Hasaels' in Amos 1, 4," *ZAW* 94(1982)413-15; H. **Hogg**, "The Starting-Point of the Religious Message of Amos," *Transactions of the 3rd International Congress for the History of Religions* (ed. P. S. Allen; Oxford: Clarendon Press, 1908) 1.325-27; W. L. **Holladay**, *The Root shubh in the Old Testament, with Particular Reference to Its Usages in Covenantal Contexts* (Leiden: E. J. Brill, 1958); E. A. **Knauf**, "Beth Aven," *Bib* 65(1984)251-53; R. P. **Knierim**, "'I will not cause it to return' in Amos 1 and 2," *Canon and Authority: Essays in Old Testament Religion and Theology* (ed. G. W. Coats and B. O. Long; Philadelphia: Fortress Press, 1977)163-75; A. **Lemaire** and J.-M. **Durand**, *Les Inscriptions Araméennes de Sfiré et l'Assyrie de Shamshi-ilu* (Genéve/Paris: Droz, 1984); L. D. **Levine**, "Menahem and Tiglath-Pileser: A New Synchronism," *BASOR* 206(1972)40-42; A. **Malamat**, "Amos 1:5 in the Light of the Til Barsip Inscriptions," *BASOR* 129(1953)25-26; J. **Morgenstern**, "Amos Studies. Part Four. The Address of Amos - Text and Commentary," *HUCA* 32(1961)295-350; N. **Na'aman**, "Looking for *KTK*," *WO* 9(1978)220-39; **Na'aman**, "Beth-aven, Bethel and Early Israelite Sanctuaries," *ZDPV* 103(1987)12-21; M. **Noth**, "Der historische Hintergrund der Inschriften von sefire," *ZDPV* 77(1961)118-72 = his *Aufsätze zur biblischen Landes- und Altertumskunde* (Neukirchen-Vluyn: Neurkirchener Verlag, 1971)1.161-210; W. T. **Pitard**, *Ancient Damascus* (Winona Lake: Eisenbrauns, 1987); J. F. A. **Sawyer**, "The Meaning of *barzel* in the Biblical Expression 'Chariots of Iron', 'Yoke of Iron', etc.," *Midian, Moab and Edom* (ed. J. F. A. Sawyer and D. J. A. Clines; JSOTSS 24; Sheffield: JSOT Press, 1983)129-34; G. **Schmitt**, "Bet-Awen," *Drei Studien zur Archäologie und Topographie Altisraels* (ed. R. Cohen and G. Schmitt; BTAVO B44; Wiesbaden: Dr. Ludwig Reichert, 1980)33-76; K. N. **Schoville**, "The Sins of Aram in Amos 1," *PWCJS* 6(1977)1.363-75;W. **Smalley**, "Translating 'Thus Says the Lord,'" *BT* 29(1978)222-24; B. K. **Soper**, "For Three Transgressions and for Four: A New Interpretation of Amos i. 3, etc.," *ET* 71(1959-60)86-87; M. **Stiles**, *The Historical Background of the Times of Isaiah the Prophet* (*Shophar* 15; Aptos, CA: Self-published, 1979); F. **Thureau-Dangin** et al., *Til Barsib* (BAH 23; Paris: Geuthner 1936); W. G. E. **Watson**, "David Ousts the City Rulers of Jebus," *VT* 20(1970)501-2; C. **Westermann**, *Basic*

Forms of Prophetic Speech (Philadelphia/London: Westminster Press/Lutterworth Press, 1967).

1:3   *Thus Yahweh has said:*
            "For three transgressions of Damascus,
                and for four, I will not recall it;
            because of their threshing of Gilead
                with iron threshing sledges.
4   *And I will send fire on the house of Hazael,*
                and it will consume the fortresses of Ben-hadad;
5   *and I will break the gate bar of Damascus,*
            and I will cut off the one ruling from the Valley of Aven,
                and the one wielding the scepter from Beth-eden;
                and the people of Aram shall be exiled to Kir,"
                                                    said Yahweh.

[3] Amos begins his speech on the nations with a declarative statement about Yahweh's future action which will affect every kingdom throughout the region (1:2). In this opening statement, the prophet speaks of the deity in a descriptive, third-person form. Beginning with v. 3, the prophet shifts to first-person address, speaking as if he were the Deity. The shift in address form follows the expression *koh 'amar YHWH* which consists of the adverb *koh* ("thus"), the verb *'amar* in third-person singular perfect form ("he said" or "he has said"), and the Hebrew personal name for God (*YHWH*).

Similar terminology is employed in Old Testament narratives (see, for example, Gen. 32:3-5; Judg. 11:14-15; 2 Kings 18:19-25; 19:1-7) where diplomatic negotiations are conducted through oral communication delivered by commissioned messengers. This similarity has led scholars to compare prophecy and prophetic preaching with aspects of official and international diplomacy (see Gunkel, 67-68). God could be seen as the sender of a message, the prophet as the ambassadorial messenger, and the words of the prophet as the diplomatic message. What began as a heuristic analogy soon became accepted, however, as established reality (see Westermann; compare Greene). Interpreters viewed the prophet as a passive recipient of divine revelation, an intermediary serving as a channel of communication between the human and divine worlds. References to the deity's having spoken were taken as formulas introducing and/or concluding direct words of God.

Expressions such as "thus Yahweh has said" were therefore understood as messenger formulas indicating that the "quotations" which followed were to be understood in light of the sender - messenger - message paradigm. When the speech was one of condemnation and coming destruction, it was assumed that the message was no more than an announcement, neither requiring nor seeking reaction from the audience.

It is probably best to understand expressions like "thus Yahweh has said" in rhetorical and metaphorical rather than realistic fashion. In so far as the prophet and his preaching were concerned, such references functioned to claim authority for the speaker and the message. "Thus has Yahweh spoken" is a way of saying both "I, as prophet, believe this is what Yahweh declares" and "if Yahweh spoke directly on the issue at hand, this is what Yahweh would say." Prophetic speech thus takes the form of assertive, authoritative address rather than rationalistic argumentation. Expressions like *koh 'amar YHWH* are better designated "attribution" than "messenger" formulas. These were employed to claim authoritative status for both the prophet and the proclamation. In so far as the audience was concerned, casting the speech material in the form of divine address confronted the hearers directly and powerfully, embodying a demand for emotional response and reaction. Ascription of the words to the Deity demanded that they be taken seriously, like the assertions of today's orators: "the Bible says"; "the church teaches"; "theology affirms."

What "for three transgressions and for four" signified to Amos's audience remains uncertain. Graduated numerical sayings (x, x + 1) are common in the Hebrew scriptures (see, for examples, Prov. 6:16-19; 30:15-16, 18-19, 21-31) and are also found in non-biblical literature (see Roth). The numbers most frequently employed in sequential enumeration are one and two (see Ps. 62:11; Job 33:14-15), two and three (see Hos. 6:2; Sirach 26:28), three and four (see Prov. 30:15-33; Sirach 26:5-6), six and seven (see Job 5:19), and seven and eight (see Mic. 5:5; Eccles. 11:2). Frequently, the elements in the numerical schemes are listed, with the last representing the climax of the series. Amos 1:3-2:5, however, repeatedly uses a stylized formula ("for three and for four") but generally specifics only one component. Therein lies an interpretive problem.

Various proposals for understanding the prophet's point have been made. A number of these are worth noting. (1) "For three and for four" is regarded as a way of referring to "the innumerable crimes" committed by the nations condemned (*Soggin). In such an interpretation, the emphasis is understood to fall on the quantity of wrongdoing. (2) The paraphrastic translation "again and again" (GNB) stresses the persistence of the wrongdoers. (3) "Three" and "four" may be seen as a way of alluding to the number seven, signifying completion or fullness (Weiss, 1967, 419; so already, Luther and Calvin). (4) Ancient rabbinic interpreters concluded that three transgressions might be forgiven but not the fourth (b. Yoma 86b; Sanh. 7a) (5) Probably the numerical reference with its staircase gradation (3 and 4) was a way of saying that a limit had been passed. Three was enough but four was beyond what could be endured; four was the last straw (see Barré, 621-22).

Whether Amos and his audience were aware of four crimes committed by the peoples condemned or whether the last was considered climactic remains unknown. The numerical expression was probably intended to function formulaically rather than realistically in any case.

The identity of the "it" in the expression 'ashibennu (a first-person hiphil imperfect of shub plus third masculine singular suffix) has engendered a number of interpretations. The following represent a sample: I will not "forgive them" (Targum), "let the deported population return" (Rashi, Ibn Ezra, Kimchi), "make the Assyrian return from attacking them" (Hogg), "revoke the punishment" (RSV), "grant them reprieve" (NEB), "revoke it (the decree of punishment)" (NJPSV), "revoke it (the anger of Yahweh)" (*Harper, 16; Knierim; *Coote, 115), "revoke the Day of Yahweh" (*Maag, 245-47), "revoke my word" (NAB), "let him [the nation involved] return (to me)" or " take him back" (Morgenstern, 314; Barré, 622), "let the matter rest" (*Gordis, 202), and "I have made my decree and will not relent" (JB; for other suggestions, see *Wolff, 128; Barton, 18). Commentators' interpretation of the expression involves not only the translation of the verb shub and the question of the antecedent of the pronominal suffix "it" but also the relationship of verses 2 and 3. If verse 2 is viewed as part of the superscription, as a late insertion, or as a motto for the entire book, and thus detached from what follows, then the suffix "has no antecedent, and hangs suspended in mysterious and threatening ambiguity" (*Mays, 24). If verse 2 comprises the introduction to 1:2-2:16, as was argued above, then the "it" refers to "the voice of Yahweh" which will sound forth from Zion/Jerusalem. Any listener having heard verses 2-3 spoken in succession by the prophet would naturally and logically have connected the unspecified "it" in verse 3 with the divine voice referred to in verse 2. A normal understanding of the hiphil of *shub* included such meanings as "recall" and the noun *qol* ("voice") is masculine singular.

The term used for the wrongdoing in the stereotypical expression "for three . . . and for four" is *pesha'*. Elsewhere the verbal form of the term is employed to describe political actions: "Israel rebelled against the house of David" (1 Kings 12:19); "Moab rebelled against Israel" (2 Kings 1:1); "the king of Moab rebelled against the king of Israel" (2 Kings 3:5). The noun is also used in contexts where it parallels the terms for "sin" and "iniquity," and denotes wrong or offensive actions of humans against one another (Gen. 31:36; 50:17; 1 Sam. 25:28) or humans against God (1 Kings 8:50; Isa. 1:2).

Amos does not stipulate the object of the offenses committed in 1:3-2:16; he only notes the subject and then provides examples of the offenses. Earlier we argued that the nations were considered guilty because of their transgression of or offense against international customary law. Yahweh was assumed to be the guardian of international customary law just as he was the guardian of Israelite customary law.

The wrongdoings of Damascus is specified in verse 3b. The construction *'al* plus infinitive construct plus third-person plural pronominal suffix could be translated as, "because they have threshed" or "because of their threshing." The "threshing of Gilead with iron threshing sledges" appears to refer to brutal and cruel treatment of the region during or following military activity. The Targum of this half verse reads "the inhabitants of the land of Gilead" and the Greek translations read "the pregnant women of Gilead" (which appears in the Qumran fragment 5QAm 1 [*hrwt hgl'd*], partially restored; see DJD III 173) as the object of the threshing. One of these expanded readings may have originally been part of the text since verse 3b is somewhat shorter than verse 3a; however, they may simply be expansive translations, perhaps influenced by verse 13b.

The term *dwsh* "to thresh" refers to the process of separating grain and seeds from the stalks. When not done by hand, this was usually performed by moving animal-drawn carts (see Deut. 25:4) or flat-bottommed sledges over the heaped-up grain. To increase the efficiency of the sledge, metal studs could be driven through the floor, with the portruding points aiding in dislodging the heads of grain. Whether Amos is speaking realistically or metaphorically about the threshing is uncertain although the latter seems more likely (see 2 Kings 13:7). Although the the Old Testament speaks of post-battle atrocities (see Judg. 8:7, 16; 11:2), these are always realistic depictions whereas threshing captives or bodies with sledges hardly seems a task one could perform. The imagery of threshing one's opponents (still sometimes employed in modern speech) occurs in a statement of the Assyrian king, Tiglath-pileser I (1114-1076), who claimed: "the land Bit-Amukkani I threshed as with a threshing instrument; all its people and its possessions I brought to Assyria" (Barton, 19). In his vassal treaty, the Assyrian Esarhaddon implores: "May Shamash plow up your cities and districts with an iron plow" (*ANET* 539[68]), which employs a similar metaphor but implies an equally impractical ordeal.

The land of Gilead which was "threshed" lay east of the Jordan. In its broadest limits, the name denoted the territory between the Arnon Gorge in the south and the Yarmuk River in the north. Through this region passed a caravan route between Damascus and the Red Sea, providing access to Arabian and African trade. Gilead was also an important source of iron ore (see Josephus, *War* IV 454; *Mishnah Succoth* 3:1). Claimed by the Israelites, this region was almost constantly a source of contention between Israel and its neighbors (Syria, Moab, and Ammon). Israel was in control of part or all of this territory only intermittently, primarily during the reigns of Saul, David, and Solomon (1 Sam. 11; 2 Sam. 2:8-9; 8; 24:1-7), the time of Omri and Ahab (1 Kings 1:17; 3:4-5), and part of the rule of Jehoash and Jeroboam II (2 Kings 13:14-19, 24-25; 1 Chron. 5:11-22). As we noted above (see Chapter 1, section 6), the latter years of Jeroboam II witnessed the beginning of Israel's loss of all Transjordanian territory. The condemnation in verse 3*b* of Damascus's brutality in warfare refers to Rezin's move to reestablish Syrian control over northern Transjordan, exercised by his predecessors, Ben-hadad I, Hazael, and Ben-hadad II (1 Kings 15:16-20; 2 Kings 10:32-33; 13:3, 24-25). Amos's reference to "iron" may have served to heighten the horror of the audience since "iron" seems to have had frightening associations in the biblical tradition (see Sawyer).

[4] In this and the following verse, Amos depicts the coming judgment for the mistreatment of Gilead. The judgment is presented, as throughout 1:3-2:5, in terms of destruction by fire (see 2 Kings 8:12). Many Assyrian royal inscriptions conclude with a list describing the destruction of enemies and their cities including "burning." In reporting his defeat of the king of Hamath, Shalmaneser III states: "I threw fire into his palaces" (*ARAB* I § 610; *ANET* 278). In the symbolic rituals accompanying the conclusion of the treaty between *KTK* and Arpad, the destruction of the king of Arpad and his city was enacted to warn against infidelity: "as this wax is consumed by fire so may Arpad and Matti'el be consumed by fire" (*ANET* 660). Given the historical situation noted in chapter one, Amos's audience must have sensed that Yahweh's sending of fire would find embodiment in an Assyrian attack.

The objects of Yahweh's fiery attacks are to be "the house of Hazael" and "the fortresses of Ben-hadad." Whether the "house" here denotes the territory of Damascus (so Höffken), the reigning house, the political alliance headed by Rezin, the Damascus king, or merely the royal palace in Damascus, remains uncertain. The ambiguity of the expression may have allowed the audience to understand the referent in various ways. The exact meaning of the term translated above as "fortresses" is also uncertain. Ancient Greek translations, for example, read "foundation walls," "large houses," "towers," and "courts." The term appears to have been used of constructions distinct from both the city wall fortifications and the royal palace per se. It appears to have been used of highly defendable structures, like fortified towers, something like a "keep," the central citadel of a medieval town.

Hazael and Ben-hadad were Syrian kings who had ruled in Damascus in the latter half of the ninth and the first part of the eighth century (see above, Chapter One, section two). The reigning king in Damascus, contemporary with Amos, was Rezin, who may or may not have been a direct descendant of Hazael and his son Ben-hadad II. An inscription of Tiglath-pileser III refers to Hadara rather than Damascus as the birthplace of Rezin (*ARAB* I § 777; *ANET* 283), which could imply that he was a usurper. A usurper, however, could be linked by outsiders with the previous ruling family. Assyrian texts, for example, associate the Israelite usurper Jehu with the preceding family of Omri (*ARAB* I § 590; *ANET* 281).

[5] Since antiquity, it has been uncertain whether "Valley of Aven" and "Beth-eden" are merely paraphrastic expressions for Damascus, or refer to other places. Some Greek manuscripts read On for Aven which interpreters identify with Heliopolis in Egypt (see Gen. 41:45, 50; 46:20) or Baalbek in Syria, and Beth-eden was understood as a reference to the city of Harran. Other ancient translations interpreted the expressions with such readings as "valley of those good for nothing" or "valley of iniquity" and "house of indulging." More recent and modern interpreters offer such translations as "Sin Valley" and "House of Pleasure" (so *Wolff, 129; JB). A straightforward reading of the text would seem to indicate that other actual places and rulers, in addition to Damascus and its king, are being spoken about.

Three apparently allied rulers are referred to in verses 4-5. The first, the ruler of Damascus, is not assigned any epithet. The prophet's frame of reference here was the old established city state with its long history culminating in the reigns of Hazael and Ben-hadad. The second is "the one ruling (*yosheb*) in the Valley of Aven." The participle *yosheb* literally means "the one sitting" but is frequently used in the Bible to designate a ruler, the one sitting in authority (see Watson and Gottwald). The third is "the one wielding the scepter in Beth-eden."

Who were these second and third rulers in addition to Rezin of Damascus and over what territory did they claim hegemony? The thesis proposed here is that these two rulers were Pekah, the Israelite rival to King Jeroboam II, and Shamshi-ilu, the powerful Assyrian *turtanu* who dominated Assyrian activity in the west for over fifty years, and that Rezin, Pekah, and Shamshi-ilu were allied as part of an anti-Assyrian front in the west. At this point, it is necessary to augment what was said in chapter one concerning the historical and political circumstances alluded to in verses 3-5.

Rezin is referred to in several biblical passages (2 Kings 15:37; 16:5-9; Isa. 7:1, 8). He is always designated as "king of Aram (Syria)" in the biblical texts and never the "king of Damascus" although it is clear that Damascus was Rezin's capital city. According to 2 Kings 15:37, Rezin and Pekah were jointly harassing Judah before the death of Jotham (759-744). No geographical area is mentioned as the object of this harassment. According to 1 Chron. 5:11-17, Jotham and Jeroboam II

at one time jointly governed part of Transjordan and it may
have been this area of Judean territory that Pekah and Rezin
attacked. Second Kings 16:6 notes that Rezin "restored" the
seaport of Elath to Aramean control although the context
would indicate that this takeover of Elath occurred at the time
of Pekah and Rezin's siege of Jerusalem (in late 734 or early
733). This seems unlikely since the siege was apparently lifted
when Tiglath-pileser III arrived in Syria-Palestine in late 734 or
early 733. Rezin spent the next three years fighting the
Assyrians with no time for any conquest of southern Transjordan. Thus the events of 2 Kings 15:37 and 16:6 were part of
Syria's conquest and harassment of Judah, already begun
before the death of Jotham.

Several inscriptions of Tiglath-pileser mention Rezin.
He appears in two versions of Tiglath-pileser's annals which
enumerate western leaders who presented tribute gifts to the
Assyrian monarch, most likely in 738 (*ANET* 283; *ARAB* I §
772). Tiglath-pileser's Iran Stela (see Levine) also notes Rezin's
presentation of tribute, probably sometime between 743 and
740 when Tiglath-pileser carried out his first western war (see
Cogan). That Rezin offered tribute gifts does not mean that he
was pro-Assyrian or uninvolved in anti-Assyrian activity but
only that he believed it expedient at that time not to oppose and
antagonize Tiglath-pileser.

Several fragmentary Assyrian texts describe Tiglath-
pileser's campaigns to the west in 734-733, 733-732, 732-731
against a major anti-Assyrian coalition headed by Syria,
Philistia, and Phoenicia. Rezin was clearly the chief architect of
this western opposition and its strongest member. Tiglath-
pileser reports that he eventually captured 592 towns in the sixteen districts directly ruled by Rezin (*ANET* 283; *ARAB* I §
777).

Like the biblical texts, Assyrian documents do not refer
to Rezin as king of Damascus. In Assyrian texts, he rules over
"the land of the ass" (*mat imerishu* or *mat sha-imerishu*)
presumably a term, like Aram, denoting a much larger territory
than the city-state of Damascus.

If Amos carried out his preaching mission in 750-749
and alluded to Rezin in verses 3-5, Rezin must have assumed
the throne before that time. Unfortunately, we do not know
when Rezin became king. Hadianu was reigning in Damascus
in 773-772 so Rezin has to have become king after that date. If

he was harrassing Judah during the reign of Jotham (759-744). Pekah, who was apparently placed in power by Rezin and killed in 731-730, reigned for twenty years (2 Kings 15:27) which means that 750-749 was his first full regnal year. While such evidence does not establish a specific date, it suggests that Rezin was king in Damascus in the 750s. No known evidence would rule out such a conclusion nor the possibility that he became king any time after 773-772.

In speaking of the "one ruling in the Valley of Aven," Amos was referring to Pekah, the son of Remaliah, who at the time was a rival claimant to the throne. The term Aven in 1:5*b* is not to be taken as either a play on the name Beth-el (as perhaps appears to be the case in Hos. 5:15 and 10:5) or as a pun employing the term "iniquity" or "evil." References to Aven in place names occur in Josh. 7:2; 18:12; 1 Sam. 13:5; 14:23; Hos. 4:15; 5:8. In Josh. 7:2, Joshua is said to have sent men "from Jericho to Ai which is near Beth-aven, east of Bethel." The northern boundary of Benjamin is described in Josh. 18:12 as extending from the Jordan River up through the hill country to the wilderness of Beth-aven. In the account of Saul's battle with the Philistines, Beth-aven is spoken of as lying west of Michmash (1 Sam. 13:5; see 14:23). In Hos. 5:8, Beth-aven is placed in the vicinity of Gibeah (probably modern *jeba'*), and Ramah (modern *er-ram*). All of these texts locate Aven and Beth-aven in the upper reaches of the Wadi es-Suweinit. This wadi forms, along with Wadi el-Qelt, the valley running up into the central hill country from the region of Jericho. Along with Wadi Farah which cuts into the hill country in the vicinity of Tirzah and just north of Shechem, this valley was one of the main avenues of entry into the central hill country from the Jordan Valley. In all probability, the Valley of Aven was the Suweinit-Qelt valley. (Other texts apparently refer to this area as the Valley of Achor; see Josh. 7:24, 26; 15:7; Hos. 2:15.)

A number of texts suggest an association of Pekah with Gilead in the Transjordan. According to 2 Kings 15:25, Pekah finally gained the throne in Samaria when he assassinated Pekahiah with the aid of fifty Gileadites. Pekah's close association with and subordination to Rezin (2 Kings 15:37; 16:5; Isa. 7:1) are best understood if Pekah was in control, under Syrian supervision, of some parts of Gilead. Hos. 6:7-10, like other texts in Hosea, probably refers to Pekah and his rival rule and does so by speaking of the "evil" of Gilead.

Pekah, with Rezin's help, led a portion of Israel, most likely initially in Gilead, to break away from Jeroboam II in 751-750. By the time Amos appeared on the scene a short time later, Pekah had gained control of some territory west of the Jordan. Perhaps the southern Jordan Valley including Gilgal (see on 4:4; 5:5) and other portions of the west bank had fallen into his hands and Pekah had begun extending his control into the hill country, westward into the Valley of Aven.

Hosea 5:8 contains a warning alarm which mentions the cities of Gibeah, Ramah, and Beth-aven and the tribe of Benjamin. In the verses that follow, both Judah and Ephraim are alternately condemned. Scholars who see this section as reflecting an actual historical situation relate it to the period of the struggle between Jerusalem and Syria-Ephraim, in the time of the so-called Syro-Ephraimitic War (734-733). One view which has received widespread acceptance argues that the text concerns a Judean counteroffensive against Ephraim and that references to Ephraim in the condemnations are later additions (Alt). An alternative view sees the text as a warning to Judah at the beginning of the Syro-Ephraimitic attack and the denunciations of Judah as secondary redactional changes (Arnold, 241-49). The text, however, is best understood as it stands and as a warning to both Ephraim and Judah of encroachment from the east, namely by Pekah and his supporters (but obviously from a time later than Amos; see Isa. 8:21-22). The towns of Gibeah (modern *jeba'*), Ramah (modern *er-ram*), and Beth-aven (unknown) lay, as we have seen, in the vicinity of the upper reaches of Wadi es-Suweinit (the Valley of Aven?).

Pekah's support among both Ephraimites and Judeans would appear to have been widespread and loyal. This is indicated by the fact that he was able to persevere as a rival claimant to the throne of Samaria for sixteen years before finally seizing power in the capital city. He was supported even in Judean circles in his campaign against Jerusalem (see Isa. 8:6), and he apparently had strong support when he led Israel in the anti-Assyrian wars of 734-732.

The most likely candidate for the third figure mentioned in 1:5, the one "wielding the scepter" or "bearing the staff" in Beth-eden, is Shamshi-ilu. This powerful leader served as *turtanu* under four Assyrian monarchs - Adad-nirari III (810-783), Shalmaneser IV (782-773), Ashur-dan III (772-755), and Ashur-nirari V (754-745). Previously known texts, and recently discovered but not yet fully published inscriptions from Antakya and Pazarcik in Turkey, indicate something of his power and role in the west. He negotiated boundary disputes between Arpad and Hamath and between Kummukh and Gurgun, led Assyrian campaigns against King Argishti of Urartu (786-764) between 781-774, conducted a campaign against Damascus in 773, fought against the land of Mushku (Phrygia) in Asia Minor, and was probably responsible for the campaigns against northern Syria in 772, 765, and 755. The eponym lists note that he was still serving as *turtanu* in 752.

Beth-eden is to be identified with Bit-Adini, a region which lay just east of the bend of the Euphrates. Shalmaneser III had conquered this region, defeated its ruler Ahuni, and transformed it into an Assyrian province in 856, renaming its main city (Til-Barsib) Kar-Shalmaneser. Shamshi-ilu's domain centered around what he called "Kar-Shalmaneser the city of my lordship." With the passage of time, Shamshi-ilu assumed more and more independence, eventually referring to himself as "governor of the land of Hatti" (northern Syria). Recently, Lemaire and Durand proposed that Shamshi-ilu is to be identified with Barga'yah, king of *KTK*, who imposed a vassal treaty on Matti'el king of Arpad in the Sefire inscriptions (*ANET* 659-61). If such an identification is correct, then it further indicates the importance of Shamshi-ilu and the Aramean coalition he forged. He set up royal-type inscriptions without any reference to the reigning Assyrian monarch. Some of his inscriptions show signs of later deliberate defacement, indicating that he ended his life out of favor with the Assyrian king (Thureau-Dangin, 142). The only monarch capable of such treatment of him was Tiglath-pileser (744-727) who came west for the first time in 743. If he was still alive after a career of over five decades, Shamshi-ilu was probably toppled from power at that time.

The historical situation reflected in this Damascus section can be reconstructed as follows. With Assyrian power under Ashur-nirari V almost nonexistent in the west, Shamshi-ilu assumed the role of ruling power in northern Syria-Palestine. Rezin in Damascus joined forces with Shamshi-ilu. In fact, Rezin may have seized power and usurped the throne with Shamshi-ilu's support and encouragement. Rezin, like Hazael before him, moved quickly to dominate all of southern Syria-Palestine. Pekah, with pro-Syrian sentiments, Syrian support, and the backing of segments of the Israelite and Judean population, became a rival to Jeroboam intent on gaining the throne in Samaria and casting Israel's lot with the anti-Assyrian coalition in the region. After Rezin's extension of his power to the Gulf of Aqaba and his seizure of the port of Elath (2 Kings 16:6), perhaps with the tacit support of Ammon, Moab, and Edom, the Beth-eden and Damascus axis controlled the territory east of the anti-Lebanon range and the length of Transjordan.

In verse 5 Amos has Yahweh proclaim a fourfold act of judgment: breaking the bar of Damascus, toppling the rulers of both the Valley of Aven and Beth-eden, and exiling the people of Aram. Since verse 4 has already spoken of the execution of judgment against the reigning dynasty and city of Damascus, one wonders if more is implied in the breaking of the bar of Damascus than merely a forthcoming attack on the city. Although "bar" (*bariah*) would normally be taken as simply a reference to the metal or wooden horizontal transom securing a gate or frame (see 1 Kings 4:13; Exod. 26:26-29), the prophet may have used the term metaphorically in this context to denote the political bond or league forged by Damascus (the Targum reads "the power of Damascus"). In Phoenician-Punic, the root *brh* seems to be used occasionally in the sense of "to control, rule over" (see Gordon and *TWOT* 2. 249-53) and this may be the case here. The two rulers, Pekah and Shamshi-ilu, will simply be "cut off," that is, removed from power since both were claimants to artificial kingdoms, ruling over personally created realms.

Finally, Amos declares that the "people of Aram" will be exiled to Kir. In all probability, Aram here refers to a larger political entity than the kingdom of Rezin. Assyrian texts never use the term Aram to refer to the kingdom of Damascus but rather employ it with reference to northern Syria (see Pitard, 12-13). The Aramaic treaty texts from Sefire speak of "all Aram" as well as "upper and lower Aram" (see Fitzmyer; *ANET* 659-61), and the so-called Bar-Hadad stela seems to refer to an Aram in northern Syria (see Pitard, 138-44). The "people of Aram" in verse 5 thus should be seen as an inclusive term referring to the people of the region extending from the Euphrates to the northern Transjordan. The location of Kir is unknown although the area is mentioned three times in the Old Testament (Isa. 22:6; Amos 1:5; 9:7; in 2 Kings 16:9 the reading is problematic and probably a gloss made on the basis of Amos 1:5).

Although Amos does not specify whom he envisions as the instrument of Yahweh's judgment, the audience must surely have associated the announced actions with Assyria. Shamshi-ilu was in reality an Assyrian official but was now playing the role of an independent monarch; Pekah was a rival claimant to the throne of the pro-Assyrian Jeroboam II; and Rezin, as history would show, was anti-Assyrian to the core.

C. Against Gaza (1:6-8)

T. **Dothan**, *The Philistines and Their Material Culture* (New Haven/London: Yale University Press, 1982); D. E. **Gowan**, "The Beginnings of Exile-Theology and the Root *glh*," *ZAW* 87(1975)204-7; M. **Haran**, "Observations on the Historical Background of Amos 1:2 - 2:6," *IEJ* 18(1968)201-12; P. **Haupt**, "Heb. *Galut Sholema*, A Peaceful Colony," *JBL* 35(1916)288-92; E. **Hindson**, *The Philistines and the Old Testament* (Grand Rapids: Baker Book House, 1971); K. A. **Kitchen**, "The Philistines," *Peoples of Old Testament Times* (ed. D. J. Wiseman; London/New York: Oxford University Press, 1973)53-78; I. **Mendelsohn**, *Slavery in the Ancient Near East* (New York/London: Oxford University Press, 1949); K. N. **Schoville**, "A Note on the Oracles against Gaza, Tyre, and Edom," *SVT* 26(1974)55-63; H. **Tadmor**, "Philistia under Assyrian Rule," *BA* 29(1966)86-102.

1:6   *Thus Yahweh has said:*
        "For three transgressions of Gaza,
            and for four, I will not recall it;
            because of their exiling a complete exile
            to deliver them to Edom.
7   *And I will send fire on the walls of Gaza,*
            and it will consume its fortresses;
8   *and I will cut off the one ruling from Ashdod,*
            and the one wielding the scepter from Ashkelon;
            and I will turn my hand against Ekron,

> *and the remnant of the Philistines will perish,"*
> *said the Lord Yahweh.*

This section, like verses 3-5, begins with a focus on a specific city but expands to include other principalities as well. The four cities mentioned - Gaza, Ashdod, Ashkelon, and Ekron - were Philistine towns in southwestern Palestine. The first three were port cities located just inland from the Mediterranean coast. Ekron, like Gath, was located inland, on the plain.

The lack of any mention of the fifth major Philistine city, Gath, has led some to deny that Amos proclaimed this Philistine material (see *Marti, 160; *Nowack, 123; *Fosbroke, 780-81). This line of argument assumes that the section must come from a time when Gath was not a viable city-state, presumably after the Assyrian king Sargon II (721-705) captured Gath about 712/11 (*ARAB* II §§ 30, 62; *ANET* 286). Such argumentation is unconvincing for three simple reasons. First, no speech against Philistia anywhere in the prophetic literature mentions all the members of the Philistine pentapolis (see Jer. 25:20; 47:5; Zeph. 2:4; Zech. 9:5-6). Second, Amos himself refers to Gath later (6:2). Third, Sargon II not only destroyed Gath in 712/11 but also Ashdod and its seaport town. Reference to Ashdod in the text would indicate that there was no connection between the content of this section and Sargon's wars in the west. The absence of Gath is best explained on the basis of current politics. Gath was probably not a participant in the anti-Assyrian coalition and thus was not involved in anti-Judean and anti-Israelite activity at the time. According to 2 Chron. 26:6-7, Uzziah had fought successfully against Gath, Jabneh, and Ashdod, but this probably occurred during the heyday of Jeroboam II rather than in the time of Amos. Thus an assumption about Gath's absence because of Judean dominance over the city seems unfounded. Gath may have been dominated by Ashdod at the time (see on 6:2) as was apparently the case in 712/11 when Sargon attacked and destroyed Ashdod, Gath, and Ashdod-by-the-sea (see *ANET* 286; *ARAB* II § 30).

[6] The denunciation of the Philistines initially mentions only Gaza, perhaps at the time the most economically and politically significant of the cities. Gaza was the southernmost

of the Philistine cities, located just north of the Wadi Besor (the Brook of Egypt) which marked the northern border of Egyptian territory. Gaza was an important commerical and caravan center located on the main north-south trade route (known as the *via maris* in later times) linking Egypt to the south with Damascus - Mesopotamia - Asia Minor to the north. Inland routes from the Judean cities of Jerusalem and Hebron as well as from Transjordan, the Gulf of Aqaba, and Arabia converged at Gaza. The commercial importance of the city is indicated by the fact that when the Assyrians conquered the Philistine region, they established a major trading center in the vicinity of Gaza. Because of its strategic location, Gaza always tended to have important connections with Egypt.

Gaza was one of the trouble spots for the Assyrians during the reigns of Tiglath-pileser and his successors. They fought and defeated the city in 734-733 and again in 720-719. Amos's statements indicate that this anti-Assyrianism in defence of Mediterannean regionalism was already characteristic of Gaza in his day.

Gaza is accused in verse 6 of exiling a *galuth shelemah*. The same charge in slightly different terminology is levelled against Tyre in verse 9. Both use the expression *galuth shelemah* which may be rendered a "complete/total captivity/exile" or "a peaceful captivity/exile" (see Haupt). The former would indicate the removal of an entire community including women and children (for this sense of *shelemah*, see Jer. 13:19). The latter would indicate the removal of people considered at peace with Gaza and Tyre (for this sense of *shelemah*, see Gen. 33:18; 34:21). That a deportation or exile is involved is indicated by the use of the hiphil of *glh* in verse 6. The verb "to hand over," used in both verses 6 and 9, is a hiphil of *sgr* employed elsewhere of extraditing escaped slaves to their lawful masters (see Deut. 23:15; see the use of the parallel verb *skr* in Sefire III 2-3 and Isa. 19:4) and of surrendering fugitives to their pursuers (Obad. 14). Amos here appears to be condemning Gaza for engaging in the wholesale removal of local populations and their sale in international slave trade although nothing is said specifically about the actual selling or commercial transaction (see *Neher, 52). (On the association of Philistia and Phoenicia see below on verses 9-10.) The taking of captives in warfare was standard practice in the ancient world (see Deut. 21:10; 2 Sam. 12:31) and the fact that the con-

sequences of warfare could be inflicted on the total population
is illustrated by the stories of David's activities (1 Sam. 27:8-12).
Amos obviously believed such practices to be inhumane and
contrary to acceptable international behavior.

In both verses 6 and 9, the expression *le'edom* suggests
that Edom was the destination or intermediary for the exiled
groups. Questions have been raised about whether Edom par-
ticipated with Philistia and Phoenicia in international slave
trade (see Haran and *Gordis, 206-10). Uncertainty arises from
three factors. (1) Both Philistia and Phoenicia, as major maritime powers, possessed considerable opportunity for disposing
of slaves through their broad contacts in the general Mediterranean world rather than having to seek markets inland, in
Edom. (2) The description of Edom's apparent humiliation at
the hands of Moab (in Amos 2:1-3) does not suggest a kingdom
sufficiently strong to play a major role in international trade.
(3) How Edom would have utilized such slaves, apparently in
sizeable numbers, is not obvious.

Gordis has proposed, since the victims are unnamed in
verses 6 and 9, that the Edomites themselves were the victims
in both cases. He suggests that the lamed in the expression
le'edom is to be understood as a *lamed accusativus* denoting the
direct object of the verbs "exiled" and "handed over." This
would translate into, "because they exiled Edom into total captivity for sale" (v. 6) and "because they exiled Edom into total
captivity" (v. 9). The use of the lamed as a direct object marker
occurs frequently in Aramaic and occasionally in biblical
Hebrew (see *BDB* 511 sec. 3). Gordis argues that the calamity
that led to the presence of Edomites on the international slave
market was either Amaziah's victory over Edom (2 Kings 14:7)
or the episode referred to by Amos in 2:1. Gaza (and Tyre)
would thus be condemned for serving as intermediaries in the
wholesale deportation of Edomites. Since both Philistine and
Phoenician states could have taken Judeans and Israelites captive as part of their harassment policy, there is no need to
resort to Gordis's proposal.

Haran argues that Edom is a scribal error for Aram
since the names are orthographically similar and since "Edom"
seems to be incorrectly written for "Aram" elsewhere in biblical
texts. He would thus see Syria and Damascus as the destination of the slaves. None of the ancient versions, however, supports the emendation of Edom to Aram.

Edom may actually have been the destination of Israelite/Judean slaves. The Edomites could have utilized slaves in copper mining operations in the Arabah south of the Dead Sea, in shipping activities on the Gulf of Aqaba, or have sold them to African and Arabian markets. Joel 3:8 mentions the Sabeans from southwest Arabia as markets for slaves.

Regardless of the destination of the presumed military captives, is it possible to understand the victims as Israelites/Judeans? Given our date for Amos, the sale of the prisoners of war would have to have occurred before the deaths of Jeroboam II and Jotham. Three biblical texts are relevant to this issue. First, in the historical review of Isa. 9:8-10:4, the prophet notes that the Syrians from the east and the Philistines on the west devoured Israel with an open mouth (9:12a). This notation occurs in the first section of Isaiah's overview, before the first appearance of the refrain (9:12b). The rest of the material in 9:8-11 relates to the earthquake which we argued above occurred before the death of Jeroboam II. In 9:13-17, the prophet spoke of the strife associated with Shallum's assassination of the son of Jeroboam II and the assassin's subsequent murder. These factors would thus allow one to interpret Isa. 9:12a as indicating Philistine military activity against Israel before the death of Jeroboam II, that is, contemporary with Amos's ministry. Second, in describing Jotham's reign, the Chronicler reports that he built cities and defense towers in the hill country, that is, in the heartland of Judah itself (2 Chron. 27:4). Such construction would indicate a strong internal or external threat. If the latter, which seems the more likely, then the Philistines would be the power most capable of striking at the heartland of Judah. Third, according to 2 Chron. 28:18, the Philistines carried out raids against cities in the Judean Negeb and Shephelah and conquered and resettled the cities of Bethshemesh, Aijalon, Gederoth, Soco, Timnah, and Gimzo and their villages. Such resettlement would obviously have necessitated the removal of the local population. Although 2 Chron. 28:18 assigns this Philistine aggression to the reign of Ahaz, it may have occurred earlier. The editors of both Kings and Chronicles depicted Ahaz in the worst light possible. Calamaties already afflicting Judah in Jotham's reign may have been deliberately written up as occurring under Ahaz's rule. In light of the evidence, it seems likely that before or during the career of Amos, the Philistines had attacked Judean and

Israelite cities, deported their populations, and settled in their territory.

[7-8] The description of the divine punishment to befall the Philistine cities closely parallels other such depictions in Amos's speech on the nations (1:4-5, 10, 12, 14-15; 2:2-3, 5). A divinely sent fire will consume the walls of Gaza, and the rulers of Ashdod and Ashkelon will be toppled from power. (Note how the expressions "the one ruling" and "the one wielding the scepter" appear in both verses 5 and 8 tying the two units together verbally in a concatenating fashion.) Ashdod was the northernmost of the coastal Philistine cities, about twenty miles north of Gaza. Ashkelon lay about halfway between the two. Ekron (both Greek translations and Akkadian texts suggest the ancient spelling was *'Aqqaron*), probably to be identified with *Khirbet 'el-Muqanna* about twelve miles inland, was to experience a swipe from Yahweh's hand. Amos portrays God taking action against the three coastal towns and then "backhanding" Ekron. The concluding statement concerning the announced judgment - "they will perish, the remnant of the Philistines" - is a way of saying "they will perish to the last person." The term "remnant" (*she'erit*) had a military origin; it was the population, the "leftovers," who had survived battle.

The closing attribution formula at the end of verse 8, "said Lord Yahweh," contains the word "Lord" (*'adonay*), not found in the attribution formula in 1:5, 15; and 2:3 and missing in most Greek texts although found in many versions and the early manuscript of Amos from *Murabba'ât* (see *DJD* II 186).

D. Against Tyre (1:9-10)

H. **Cazelles**, "L'arrière plan historique d'Amos 1. 9-10," *PWCJS* 6(1977)1.171-76; F. C. **Fensham**, "The Treaty Between the Israelites and Tyrians," *SVT* 17(1969)71-87; E. **Gerstenberger**, "Covenant and Commandment," *JBL* 84(1965)38-51; D. J. **McCarthy**, *Treaty and Covenant* (AB 21A; Rome: Pontifical Biblical Institute, 1978); B. **Peckham**, "Israel and Phoenicia," *Magnalia Dei: The Mighty Acts of God* (ed. F. M. Cross et al.; Garden City: Doubleday & Co., 1976)224-48; J. **Priest**, "The

Covenant of Brothers," *JBL* 84(1965)400-406; H. J. **Katzenstein**, *The History of Tyre, from the Beginning of the Second Millenium B.C.E. until the Fall of the Neo-Babylonian Empire in 538 B.C.E* (Jerusalem: Schocken Institute for Jewish Research of the Jewish Theological Seminary of America, 1973)193-205; L. D. **Levine**, "Menahem and Tiglath-Pileser: A New Synchronism," *BASOR* 206(1972)40-42.

1:9   *Thus Yahweh has said:*
       "For three transgressions of Tyre,
          and for four, I will not recall it;
       because of their delivering up a total exile to Edom,
          and did not remember the covenant of brothers.
10   *And I will send fire on the walls of Tyre,*
       and it will consume its fortresses."

With verse 9, Amos turns to a denunciation of Tyre, the prosperous Phoenician maritime power to the northwest of Israel proper. Tyre, with its rocky island fortress, was located about thirty miles north of Mt. Carmel. In the mid-eighth century, Tyre was by far the strongest of the Phoenician cities. The Phoenicians and Philistines are associated in several passages in the Old Testament (see Jer. 47:4; Joel 3:4-8; Zech. 9:3-6; Ps. 83:7) and this along with geographical considerations may help explain the prophet's denunciation of Tyre immediately following that of Philistia. The repetition of terminology in verses 6*b* and 9*b* links the two units verbally. Speeches criticizing Tyre are common in the prophetic books (Isaiah 23; Jer. 25:22; 27:3; 47:4; Ezek. 26:1-28:19; Joel 3:4-8).

[9] Amos condemns Tyre for two wrongs: (a) the handing over of a complete exile to Edom and (b) the failure to remember a covenant of brothers.

(a) Unlike Gaza in verse 6, Tyre is not unequivocally condemned for the actual seizure and deportation of captives but only for handing them over, that is, engagement in slave trade. The difference between what is being described in verses 6 and 9, however, may be more apparent than real. The statement in verse 9 may simply be an abbreviated form of what is said more fully in verse 6. Edom is again said to be the destination of this trade in humans although Phoenicia's geographical proximity to Aram and Damascus would make Aram a more logical trading partner than Edom. No textual evidence, however, reads "Aram" instead of "Edom."

Tyre's involvement in slave trade is noted elsewhere in Scripture. In Joel 3:4-8, Tyre and Sidon are accused, along with the Philistines, of selling the people of Judah and Jerusalem to the Greeks. When this occurred is not known. Greeks are mentioned in an Assyrian text as raiding and plundering along the eastern Mediterranean coast and as far south as Phoenicia as early as the eighth century (*CAH* 3/3, 15). Greek colonies were also established in Syria, for example, at Sukas, by the time of Amos. Thus the sale of slaves to the Greeks by Tyre in the eighth century is within the realm of possibility. Ezek. 27:13 also notes Tyre's trading in slaves.

As in verse 6, the prophet does not specify who the victims were. Unlike the case of the Philistines, however, there is no direct evidence indicating Phoenician encroachment on Israelite/Judean territory at the time of Amos. Any attempt at identifying the victims in this case also involves speculating about the participants in "the covenant of brothers."

(b) The expression "covenant (or "treaty") of brothers" is not only unique to the Bible but apparently to the literature of the Near East. A treaty or covenant agreement between states establishing a legal relationship with recognized obligations had been common in the Near East for centuries before Amos. The content of such covenants varied depending upon whether the relationship was imposed, as in vassal treaties, or entered into by equals, as in parity treaties. Although the expression "covenant of brothers" is without parallel, the idea it expresses was common in near eastern diplomacy (see Gerstenberger and Priest). A covenant/treaty between two independent states created a relationship that could be described in terms of "brotherhood" between the participants (see 1 Kings 9:13; 20:32). Vassal kingdoms subordinate to a common overlord could speak of themselves as "brothers."

There is no need to see the reference to a covenant of brothers in the Tyre section as either a late gloss or as originally referring to a covenant between Edom and Israel (so *Fosbrooke, 781 and others). The brotherhood was probably one existing between Israel and Tyre. The question that remains, and which may be unanswerable, is whether the brotherhood was based on a treaty between Tyre and Israel or whether the two nations were brothers as a consequence of a common treaty with Assyria.

Close relationships existed between Israel/Judah and Tyre throughout much of their history. This was especially the case in the tenth and ninth centuries. Hiram of Tyre and Solomon entered covenant relations (1 Kings 5:12) and are referred to as brothers (1 Kings 9:13). According to 2 Sam. 5:11-12, David had already established close relations with Hiram although nothing is said about a treaty between the two states. The Greek text of 1 Kings 5:1 declares that "Hiram king of Tyre sent his servants to anoint Solomon in place of David, his father, because Hiram loved David all the days" (3 Kings 5:15 in Greek). If this text accurately reflects historical conditions, then the Israelite king would appear to be subordinate to the king of Tyre. Solomon's trading ventures on the Red Sea with Tyre (1 Kings 9:26-28; 10:11-12, 22) also seem to presuppose Israel's subordinate relationship to Tyre since Israel was clearly the secondary partner in maritime commerce. In the ninth century, during the reigns of Omri and Ahab, a coalition between Phoenicia and Israel was sealed with Ahab's marriage to Jezebel, a Phoenician princess, again no doubt involving treaty arrangements and renewed cooperative maritime commerce.

Was there a renewal of treaty relations between Israel and Tyre in the eighth century during the reign of Jeroboam II? The description of Jeroboam's reign in 2 Kings 14:23-29 contains no explicit reference to this effect. The only evidence pointing in this direction is circumstantial. Under Jeroboam and Uzziah, the Israelites/Judeans again had control of the seaport at Elath and thus were again engaged in commercial enterprises on the Red Sea (2 Kings 14:22). If, as on former occasions, this maritime activity was carried out with Phoenician cooperation and naval expertise, then treaty arrangements with Tyre were probably resumed. Finally, when Pekah and Rezin sought to replace Ahaz on the throne in Jerusalem (2 Kings 16:5), it appears that they intended to enthrone a prince of Tyre as king of Judah and Jerusalem. A son of Tabeel was to be installed as the new ruler (Isa. 7:6). In the 740s, the king reigning in Tyre was a certain Tubail, now known from an inscription of Tiglath-pileser (see Levine). Tubail and Tabeel are probably variants of the Phoenician name Ethbaal (see 1 Kings 16:31). That a Tyrian prince was viewed as a likely candidate for the Jerusalem throne could indicate popular support in Judah and the possibility that such support was based on a policy of cooperation between Tyre and Israel/Judah. Amos's condemnation of Tyre in 750-749 for breaking the covenant of brothers could be interpreted as follows. Under Jeroboam II, Israel and Tyre had again undertaken joint commercial ventures and entered a treaty alliance. When Tyre became involved in the western anti-Assyrian coalition and Israel remained pro-Assyrian, Tyre moved to possess some Israelite territory and sold Israelites as slaves. Such actions involved the repudiation of treaty arrangements, and thus a failure to remember (to remain faithful to) the covenant.

Another way of viewing Amos's denunciation, and it must be remembered that we are dealing very much in the realm of conjecture, is to assume that both Israel and Tyre were still bound to Assyria with treaty obligations and that Tyre's encroachment on Israelite territory was disloyalty to a covenant associate. Tyre seems to have offered loyal submission to Assyria for over a century. Three Assyrian kings - Ashurnasirpal II (883-859), Shalmaneser III (858-824), and Adad-nirari III (810-783) - mention Tyre's submission and the payment of tribute (*ANET* 276, 280, 281; *ARAB* I §§ 479, 672, 739). Tyre is conspiciously absent from the list of anti-Assyrian forces that fought Shalmaneser at Qarqar in 853 (*ANET* 278; *ARAB* I § 610). Tyre's first known anti-Assyrian activity was the town's involvement with Rezin's anti-Assyrian exploits. If this be the case, then Tyre and Israel would technically have been brother vassals to Assyria at the time of Amos although Tyre was already casting its lot with anti-Assyrian forces and taking hostile actions against Israel. They no longer remembered the covenant of brotherhood.

[10] The anticipated punishment to befall Tyre is expressed in Amos's repetitive picture of fiery destruction.

E. Against Edom (1:11-12)

M. L. **Barré**, "Amos 1:11 Reconsidered," *CBQ* 47(1985)420-27; J. R. **Bartlett**, "The Brotherhood of Edom," *JSOT* 4(1977)2-27; C.-M. **Bennett**, "Excavations at Buseirah (Biblical Bozrah),"

Midian, Moab and Edom (ed. J. F. A. Sawyer and D. J. A. Clines; JSOTSS 24; Sheffield: JSOT Press, 1983)9-17; I. **Beit-Arieh**, "New Light on the Edomites," *BARev* 14/2(1988)28-41; R. B. **Coote**, "Amos 1:11 *rhmyw*," *JBL* 90(1971)206-8; M. **Fishbane**, "The Treaty Background of Amos 1:11 and Related Matters," *JBL* 89(1970)313-18; **Fishbane**, "Additional Remarks on *rhmyw* (Amos 1:11)," *JBL* 91(1972)391-93; R. **Gordis**, "Amos, Edom and Israel - An Unrecognized Source for Edomite History," *Essays on the Occasion of the Seventieth Anniversary of the Dropsie University* (ed. A. I. Katsh and L. Nemoy; Philadelphia: Dropsie University, 1979)109-32; M. **Haran**, "Observations on the Historical Background of Amos 1:2-2:6," *IEJ* 18(1968)207-12; M. **Held**, "Studies in Biblical Homonyms in the Light of Akkadian," *JANESCU* 3(1970-71)47-55; S. M. **Paul**, "Amos 1:3 - 2:3: A Concatenous Literary Pattern," *JBL* 90(1971)397-403; G. **Schmuttermayr**,"*rhm* - Eine lexikalische Studie," *Bib* 51(1970)499-532.

1:11   *Thus Yahweh has said:*
           "For three transgressions of Edom,
                  and for four, I will not recall it;
           because of his pursuing his brother with the sword,
                  and destroyed his maidens;
           and his anger tore without subsiding,
                  and his rage stood guard without faltering.
  12   *And I will send fire on Teman,*
                  and it will consume the fortresses of Bozrah."

The fourth nation denounced by the prophet was Edom, a kingdom lying south and southeast of Judah, spanning both sides of the Arabah depression south of the Dead Sea. The close kinship of Israelites and Edomites is reflected in the patriarchal narratives of Genesis where Jacob (= Israel) and Esau (= Edom) are described as twins (Gen. 25:19-34). Their hostilities and animosities conjoined with their brotherhood were prefigured, according to legend, in the twins' prenatal struggle in their mother's womb (Gen. 25:22-23).

Second Samuel 8:13-14 and 1 Kings 11:15-16 indicate that David brought Edom under Israelite control. During Solomon's rule, the Edomites apparently asserted their freedom and harassed Israel (1 Kings 11:14-25). During the reigns of Ahab of Israel (868-854) and Jehoshaphat of Judah (877-853) when Israel/Judah again exercised control over the port of Elath, the Edomites were again subjected to vassal status (1 Kings 22:47; 2 Kings 3:9). After the death of Jehoshaphat, the Edomites reasserted their independence (2 Kings 8:16-22). We next hear of Edom in the days of King Amaziah (802-786) who attacked the Edomites in the Valley of Salt (*Wadi el-Milh* east of Beer-sheba) slaying great numbers of them (2 Kings 14:7).

[11] The exact status of relations between Israel/Judah and Edom in the days of Amos remains uncertain. Edom paid tribute to Assyria early in the reign of Adad-nirari III (810-783; *ANET* 281; *ARAB* I § 739) but goes unmentioned in Assyrian texts until after Tiglath-pileser's 734 campaign when Edom under King Kaushmalaku, along with other Syro-Palestinian states, paid him tribute (*ANET* 282; *ARAB* I § 801). Some of these states, like Ashkelon and Gaza, had clearly sided with Rezin's anti-Assyrian coalition. Thus the fact that Edom paid tribute in 734-733 provides no indication of its political posture vis-à-vis Assyria before that date. Neither Edom nor Moab is listed as paying tribute during Tiglath-pileser's earlier 743-740 and 738 western campaigns.

Only two biblical texts mention Edom in contexts that may refer to historical situations at the time of Amos. Both texts occur in narratives describing the reign of Ahaz but, as we noted earlier, conditions attributed to the time of Ahaz may have existed before his day, that is, in the reign of Jotham contemporary with Amos's activity.

Second Kings 16:6 reads: "At that time, Rezin king of Aram recovered Elath for Aram and drove the Judeans from Elath and the Arameans came to Elath and they dwelt there until this day." The Masoretic scribes suggested that the term Arameans should be read Edomites. If one makes this change in the consonantal text then we have the following scenario. Rezin, in cooperation with Edom (see 2 Kings 15:37), recovered the seaport of Elath which Hazael had earlier controlled, and allowed the Edomites to settle there forcing out the Judeans. Some scholars have suggested that all the references to Aram in 2 Kings 16:6 should be changed to Edom and the reference to Rezin dropped (see RSV) so that the Edomites alone wrest control of Elath from Judah. Such extensive surgery on the text is unnecessary and actually creates a

redundancy: "the king of Edom recovered Elath for Edom . . .
and Edomites came to Elath. . . ."

Second Chronicles 28:16-17 claims that Ahaz sent to the
Assyrian kings for help since the Edomites had again invaded
Judah and carried away captives. The description of this aspect
of Ahaz's troubles is part of a depiction of his difficulties with
Syria (28:5), Israel (28:6-8), and Philistia (28:18-19) as well as
with Edom. All of these states plus Tyre and Ammon appear
as enemies to Israel/Judah in the book of Amos.

These two texts indicate that relationships between
Edom and Israel/Judah had deteriorated to the level of open
warfare. Does Amos 1:11 indicate a similar situation?

As in the previous sections, it seems best to understand
Edom's actions as carried out against Judah/Israel rather than
as events in an Edomite civil war (*Gordis, 211) or engage-
ments with some other country. In the one section where
hostile action against non-Israelites/Judeans is described, the
object of the enmity is clearly identified (see 2:1). "His brother"
in v. 11 thus probably denotes the house of Israel/Jacob. The
expression $rhmyw$ which parallels "his brother" has presented
interpreters with difficulties since antiquity. Terms built on the
root rhm may mean "womb/entrails," "compassion,"
"friend/relative," and "girl/young woman."

For $rhmyw$ ancient Greek translations read "womb,"
"mother," and "mother upon the ground" (see Gen. 38:9). The
rabbinic tradition traced an interpretation to Rabbi Judah
which noted that "when Esau was about to be born he severed
his mother's womb so that she would not be able to bear any
more children," an interpretation of the birth of Jacob and Esau
based on Amos 1:11 (*Routtenberg, 38). Modern translations
vary enormously: "he cast off pity" (RSV following KJV), "sti-
fling their natural affections" (NEB), "repressed all pity"
(NJPSV).

The verbs in the first line of verse 11b were at home in
the realm of warfare (see Barré); rdp indicating "chase/pursue"
and $shht$ describing the consequences, "destroy/annihilate,"
once the enemy was apprehended. Thus both verbs demand a
very specific and concrete object, not something like "pity,"
"natural affections," or "covenant mercy" (the latter in *Coote,
208). Assuming that "brother" and rhm are terms denoting
treaty relationships, Fishbane (1970, 316-17) translates the half
verse:

> For he pursued his brother by the sword,
> > and utterly destroyed his allies/friends;
> because he nurtured his ire e'er,
> > and kept his wrath beyond measure.

*Gordis (p. 211) surrenders any effort to associate the term *rḥm* with treaty conceptions and translates, "He pursued his brothers with the sword and destroyed his kinsmen."

The translation given above is based on the fact that *rḥm* is occasionally used to mean "young female/girl." This usage appears in Ugaritic texts where in one case *rḥm* parallels *btlt* ("a prepubescent female"). The term also occurs in the Mesha inscription (line 17; see *KAI* no. 181) where it appears in a list: "slaying all, seven thousand men, boys, women, girls and maidservants (*rḥmt*), for I had devoted them to destruction for the god Ashtar-Chemosh" (*ANET* 320). In Judg. 5:30, *rḥm* is used with reference to women taken in battle, subsequently to be divided among the soldiers as spoil. The manner in which Amos ties together the sub-units in 1:2-2:3 through repetitive terms and themes also supports reading *rḥm* as "maiden" since the Edom section then shares the theme of the unnecessary slaughter of women with the following Ammon section (Paul, 402-3).

In the final two parts of verse 11*b*, the language shifts so that the country's rage and anger are the subjects of the sentences rather than Edom. Some ancient versions, the Syriac and Vulgate, apparently understood the verbs so as to preserve Edom as the subject. Thus *wayiṭṭor* (from *nṭr* "to watch, maintain") was read for *wayiṭrop* ("to tear," like a wild beast; see Hos. 5:14) and *shamar* "he kept" for *shemarah* "(his wrath) kept." The standard Hebrew text should be retained.

The fourfold denunciation in verse 11*b* thus focuses on Edom's harsh treatment of Israelites/Judeans which the prophet understood as hideously extravagant. The specific events alluded to remain uncertain but should be seen against the background of the episodes noted in 2 Kings 16:6 and 2 Chron. 28:17.

[12] In his proclamation of Yahweh's coming judgment, Amos refers to Teman, apparently a district rather than a city in Edom (see Gen. 36:31-42; Jer. 49:7, 20; Ezek. 25:13; Obad. 1, 12; Hab. 3:3), and Bozrah (see Gen. 36:33; Isa. 34:6; 63:1; Jer.

49:13, 22), located at the impressive site of *Buseirah*, twenty-one miles southeast of the Dead Sea, where British excavations suggest major construction in the eighth century.

F. Against Ammon (1:13-15)

M. **Cogan**, "'Ripping open Pregnant Women' in Light of an Assyrian Analogue," *JAOS* 103 (1983) 755-57; F. M. **Cross**, "Epigraphic Notes on the Amman Citadel Inscription," *BASOR* 193(1969)13-19; S. H. **Horn**, "The Amman Citadel Inscription," *BASOR* 193(1969)2-13; P. **Machinist**, "Assyria and Its Image in the First Isaiah," *JAOS* 103(1983)719-37; E. **Puech**, "Milkom, le dieu ammonite, en Amos I 15," *VT* 27(1977)117-25; J. de **Waard**, "A Greek Translation-Technical Treatment of Amos 1:15," *On Language, Culture and Religion: In Honor of Eugene A. Nida* (ed. M. Black and W. A. Smalley; The Hague/Paris: Mouton, 1974)111-18; G. **Widengren**, "Quelques remarques sur l'émasculation rituelle chez les peuples sémitiques," *Studia Orientalia Ioannii Pedersen* (Hauniae: Einar Munksgaard, 1953)377-84.

1:13   *Thus Yahweh has said:*
      "For three transgressions of the Ammonites,
         and for four, I will not recall it;
      because of their ripping open pregnant women of
         Gilead, in order to enlarge their territory.
  14   *And I will set fire to the wall of Rabbah,*
      and it will consume its fortresses;
      amid shouting on a day of battle,
      with a windblast on a stormy day.
  15   *And their king will go into exile,*
      he and his officials together,"
                                said Yahweh.

     The land of Ammon skirted the Arabian Desert east and south of Gilead. The usual biblical designation, as here, speaks of the "children of Ammon" and Akkadian texts of the "house of Ammon" (*bit-Ammon*, see *ANET* 282, 287) rather than just of "Ammon," but for reasons unknown.

The Israelites viewed themselves as rather close relatives to the Ammonites. The rather coarse story in Gen. 19:30-38 ascribes the latter's (and the Moabites') origin to a drunken, incestuous relationship between Lot, Abraham's nephew, and one of his daughters after the destruction of Sodom. The biblical texts frequently note the hostile relations between the Ammonites and Israelites. Jephthah, Saul, and David are described as fighting Ammonites (see Judg. 10:7-11:33; 1 Samuel 11; 2 Sam. 8:12; 10:1-11:1; 12:26-31).

[13] The Ammonites are condemned for war atrocities carried out in expanding their territory into Gilead. No known evidence can be related to the events alluded to by Amos. Presumably, the Ammonites were encroaching on Israelite holdings in Gilead, perhaps in moves coordinated with Rezin's advance into Transjordan (see on 1:3). In 2 Sam. 10:6-19, Ammon and Aram are pictured as confederates against David suggesting that the two powers were accustomed to cooperation.

The criminal act scorned by Amos was the slitting open of pregnant women. (The medieval Jewish scholars, Kimchi and Ibn Ezra suggested reading "mountains" [harim] instead of "pregnant females" [harot] perhaps because of the repugnance of the plain sense. This verse, perhaps because of its repulsive content, is not quoted anywhere in Talmudic - Midrashic literature; see *Routtenberg, 39.) The practice of ripping open pregnant women was either a means of slaughtering unborn males or else the symbolic emasculation of males carried out by ripping apart the bodies of dead pregnant females (for the latter view see Widengren). The practice of slaughtering the unborn during warfare is mentioned in Akkadian (see Cogan; *Wolff, 161) and Arabic (*Wellhausen, 70-71) literature. In the Iliad, Agamemnon pleaded with Menelaus to slaughter a Trojan captive: "Let us not spare a single one of them - not even the child unborn and in its mother's womb; let not a man of them be left alive, but let all in Ilius perish, unheeded and forgotten" (VI 57-58). Three biblical texts refer to this practice (2 Kings 8:12; 15:16; Hos. 13:16). Second Kings 15:16 reports that when Menahem took over the throne in Israel, he had to force a region or city to submit to his authority: "Because they did not open it to him, he attacked it and ripped open all its pregnant women." In describing the overthrow of reigning families, several biblical texts note that all the males of the line were

killed (see 1 Kings 14:10; 16:11; 21:21; 2 Kings 9:8). No
reference is made in these texts to the slaughter of the unborn
but this may have been the case, especially when the goal was
to exterminate all the royal line. (Such a situation is the background to Isaiah's promising Ahaz in Isaiah 7 that the unborn
child, Immanuel, will not be killed.)

The slaughter of the unborn and the ripping apart of
pregnant women probably occurred under extraordinary military conditions: when extreme brutality was resorted to in order
to exact vengeance or to teach the enemy a lesson and when
there was a desire to eradicate a particular element in society,
such as the members of a royal line. No biblical law explicitly
forbids such carnage. In fact, David is described as wiping out
the entire populations of villages to prevent anyone from expos-
ing his scheming (1 Sam. 27:8-12). Amos however clearly
seems to have understood the Ammonite slaughter of mothers-
to-be and their unborn in the course of extending territory as
being unwarranted and a criminal act contrary to customary
behavior.

[14-15] These verses describe the coming judgment
upon the Ammonites: divine action against the capital city and
deportation of the Ammonite king and his staff. Rabbah was
the chief city of Ammon, in fact, the only Ammonite city mentioned in the Old Testament (2 Sam 11:1, 12:27, 29; Ezek. 21:20
and elsewhere). Rabbah was situated on the upper reaches of
the Jabbok River about twenty-five miles northeast of the Dead
Sea. Known as Philadelphia during classical Greco-Roman
times, the city has borne the name Amman since the Muslim
conquest of the region. The fiery destruction of the city wall is
spoken of in terms of Yahweh's "kindling a fire on/in the wall"
rather than sending fire as in the other nation oracles. The
igniting of the wall in verse 14*a* is elaborated by two further
images in verse 14*b*, a war-cry on a day of fighting and a wind-
blast on a stormy day. All three expressions could be
understood as referring to military action against Ammon. In
Isa. 28:2, an Assyrian attack is described as a destructive storm,
a common image used by Assyrian kings themselves to describe
their military campaigns (see Machinist, 726-28).

Verse 14 speaks of a future military onslaught against
Ammon; v. 15 anticipates the exile of the Ammonite king and
his entourage. The reference to "their king" (*malcam*) was
understood by some ancient translations as a reference to the

Ammonite god Milcom mentioned elsewhere in the Old Testament (1 Kings 11:5, 33; 2 Kings 23:13; but see Judg. 11:24 where Chemosh is named as the people's deity) and in Ammonite inscriptions (for example, see Cross and Horn). Most Greek manuscripts read verse 15 as referring to "its (Rabbah's) kings . . . their priests and political leaders" although this probably reflects a translation technique rather than a different reading in the source text (see de Waard and compare Jer. 49:3b).

G. Against Moab (2:1-3)

K.-H. **Bernhardt**, "Beobachtungen zur Identifizierung moabitischer Ortslagen," *ZDPV* 76(1960)136-58; T. J. **Mafico**, "The Usage of the Root *šāpiṭum* in Akkadian Documents," *JNSL* 13(1987)69-87; W. **Richter**, "Zu den 'Richtern Israels,'" *ZAW* 77(1965)40-72; N. J. **Tromp**, *Primitive Conceptions of Death and the Nether World in the Old Testament* (BibOr 21; Rome: Pontifical Biblical Institute, 1969); A. H. **van Zyl**, *The Moabites* (Leiden: E. J. Brill, 1960).

2:1 *Thus Yahweh has said:*
  "For three transgressions of Moab,
   and for four, I will not recall it;
  because of its burning the bones
   of the king of Edom to lime.
2 *And I will send fire on Moab,*
   and it will consume the fortresses of Kerioth;
  and Moab will die amid uproar,
   amid shouting, amid the sound of the trumpet.
3 *And I will cut off the one ruling from her midst,*
   and all her officials I will kill with him,"
     said Yahweh.

Amos concluded his denunciations of the nations to Israel's southeast and east with Moab, the "brother-nation" to Ammon (see Gen. 19:30-38). The heartland of Moabite territory was the lofty tableland directly east of the Dead Sea. Bounded on the south by the River Zered, the east by the Arabian Desert, and the west by the Dead Sea, Moab struggled

throughout much of its history to extend and control its northern border, often in conflict with Israel (note the anti-Moabite
sentiment in Deut. 23:3-6; Isa. 16:12-14).

Israel and Judah had a long history of varied relationships with Moab. Although tradition traced his ancestry to
Moabite roots (see Ruth 4:17*b*-22; 1 Sam. 22:3-4), David is said
to have treated Moab cruelly (2 Sam. 8:2). After a time of
independence following the reign of either David or Solomon,
Moab was again subjected to Israel by King Omri (879-869),
but rebelled following the death of Omri's son and successor
Ahab (868-854; see 2 Kings 1:1; 3:5). Mesha, the Moabite king
at the time, commemorated his victory in a memorial stela, one
of the most famous non-biblical inscriptions (see *ANET* 320-
21). Immediate attempts by Israel to reconquer Moab failed
(see 2 Kings 3). During the reign of Hazael (about 843-806),
Transjordan was overrun by Damascus (2 Kings 10:32-33).
Jeroboam II appears to have temporarily retaken portions of
Transjordan, perhaps including some territory held or claimed
by Moab (2 Chron. 5; note v. 17), but apparently had lost most
of this before the end of his reign.

[1] Moab is not condemned for anti-Israelite activity but
for desecration of an Edomite monarch's remains. The per-
petrator of the criminal act would appear to be the nation as a
whole since the only antecedent to the pronominal suffix "it" in
verse 1*b* is the country or the people of Moab. Just as the
Ammonites were condemned for destroying the unborn (1:13)
so the Moabites were denounced for desecrating the deceased.
The reference to bones would indicate the desecration of a
tomb rather than a corpse.

Despite the aversion to tomb desecration and looting in
the ancient world, no doubt such practices occurred. Palestinian
sepulchral inscriptions plead with and warn the would-be
intruder about desecrating the tomb.

> Whoever you are who shall do wrong and remove
> me, may [the gods] Sahr, Nikkal, and Nusk cause him
> to die a miserable death, and may his posterity
> perish!

> Don't, don't open it, and don't disturb me, for such a
> thing would be an abomination to [the goddess]
> Astarte! But if you do open it and if you do disturb

me, may you not have any seed among the living under the sun or resting-place together with the shades!

Whoever you are, ruler or ordinary person, may he not open it and may he not uncover me and may he not carry me away from this resting-place and may he not take up the casket in which I am resting, lest these Holy Gods abandon them and cut down that ruler and those persons and their seed forever! (*ANET* 505)

After a lengthy and bitter vindictive war with the Elamites and their allies, the Assyrian monarch, Ashurbanipal, noted severe measures he took against his enemies following his victory. Property was seized; palaces were looted; temples were destroyed; leaders were killed; and citizens were deported. In addition, Ashurbanipal noted his treatment of the skeletal remains of his enemies' rulers.

The rest of the sons . . . , his family, the seed of his father's house, . . . and the bones of the father who begot them, . . . I carried off from Gambulu to Assyria. (*ARAB* II § 788)

The sepulchers of their earlier and later kings, who did not fear [the Assyrian gods] Assur and Ishtar, my lords, and who had plagued the kings, my fathers, I destroyed, I devastated, I exposed to the sun. Their bones I carried off to Assyria. I laid restlessness upon their shades. I deprived them of food-offerings and libations of water. (*ARAB* II § 810)

The bones of Nabu-shum-eresh, which they had brought from Gambulu to Assyria, these bones I had his sons crush in front of the gate inside Nineveh. (*ARAB* II § 866)

From Ashurbanipal's statements, one could conclude that his treatment of the skeletal remains of these rulers was an extremely humiliating act. The dead rulers were deprived of their resting places - cut off from their ancestors in the realm of the dead - were denied the benefits of the cult for the dead (food-offerings and water libations), and were symbolically eradicated from memory in the crushing of their bones by their own descendants which removed the final traces of their existence.

Similar motives probably lay behind the burning of the bones of the king of Edom by the Moabites. "Burning to lime" transformed the human remains into a non-human substance (see Isa. 33:12). The Targum asserts that the ashes were subsequently used in plaster for a house; perhaps burned non-human bones were normally used in such mixtures. When the Moabites burned the bones of the Edomite king cannot be determined but presumably it was an occurrence known to Amos's audience. Jeremiah (8:2-3) later threatened the Judeans with a description of the profanation of their royal tombs (on the burning of corpses, see below on 6:9-10).

[2-3] The description of the announced punishment against Moab stipulates action against both the nation (v. 2) and its leadership (v. 3). The fire to be sent against Moab will destroy the strongholds of Kerioth. Although a place name Kerioth appears in line 13 of the Mesha inscription and in Jer. 48:24, the expression here, with the definite article, could be read as "the cities" as was done in ancient Greek translations. (See Jer. 48:41 where the expression is normally translated "the cities.") The Moabite city of Kerioth is generally identified today with the modern site of *el-Qereiyat* primarily on the basis of the similiarity of the names. The Mesha inscription implies the existence of an important sanctuary in Kerioth dedicated to Chemosh, the national god of the Moabites (see Num. 21:19; 1 Kings 11:7).

The second half of verse 2 associates the "death" of Moab with military imagery: the uproar of a military campaign, the shouting in battle, and the sound of the trumpet (or ram's horn) used to direct the movement and attack of troops.

In speaking of the leadership of Moab destined for destruction, Amos refers to the "one ruling" or the *shopet* (judge) and the nation's officials. Elsewhere in speaking of the rulers over various states (in 1:5, 8), he used terminology indicative of a native monarchy. The reference to the judge of Moab could indicate that, at the time, Moab was ruled over by another state under whose supervision the *shopet* exercised authority. If this were the case, then one should think of

Damascus and Rezin as the foreign overlords. After Mesha, no king of Moab is mentioned by name in the Old Testament. In 734, Salamanu of Moab paid tribute to Tiglath-pileser after the latter had moved into Syria-Palestine in force (*ANET* 282). The status of Moab in the middle of the eighth century is unknown but Rezin was clearly active in Transjordan at the time or shortly thereafter (see 2 Kings 15:37; 16:6).

H. Against Judah (2:4-5)

H. **Gottlieb**, "Amos und Jerusalem," *VT* 17(1967)430-63; S. M. **Paul**, "A Literary Reinvestigation of the Authenticity of the Oracles against the Nations of Amos," *De la Tôrah au Messie* (ed. M. Carrez et al.; Paris: Desclée, 1981)189-204; H. **Robscheit**, "Die Thora bei Amos und Hosea," *EvTh* 10(1950-51)26-38; W. H. **Schmidt**, "Die deuteronomistische Redaktion des Amosbuches. Zu den theologischen Unterschieden zwischen dem Prophetenwort und seinem Sammler," *ZAW* 77(1965)168-93; S. **Wagner**, "Überlegungen zur Frage nach den Beziehungen des Propheten Amos zum Südreich," *TLZ* 96(1971)653-70; M. **Weinfeld**, *Deuteronomy and the Deuteronomic School* (London: Oxford University Press, 1972).

2:4   *Thus Yahweh has said:*
        "For three transgressions of Judah,
                and for four, I will not recall it;
        because of their rejecting the instruction of Yahweh,
                and they have not obeyed his decrees;
        and their lies have led them astray,
                those after which their fathers walked.
5   *And I will send fire on Judah,*
                and it will consume the fortresses of Jerusalem,"
                                        said Yahweh.

Many scholars during the past century have concluded that this Judah section is a late addition to the authentic words of Amos. The main arguments for this conclusion are as follows. (1) Outside of this section, the prophet shows no special interest in Judah and makes only passing references to the southern kingdom (only in 6:1; 7:12; 9:11). (2) The accusations against Judah are not only couched in theological terms which sharply contrast with the ethical and moral aspects of the other national denunciations but also are expressed in insipid generalities rather than in the concrete and vivid language used about the other nations. (3) The material contains internal inconsistencies since it begins as a divine speech but in verse 4b utilizes third-person references to God. (4) Elimination of the Judah section would leave speeches against seven nations, a more likely pattern than a sequence of eight nations. (5) The ideas and terminology of the section reflect special deuteronomic nomenclature and therefore must derive from a time after the appearance of the book of Deuteronomy, a period considerably later than Amos (see Schmidt). Some of these assertions and assumptions have already been discussed (see above, pp. 54-58) and in the following treatment all of these arguments will be contested (see Paul, 194-97).

[4] Like the material on Tyre and Edom, this subportion on Judah contains a longer description of the wrongs than of the coming punishment. The descriptions of the wrongs in these oracles follow an a + b pattern in the case of Tyre (enumerating two wrongs), an a + b + c + d pattern in the case of Edom (enumerating four wrongs), and an a + b + c pattern in the Judah section. The three wrongs listed for Judah are rejection of the torah of Yahweh, failure to keep Yahweh's statutes, and being led astray by the lies in which their parents had walked.

Although the shift from direct divine address in the first person to references to Yahweh in the third person (in verse 4b) is a bit jarring, it is hardly without precedence in prophetic speech. In Amos 1:2, the prophet begins with third-person references and then shifts to direct address in v. 3 while 3:1-2 and following reflect the opposite, a movement from first- to third-person references. In addition, the expression "torah of Yahweh" may have been used since it had something of a technical quality about it which carried more impact rhetorically than a simple "my torah."

The expression "torah (instruction) of Yahweh" is generally taken to reflect later deuteronomic or deuteronomistic material where emphasis on torah is strong. This particular expression, however, never occurs in the book of Deuteronomy nor in literature closely related to it. "To keep (obey) his decrees (statutes)" is a common expression in deuteronomic and related material (Deut. 4:5-6, 40; 5:1; 6:17; 7:11; 11:32; 16:12; 17:19; 26:16-17; 1 Kings 3:14; 8:58; 9:4; 2 Kings 17:37; 23:3). It also occurs, however, in non-deuteronomic contexts (see Weinfeld, 336). If the term "decree" was used of official or royal edicts (see Isa. 10:1-4), one would assume that an expression like "to (not) obey a decree(s)" would have been a part of common, everyday speech. "To be led astray by lies" is also not a deuteronomic idiom; the expression is unique to this text. The case for a deuteronomic or deuteronomistic origin for this section, therefore, does not stand the test of close scrutiny. If an editor had added a deuteronomistic-type statement on Judah after the fall of the southern kingdom, one would expect the text to reflect more characteristic terminology and a more concrete statement on the "sins" of Judah (see 2 Kings 17:7-41 for a characteristically deuteronomistic example).

The generality of the statements concerning Judah's wrongdoings make it difficult to know to what Amos was referring. Were the wrongdoings religious, legal, political, or some combination of these in nature?

The ancient Greek translators of the text understood the "lies" to refer to apostasy, false gods, or idol worship, adding the expression "which they made." This view is almost universally accepted by modern interpreters. Three factors argue against such an interpretation. First, the term "lies" is nowhere else used to refer to other or false gods. Second, Isaiah, a younger contemporary of Amos, never condemned the Judeans and Jerusalemites for religious apostasy or the worship of other gods, a surprising silence if apostasy was a burning issue in the south. Third, the term is employed in contexts which suggest a political rather than a religious connotation (see Weinfeld on the Akkadian parallel with political nuances). In Isa. 28:15-17, the expression is used to denounce the plan of supporters of rebellion against Assyria. In Hos. 7:13 and 12:1, the term describes political plans involving revolt against Assyria with Egyptian assistance. This usage points to political rather than religious concerns.

The term "decree" (*ḥuqqah/ḥoq*) appears in many contexts in the Hebrew scriptures but seems to indicate some officially proclaimed decree, regulation, or ordinance (see *TDOT* 5, 139-47). In Ps. 2:7, Yahweh's decree includes the affirmation of the Davidic monarch's divine sonship and dominion over the nations of the world. In Isa. 10:1-4, the term is applied to official decrees, perhaps to Pekah's orders after he had seized the throne in Samaria in 734 (see 2 Kings 15:23-26).

Again the expression "torah of Yahweh" was utilized in a number of contexts. "Ruling, decision, or instruction of Yahweh" appears as appropriate a translation as "law of Yahweh." In Isa. 1:10 ("torah of God"); 5:24; and 30:9, the torah of Yahweh is related to ethical and political matters and is used as an equivalent to the "word of God" or "word of the prophet" (see also 8:16, 20).

Thus it appears that Amos may have condemned Judah for ethical/political and not just for religious/theological sins. If so, then the people were guilty of a political/ethical course of action that had gone on for some time since the prophet describes the action with reference to the preceding generation ("after which their fathers walked"). One should take into consideration that Amos was referring to the Judean and Davidic policy of subordination to Israelite dominance and to Israel's program and policies. As was noted in Chapter 1, section 4, Judah's subordination to Israel had been a longstanding policy by the time of Amos but obviously not one shared by all southerners (see 2 Kings 14:8-14) and certainly not consistent with the Davidic ideology.

[5] The punishment declared against Judah parallels that found in the Tyre (1:10) and Edom (1:12) sections. These three kingdoms are threatened with the ravaging fire of a military conquest but no reference is made to the slaughter or exile of their rulers as is the case in the Damascus, Philistia, Ammonite, and Moabite material. Perhaps it was these latter powers that were most aggressive in the strong western regionalism, and thus anti-Assyrianism, at the time of Amos. Eventually, Tyre would become one of the strongest supporters of Rezin's policies (see above on 1:9-10).

I. Against Israel (2:6-16)

R. Bach, "Gottesrecht und weltliches Recht in der Verkündigung des Propheten Amos," *Festschrift für Günther Dehn* (ed. W. Schneemelcher; Neukirchen Kreis Moers: Verlag der Buchhandlungen des Erziehungsvereins, 1957)23-34; H. M.

Barstad, *The Religious Polemics of Amos: Studies in the Preaching of Am 2, 7B-8; 4, 1-13; 5, 1-27; 6, 4-7; 8, 14* (SVT 34; Leiden: E. J. Brill, 1984)11-36; M. A. **Beek**, "The Religious Background of Amos II 6-8," *OTS* 5(1948)132-41; G. H. **Box**, "Amos 2:6 and 8:6," *ET* 12(1900-01)377-78; C. M. **Carmichael**, "A Ceremonial Crux: Removing a Man's Sandal as a Female Gesture of Contempt," *JBL* 96(1977)321-36; S. **Cox**, "The Harvest Cart; or, the Oracle of Amos against Israel," *Expositor* 2d series 8(1884)321-38; M. **Dahood**, "'To Pawn One's Cloak,'" *Bib* 42(1961)359-66; J. A. **Dearman**, *Property Rights in the Eighth-Century Prophets: The Conflict and its Background* (SBLDS 106; Altanta: Scholars Press, 1988)18-25; H. **Gese**, "Kleine Beiträge zum Verständnis des Amosbuches," *VT* 12(1962)417-38; H. L. **Ginsberg**, "'Roots Below and Fruit Above' and Related Matters," *Hebrew and Semitic Studies Presented to G. R. Driver* (ed. D. W. Thomas and W. D. McHardy; London: Oxford University Press, 1963)59-71; O. **Happel**, "Amos 2, 6-16 in der Urgestalt," *BZ* 3(1905)355-67; D. R. **Hillers**, "*Hôy* and *Hôy*-Oracles: A Neglected Syntactic Aspect," *The Word of the Lord Shall Go Forth: Essays in Honor of David Noel Freedman in Celebration of His Sixtieth Birthday* (ed. C. L. Meyers and M. O'Connor; Winnona Lake: Eisenbrauns, 1983)185-88; E. R. **Lachmann**, "Note on Ruth 4:7-8," *JBL* 56(1937)53-56; B. **Lang**, "Sklaven und Unfreie im Buch Amos (II 16, VIII 6)," *VT* 31(1981)482-88; **Lang**, "The Social Organisation of Peasant Poverty in Biblical Israel," *JSOT* 24(1982)47-63; I. **Mendelsohn**, *Slavery in the Ancient Near East* (London/New York: Oxford University Press, 1949); J. **Milgrom**, *Cult and Conscience: The Asham and the Priestly Doctrine of Repentance* (SJLA 18; Leiden: E. J. Brill, 1976); J. **Morgenstern**, "Amos Studies: Part IV," *HUCA* 32(1961)295-350; H.-P. **Müller**, "Die Wurzeln '*yq, y'q* und '*wg*," *VT* 21(1971)556-64; S. M. **Paul**, "Two Cognate Semitic Terms for Mating and Copulating," *VT* 32(1982)492-94; R. **Rendtorff**, "Zu Amos 2, 14-16," *ZAW* 85(1973)226-27; H. N. **Richardson**, "Amos 2:13-16: Its Structure and Function," *SBLSP* (ed. P. Achtemeier; Missoula: Scholars Press, 1978)361-68; E. A. **Speiser**, "Of Shoes and Shekels, (I Samuel 12:3; 13:21)," *BASOR* 77(1940)15-20 = his *Oriental and Biblical Studies* (Philadelphia: University of Pennsylvania Press, 1967)151-59; J. **Wijngaards**, "*hwṣy'* and *h'lh*. A Twofold Approach to the Exodus," *VT* 15(1965)91-102.

2:6   *Thus Yahweh has said:*
        "For three transgressions of Israel,
            and for four, I will not recall it;
        because of their selling the righteous for silver,
            and the poor for a pair of sandals;

7   *those who pant over the dust of the earth on the*
            head of the weak,
            and the way of the afflicted they turn aside;
        and a man and his father have sex with the same maiden,
            and thereby profane my holy name;

8   *and upon garments taken in pledge they stretch out,*
            beside every altar,
        and wine taken in exaction they drink
            in the temple of their God.

9   *Yet I destroyed the Amorite for their benefit,*
            whose height was like the height of the cedars,
            and whose strength was like the oaks;
        and I destroyed his boughs above,
            and his roots below.

10   *And I brought you up from the land of Egypt,*
            and led you in the wilderness forty years,
            to possess the land of the Amorite.

11   *And I raised up prophets from your sons,*
            and nazirites from your young men.
        Is this not so, O children of Israel?" declares Yahweh.

12   *"But you made the nazirites drink wine,*
            and the prophets you commanded, saying,
            'Do not prophesy.'

13   *Behold, I am pressing (you) down in your place,*
            like the cart overburdened with cut grain presses down.

14   *And flight shall fail the swift,*
            and the strong shall not retain his strength,
        and the warrior shall not save his life,

15   *and the bowman shall not stand (his ground),*
        and the fleet of foot shall not escape,
            and the horseman shall not save his life,

16   *and the stouthearted among the warriors*
            shall flee unarmed on that day,"
                            declares Yahweh.

After having noted the wrongs of and described the
judgment coming upon seven nations, Amos completes his sur-

vey of the kingdoms in the region by focusing on the central object of his proclamation - Israel. In his preaching, Amos has moved from the northeast (Damascus), to the southwest (Philistia), to the northwest (Tyre), to the southeast (Edom, Ammon, Moab), to the south (Judah), and, after this rhetorical and geographical circumambulation, hones in on the center, his actual audience.

This Israel section differs from those on the other nations in several ways. (1) Both the general description of the wrongs (vv. 6-8, 12) and the depiction of the coming judgment (vv. 13-16) are greatly expanded. (2) The accusations no longer concern matters of international relations but instead address domestic matters. (3) Reference is made to specific events of the people's past. (4) Second-person, direct address to the audience becomes interspersed with third-person, indirect address. (5) The stylized announcement of judgment - "I will send (set on) fire the fortresses (wall)" - is dropped.

[6-8] The enunciation of wrongs contains the same opening formula used in the other sections - "for three trans gressions and for four." Only the Edom section among the preceding sections lists what could be interpreted as four trans-gressions. The enumeration of Israel's wrongdoings in verses 6-8 can be understood as stipulating either four or seven depending on how the text is divided. One way of reading the text is to see the two statements in verse 7*a* as parallel to and a repetition of the charge in verse 6*a* which is already spelled out in two parallel statements. Verses 7*b*, 8*a*, and 8*b* would then contain the second, third, and fourth charges. Such an interpretation assumes that the prophet was listing the four trans-gressions alluded to in the opening formula.

Another approach is to read each of the elements in verses 6*b*-8 as an independent accusation. This provides a total of seven charges, giving the three plus four noted in the opening formula. This seems to be the better line of approach since the various elements are not identical and therefore no two are quite parallel. None of the charges in verses 7*b*-8 is stated in parallelism; perhaps those in verses 6*b*-7*a* were also to be heard as separate accusations. If this be the case, then the prophet was expressing the completeness of Israel's sinfulness, seven being the number of totality or fullness. Verse 12, also an accusation, would then constitute the eighth wrong, giving a sense of going beyond all limits. Reading the accusations as seven/eight in number thus seems more in line with the straightforward sense of the text. Verses 14-16 also seem to enumerate seven consequences to result from divine judgment.

"Because they have sold the righteous for silver" points to the selling of human beings for a monetary value (see 8:6). Presumably the term "righteous" here has a legal meaning and thus would correspond to our designation "innocent" (see Exod. 23:7; Deut. 25:1). Or it may mean nothing more than our expression "an honest person." It is impossible to know whether Amos was here condemning a matter "legally" wrong or only one that he and some fellow Israelites felt was "morally" wrong. How the innocent came to be in a position where they could be sold and who were the buyers and sellers go unexplained in the text. Two possibilities have been considered most likely. (1) Corrupt judges/jurors were deciding cases against the innocent in return for bribes (see Exod. 23:6-8) or to profit from a conviction. In this case, the abuse of the legal system was the condition which made it possible to "sell out" the innocent (see * Sellin, 206-7; *Robinson, 78-79). (2) The innocent, who may have been a property owner, was sold into slavery for non-payment of a debt. In this case, the wrong would be the rapacity of the creditor, a view held by many interpreters (see *Mays, 45; *Rudolph, 141; *Wolff, 165).

Several references to persons, guilty of no crime, but sold or selling themselves into slavery for debts occur in the Old Testament (see Exod. 21:7; Lev. 25:39; 2 Kings 4:1; Neh. 5:5, 8). Such debts were not necessarily the result of a creditor's charging interest, either normal or excessive, on loans, a practice prohibited in the Old Testament (Exod. 22:25; Lev. 25:35-37; Ps. 15:5a; Ezek. 18:8, 17) but exercised at least on occasion (see Neh. 5:1-13). Only the principle of the loan may have been involved. To sell a debtor into slavery to recover the value of a loan would have been quite "legal" in ancient Israel. If the creditors were themselves officials responsible for the administration of justice, then corruptors of the legal system and rapacious creditors could have been the same group (see Dearman).

Most of the citizens of ancient Israel were probably farmers who owned only small plots of land. Such peasant farmers always lived rather precarious existences since any crop failure (see 4:6-9) could force one into debt. When debts became great or loans could not be repaid, a farmer could be forced to sell members of his family (Exod. 21:7; Neh. 5:15) or even himself (Lev. 25:39-40a) into debt servitude. Apparently the children of a debtor were or could be treated as collateral for a loan and forced into slavery for non-payment (see 2 Kings 4:1-2). Such indebtedness no doubt lay behind much of ancient Near Eastern slavery (see Mendelsohn, 23).

Persons convicted of negligence, bodily injury, or crimes were required to make restitution (see Exod. 21:18 - 22:17). The thief, when convicted, could be sold into slavery to recover funds if personal resources were not available (Exod. 22:1). Other cases of inability to make restitution may have been treated similarly. Whether Amos would have referred to such persons as "innocent" or not is uncertain but unlikely.

The expression "the poor for a pair of sandals," in the prophet's second accusation, has generated a number of interpretations. In the first place, Amos used three designations in verses 6b-7a whose exact meanings are uncertain. These are 'ebyon, dallim, and 'anawim which we have translated as "poor, weak, and afflicted." Given the nature of the biblical evidence and our present knowledge, it is impossible to know how these differed from one another. Persons in these categories seem to have shared a state of weakness, oppression, and exploitation. Second, the reference to a pair of sandals is even more ambiguous. The following are some interpretations that have been proposed. (1) Reference to the pair of sandals or the price of such items stressed the insignificance of the bribe for which judges/jurors were willing to pervert legal cases. (Judges and arbitrators may have been paid by the litigants in ancient times.) (2) Debtors may have owed no more than the equivalent or the price of a pair of sandals yet were still sold into debt slavery. (3) The property of the poor being described was worth no more than a pair of sandals. (4) The transfer of a shoe or sandal represented or symbolized taking possession and the confirmation of property exchange (see Deut. 25:7-10; Ruth 4:7-8; Ps. 60:8; 1 Sam. 12:3 [Greek; see Box]; Lachmann; Speiser). (5) The expression was used to indicate the ridiculously low payment required to "purchase" the poor.

Others have argued that the text has nothing to do with sandals. The Aramaic Targum understood the text to mean "the needy in order to take possession of them." The medieval Jewish exegete Rashi understood the Targum to suggest that a judge forced a poor person to sell a field located between two fields owned by the judge so that the latter might then secure the property and "lock" it in. This, Rashi suggested, indicated that the noun *na'alaim* (a dual form from which is derived the reference to "pair") was derived from the root *n'l* meaning "to lock, close" not from its homonym meaning "sandal." Another explanation traces the term back to the root *'lm* meaning "hide or conceal" and thus refers to some "hidden gift" or bribe (see 1 Sam. 12:3 [Greek]; Sir. 46;19; *Gordis, 213-15).

In relating the trading of the poor to a pair of sandals, Amos was emphasizing how lightly human life was being treated by drawing upon the imagery one might use in describing a good bargain purchased cheaply. Kilamuwa of Sam'al who ruled in northwest Syria in the ninth century set up an inscription bragging about his achievements. In it he notes that "the king of the Danunites tried to overpower me, but I hired against him the king of Assyria, who gave a maid for a lamb, a man for a garment" (*ANET* 654). In other words, he secured assistance at a very low cost. He could have written, "a human for a pair of sandals."

Two differing translations have been proposed for the opening part of verse 7a, the third of Amos's accusations against Israel. The KJV reflects one option: "that pant after the dust of the earth on the head of the poor." The RSV reflects the other: "that trample the head of the poor into the dust of the earth." The former provides a literal reading of the Hebrew while the latter alters the text slightly and treats the verb *sh'p* ("to pant, yearn for") as derived from or a synomym of *shup* ("to trample, tread upon"; see Gen. 3:15). The translation offered above agrees with the KJV (see 8:4).

The reference to those panting (the form is a participle) over the dust on the head of the weak is a satirical comment about the greed and avarice of the ruling classes in Israelite society. The term "pant after" is a graphic way of referring to this greed. Jeremiah later spoke of the wild ass in breeding season panting for a mate (2:24) or gasping air while suffering from heat and drought (14:6). Amos paints a picture of land hungry upperclass citizens, perhaps government officials, so desirous of accumulating ever larger estates that they were envious of even the dust (used as a sign of mourning?) on the heads of the embattered peasantry.

The fourth of Amos's charges is again expressed in rather cryptic language: "the way of the afflicted they turn aside" (or "make long, extend"). Although the specifics in this accusation remain unclear, it points to a deliberate circumvention of justice. The designation "way" (*drk*) can refer to one's journey, undertaking, situation, behavior, and so on. Whether the term could designate a court case or legal complaint remains uncertain. At any rate, the meaning of the statement here probably parallels what is described in Prov. 17:23 - "A wicked man accepts a bride from the bosom to pervert (to turn aside) the ways (*'rḥ* not *drk*) of justice" (see Prov. 18:5). The verb "turn aside" or "extend, stretch out" is frequently used in contexts describing the perversion of justice (Exod. 23:2, 6; Deut. 16:19; 1 Sam. 8:3; Isa. 10:2; 29:31; 30:11). It remains uncertain whether Amos is referring to undue, lengthy conditions of servitude placed on the afflicted or to practices and procedures used to derail justice or to delay hearing legal complaints.

The fifth accusation concerns sexual relations with the same female by father and son. The Hebrew actually reads "to go in to" which is a euphemism for intercourse (see Paul). The Hebrew expression for the female is "the *na'arah*." Presumably the definite article is used to indicate that the two males were involved sexually with the same female. Two questions are at issue in the interpretation of this charge. What was the status of the female? What was the nature of the sexual relationship that profaned the name of God?

The term *na'arah* in the Old Testament denotes a young female without reference to social status. Thus the term here does not aid in identifying the particular class of the woman alluded to. Interpreters have assumed she is a secular prostitute (for example, *Gordis, 216), a temple prostitute (for example, *Soggin, 48), or a waitress at a house of feasting (Barstad, 11-36, who provides a survey of modern interpretations) but such connotations are neither indicated by the text nor necessary for its interpretation.

The sexual relations of a father and son with the same female are said to profane God's holy name. "To profane (*ḥll*) the name of God" is a technical term in the Old Testament used to denote transgression or trespass directed against the Deity (see Milgrom, 86-89). Profanation involved either desecration of something especially dedicated to God, that is, trespass on or the violation of the "holy" sancta, the transgression of a relationship especially protected by God, or the violation of the name of God through breaking or falsely swearing an oath in the name of God. (Lev. 18:21; 19:12; 20:3; 21:6, 12; 22:2, 32: Jer. 34:16). The penalty for profaning the name of God or desecration of sancta was a reparation offering (an *'asham*). For sexual relations to have defiled the name of God, the female had to stand in some particular relationship to the Deity. For a father and son to have consorted sexually with a common or cultic prostitute or for a father to have "intruded upon his son's love affair" (*Wolff, 167) would not have profaned the name of God.

Old Testament laws prohibited sexual relations by a son with the wife of his father (Lev. 18:8; 20:11; Deut. 22:30; 27:20), a father with the wife of his son (Lev. 18:15; 20:12), and a man with a woman and her daughter (Lev. 18:17; 20:14) or two sisters (Lev. 18:18), but probably none of these is referred to by Amos since he uses such a general term for the female. The situation condemned by the prophet can best be understood in light of Exod. 21:7-11 and Lev. 19:20-23. According to the Exodus text, a person might purchase a female slave (one of the possible meanings of *na'arah*; see *Maag, 177, note 9) and designate her for himself or his son as a sexual partner. If he designated her for his son then he had to treat her as a daughter; presumably if designated for himself, the son had to treat her as his father's wife. In both cases, sexual relations with her by both father and son would have broken a taboo.

Throughout much of the ancient Near East, marriage, betrothal, and officially sanctioned sexual arrangements were considered under the special protection of the divine. Adultery was considered the "great sin" (see Milgrom, 131-33). Thus betrothals, marriages, and concubinage were understood as covenanted relationships divinely protected as if the Deity were the third party in such relationships. According to Lev. 19:20-23, sexual intercourse with a "designated" female, even a slave, by a male other than the intended husband required a reparation offering (*'asham*) as a penalty to the Deity. Such activity was a desecration of the name of Yahweh, a trespass on a divinely protected relationship.

Verse 7b should therefore be understood as a condemnation of not just the acquisition of females but male utilization of such women in a manner that transgressed a sexual taboo, infringing on a relationship under divine sanction, and thus profaning the name of God.

The sixth wrongdoing has to do with the use of garments taken as pledges against a loan. The practice of pawning personal possessions is regulated in Old Testament laws in terms of the items to be used as collateral, the person affected, and certain time stipulations. Hand-mills and grindstones, essential to food production, were not to be pawned (Deut. 24:6); a widow's garment was not to be taken (Deut. 24:17); and a man's cloak, his outer garment, was not to be kept overnight (Exod. 22:26-27; Deut. 24:12-13).

Most interpreters have understood the abuse referred to in one of three ways. (1) The garments were spread out in "the preparation of a place in which to bed down for the night" (*Wolff, 167) thus breaking the regulation about returning a cloak before nighttime (Exod. 22:26-27; Deut. 24:10-13). (2) The garments had been taken by temple personnel as pledges for sacrifices purchased on credit by poor Israelites (*Maag, 235, note 22). (3) Special cultic garments were worn in the sanctuary precincts (see 2 Kings 10:22; 22:14), as in modern Muslim pilgrimages at Mecca. Normal clothing worn inside the sanctuary precincts would have become holy and thus temple property. Creditors were dedicating and contributing others' clothing to the sanctuary (so Morgenstern, 316).

None of these three interpretations, however, seems to be implied by the text. Nothing suggests that the people lying on the garments were spending the night, certainly not beside the altar. Temple personnel are not mentioned, and no Old Testament text explicitly mentions wearing special clothing in the temple precincts.

Amos seems merely to be condemning wealthy creditors who rather than providing their own lounging materials while attending worship and enjoying a meal of sacrificial flesh were using pledged garments with no respect and much disdain for their poor owners who could not afford the pleasure of such sacrifices.

The final accusation in verses 6-8 concerns the consumption of wine in the temple. The simple act of drinking wine in the temple precincts, that is, where one consumed the wine, was not the issue since one would assume that wine consumption at sacrificial meals was the norm. Even priests were prohibited from drinking wine and strong drink in the temple precincts only when they were on duty and actually officiating in the sacrificial services (Lev. 10:9). The source of the wine was either fines for misconduct or taxes. The term *'anushim* designating those from whom the wine was secured occurs nowhere else in the Hebrew Bible. The verb *'nsh*, however, is used in Exod. 21:22 in speaking of the penalty to be imposed on a man who, while struggling with another, bumps a pregnant woman causing her to miscarry, and in Deut. 22:19 where a man is convicted of slander against his new bride and her parents (see also Prov. 22:3; 27:12). The noun form *'onesh* occurs in 2 Kings 23:33 as a penalty or tribute imposed on Judah by Egypt. In non-biblical texts, the noun *'nshm* can refer to taxes or tariffs. (This usage may be reflected in the Greek form of 1 Kings 10:15.)

If the wine was a fine, with alcoholic beverages used as a medium of exchange, then, according to Exod. 21:22 and Deut. 22:19, the victim should have received the fine. (The basic principle in the administration of justice in ancient Israel was restitution of the victim rather than punishment of the offender [see Lev. 6:5; Num. 5:7].) If the wine was collected as taxes or exactions from the peasant farmers (see on 5:11), then it was most likely the government officials whom Amos condemns. There is nothing to suggest that the fines were imposed by the temple hierarchy nor that the use of the wine was part of a temple service involving cultic prostitution, all-night orgies, and drinking bouts (so *Hammershaimb, 47-50).

Amos's condemnation implies two things. (1) The acquisition of the wine, whether as a tax, a fine, or even as payment or interest on debts, was considered an oppressive act. The *'onesh* was always imposed on someone by another, whether legitimately or illegitimately. (2) The use of this particular wine in cultic meals, where persons would normally utilize and enjoy the products of their own labors, was apparently especially odious to the oppressed and to Amos.

[9-12] In verses 9-10, Amos has God remind the audience of divine actions which resulted in the Israelite possession of the land. Three actions are noted. (1) The destruction of the Amorite population is given priority probably because it was the event which made possible the actual possession of the land. The term Amorite, derived from the Semitic term Amurru used in Akkadian texts to refer to the west in general, was also the name of a territory in northwestern Syria. Amos uses the term to denote the population of Palestine before the arrival of the Israelites. (On the motif of "migration

from another land," see below on 9:7.) In describing the Amorite population, Amos gives expression to a motif found elsewhere in the scriptures, namely, that the indigenous population of Israel's future land was abnormal and strong (see Num. 13:28; Deut. 1:28; 9:2). Here they are described as being as tall as cedars and as powerful as oaks. The completeness of the Amorite destruction is expressed in an idiomatic expression using two extremes to denote "everything" - "boughs (or "fruit") above and roots below" (see Isa. 37:31; *ANET* 662; Ginsberg).

(2) Reference is made to God's having brought the people up from the land of Egypt (see 3:1; 9:7). Amos's formulation of this statement is worded so as to focus on the goal of the exodus, namely, the acquisition of the land (note the last part of v. 10). Old Testament texts sometimes use the expression "to bring out" (hiphil of the verb *yṣ'*) and at other times "to bring up" (hiphil of *'lh*) depending primarily upon whether the focus is on the redemptive act of liberation from slavery or the possession of the land (see Wijngaards). Amos here uses *'lh*.

(3) Divine guidance in the wilderness for forty years (probably a symbolic number indicating a lengthy period) is also mentioned. Although reference to the long stay in the wilderness is mentioned by no other eighth-century prophet (see Amos 5:25), Amos's contemporary Hosea utilized the wilderness motif in his preaching (see Hos. 2:14).

References to the exodus and to the guidance in the wilderness are subordinated to the last statement in verse 10, namely, the possession of the land. They are treated as preliminary phases which culminated in the acquisition of the land. Amos highlighted this element because the abuses he condemned in verses 6-8 had to do with land possession, usage, and distribution. Amos implies that, since the possession of the land was a consequence of divine favor, the Israelites were not free to deal with it however they wished. This was not actually stated by the prophet, who drew no overt conclusion on the basis of the evidence supplied in verses 9-10. Presumably he left the conclusion to be drawn by his audience.

Beginning with verse 10, the prophet uses second-person address in the remainder of this section (v. 10-16). In verses 6-8, Israel was spoken of in the third person. This shift in address is found frequently in prophetic address and does not indicate the presence of secondary additions (see Hillers who examines the phenomenon in woe oracles).

A fourth piece of evidence in addition to the threefold declaration about the divine favor in granting the land to the people (in verses 9-10) is supplied by the prophet in verse 11 to substantiate the logic of his case against his audience. In this instance Amos overtly describes the people's acts as frustrating the divine purpose (verse 12).

The raising up of prophets and Nazirites is depicted as a divine action comparable to the destruction of the Amorite population, the exodus from Egypt, and the guidance in the wilderness. Apparently for Amos, the work of the prophets and the nazirites constituted divine guidance supplied by God for life in the land. The fact that Amos nowhere refers to the priests could indicate that he considered them part of the corrupt establishment along with the monarch and the officialdom of the state. (Note his condemnation of Amaziah in 7:16-17 and the parallels between 2:12 and 7:16.)

The fact that the two groups mentioned in verse 11 are described as "raised up" by God indicates that Amos viewed prophets and Nazirites as special instruments of the divine whose functions were carried out for the welfare of society. In this text, Amos clearly views the prophets in a favorable light (see below on 7:14-15). Unfortunately he supplies no indication of the nature and function of the prophets and nazirites in Israelite culture since he could assume that his audience was acquainted with these.

If Amos viewed his own activity as prophetical, as appears to have been the case (see 3:8; 7:15), he must have seen one of the functions of prophets to be social criticism. The context within which he first refers to prophets, namely, in 1:2-2:16, would suggest this. A second function of prophets, given the context of Amos's reference, was the task of envisioning the future in terms of the divine reaction to conditions in the present.

No Old Testament texts discuss the nature and function of prophecy in theoretical terms. Two passages in non-prophetical books, however, provide some insight. Lam. 2:14 declares:

> Your prophets envisioned (or proclaimed) for you
>   delusion and folly;
> and they did not expose your iniquity
>   in order to reverse your fate (or restore your

> fortunes);
> but they envisioned (or proclaimed) for you oracles
>   of delusion and deception.

Similarly, Prov. 29:18 asserts:

> where there is no (prophetic) vision
>   a people cast off restraint;
> but the one keeping torah
>   is blessed.

These texts highlight two functions of the prophet, namely, the exposure of the wrongs and ills of a society and the envisionment of the future state of a society. In both, the goal of prophetic activity is right order in society, related to either proper obedience or to repentance from wrong.

The functions of the Nazirite in Israelite society are less certain. Apparently a child could be dedicated to God as a lifelong Nazirite. Two cases of this are known from the Bible, namely, Samson (Judg. 13:2-8) and Samuel (1 Sam. 1:3-11), both of whom were vowed before conception. A person, either male or female, could become a temporary Nazirite voluntarily (see Num. 6:1-21).

A Nazirite was required to abstain from any contact with grapes or products made from them, from cutting the hair, and from any contact with a corpse (Num. 6:1-8). A vow was required to become a Nazirite (Num. 6:2) and a desacralization ritual was undergone when the person reentered ordinary life (Num. 6:13-20). While a Nazirite, the person belonged to the realm of the "holy" (Num. 6:6, 8) and to this extent resembled a priest. (Only in 2 Kings 4:9, part of a prophetic legend about Elisha, is a prophet ever called holy *qadosh*.) Unlike a Nazirite, a prophet could presumably assume a prophetic role without a vow and give up the function without a desacralization ritual.

The Old Testament nowhere discusses the role and function of a Nazirite nor the motivations which compelled people to assume such a vow. A Nazirite appears to have been an ascetic with a somewhat restricted lifestyle but not a monastic. Perhaps they, like the Rechabites (see Jer. 35:1-11), shared and gave testimony to a simple lifestyle and thus presented a living challenge to aspects of the culture of their day.

At any rate, Amos accused his audience of either supplying the
Nazirites with wine, encouraging them to drink, or altering the
requirements associated with the vow. Both the prophets, who
were probably considered persons especially called by God to
their tasks, and the Nazirites, who voluntarily assumed their
roles, were interfered with by the people whom Amos thus
accused of perverting and hindering the special roles of these
functionaries.

[13-16] In these verses, Amos describes the judgment to
befall the Israelites. Only in intent does this section parallel the
proclamations of judgment in the other oracles on the nations
in 1:2-2:6. In verses 13-16, the description of the coming judgment is greatly expanded and no reference is made to a
destruction by fire.

In verse 13, which introduces the judgment section,
Amos employs a simile using verbal forms which occur
nowhere else in the Old Testament. The verse, therefore, presents scholars with problems of interpretation and has
engendered a variety of translations. The following is a sample
of such translations (for others, see *THBA*, 55-56).

> Listen, I groan under the burden of you,
>   as a wagon creaks under a full load (NEB; see KJV).

> Ah, I will slow your movements
> As a wagon is slowed
> When it is full of cut grain (NJPSV).

> Behold, I will press you down in your place,
>   as a cart full of sheaves presses down (RSV).

The translation proposed above is based on the following considerations. (1) The verb *'uq* is an Aramaism equivalent
to the Hebrew *ṣuq* meaning "to press upon, oppress" (see Pss.
55: 3; 66:11; *Gordis, 217). (2) God is the active agent in verse
13*a* (see RSV); the verbal form is not to be understood in an
intransitive sense (as in NEB and KJV). (3) The imagery of
the simile does not point to the prediction of an earthquake (so
*Wolff, 171; *Soggin, 49). (4) The use of the participle form in
verse 13*a* (*me'iq*) with the first person pronoun is not to be
read in a future sense ("I will press down"; so RSV) but in a
present sense ("I am pressing down") descriptive of an action

already begun. (5) The term *hml'h*, understood and pointed as from *ml'* "to be full," may be a participial form of the verb *l'h*.

The "pressing down" of the Israelites in their place probably refers to the aggressive military action already underway against Israel and spoken of in 1:3-15. Surrounding nations were aggressively encroaching on Israelite territory and Amos announces that the situation will worsen, with frightening effects on the Israelites (see on 3:11 and 6:12).

In verses 14-16, Amos describes the panic that will overwhelm the Israelite military. In the day of battle, the elite and most qualified of the foot soldiers and chariot corps will lose all those qualities that made for effectiveness in battle. Utilizing a sevenfold scheme, Amos enumerates the consequences that will overcome the swift, the strong, the warrior, the bowman, the fleet of foot, the horseman, and the stouthearted.

3. AN ADVERSARY ALL AROUND
THE LAND (3:1-11)

W. **Baumgartner**, "Amos 3, 3-8," *ZAW* 33(1913)78-80; M. O. **Boyle**, "The Covenant Lawsuit of the Prophet Amos: III 1-IV 13," *VT* 21(1971)338-62; H. **Gese**, "Kleine Beiträge zum Verständnis des Amosbuches," *VT* 12(1962)417-38; Y. **Gitay**, "A Study of Amos's Art of Speech: A Rhetorical Analysis of Amos 3:1-15," *CBQ* 42(1980)293-309; T. R. **Hobbs**, "Amos 3, 16 and 2, 10," *ZAW* 81(1969)384-87; H. **Huffmon**, "The Treaty Background of Hebrew *yada'*," *BASOR* 181(1966)31-37; H. **Junker**, "*Leo rugiit, quis non timebit? Deus locutus est, quis non prophetabit?* Eine textkritische und exegetische Untersuchung über Amos 3:3-8," *TTZ* 59(1950)4-13; F. **Lindström**, *God and the Origin of Evil: A Contextual Analysis of Alleged Monistic Evidence in the Old Testament* (CBOT 21; Lund: CWK Gleerup, 1983)199-214; R. F. **Melugin**, "The Formation of Amos: An Analysis of Exegetical Method," *SBLSP* (ed. P. J. Achtemeier; Missoula: Scholars Press, 1978)369-91; S. **Mittmann**, "Gestalt und Gehalt einer prophetischen Selbstrechtfertigung (Am 3, 3-8)," *TQ* 151(1971)134-45; M. J. **Mulder**, "Ein Vorschlag zur Übersetzung von Amos III 6b," *VT* 34(1984)106-8; S.M. **Paul**, "Amos 3:3-8: The Irresistible Sequence of Cause and Effect," *HAR* 7(1983)203-20; H. **Pelser**, "Amos 3:11 - A Communication," *OTWSA* 7-8(1964-65)153-56; G. **Pfeifer**, "Unausweichliche Konsequenzen: Denkformenanalyse von Amos III 3-8," *VT* 33(1983)341-47; **Pfeifer**, "Die Denkform des Propheten Amos III 3-8," *VT* 33(1983)341-47; **Pfeifer**, "Die Denkform des Propheten Amos (III 9-11)," *VT* 34(1984)476-81; B. **Renaud**, "Genèse et théologie d'Amos 3, 3-8," *Mélanges bibliques et orientaux en l'honneur de M. Henri Cazelles* (ed. A. Caquot and M. Delcor; AOAT 212; Kevelaer/Neukirchen-Vluyn: Butzon & Bercker/Neukirchener Verlag, 1981)353-72; A. **Schenker**, "Steht der Prophet unter dem Zwang zu weissagen, oder steht Israel vor der Evidenz der Weisung Gottes in der Weissagung des Propheten? Zur Interpretation von Amos 3,3-8," *BZ* 30(1986)250-56; D. **Shapiro**, "The Seven Questions of Amos," *Tradition* 20(1982)327-31; L. A. **Sinclair**, "The Courtroom Motif in the Book of Amos," *JBL* 85(1966)351-53; D. W.

Thomas, "Note on *nô'adû* in Amos 3:3," *JTS* 7(1956)69-70; T. C. Vriezen, "Erwägungen zu Amos 3, 2," *Archäologie und Altes Testament: Festschrift für Kurt Galling* (ed. A. Kuschke and E. Kutsch; Tübingen: J. C. B. Mohr [Paul Siebeck], 1970)255-58.

3:1 *Hear this word which Yahweh has spoken concerning you,*
        O people of Israel, concerning the whole family which I
        brought up from the land of Egypt, saying,
2 *"Only you have I known*
                of all the families of the earth;
            therefore, I will hold you accountable for all your
                iniquities."
3 *Do two people walk together,*
            without having met?
4   *Does a lion roar in the forest,*
            when there is no prey for it?
        Does a young lion give forth his voice from its liar,
            without having made a catch?
5 *Does a bird swoop down upon a trap on the ground,*
            when there is no bait for it?
        Does a trap spring up from the ground,
            unless it has caught something?
6 *Or is a ram's horn sounded in the city,*
            without the people being alarmed?
        Or does evil befall a city,
            unless Yahweh has caused it?
7 *Surely, my Lord Yahweh does not do a thing,*
            unless he has revealed his purpose to his servants
                the prophets.
8 *A lion has roared,*
            who cannot be afraid?
        My Lord Yahweh has spoken,
            who cannot prophesy?
9 *Proclaim upon the fortresses of Ashdod,*
            and upon the fortresses of the land of Egypt;
        and say, "Gather on the hills of Samaria;
            and observe the great outrages within her,
            and the oppression in her midst."
10 *"They have not known how to do right," says Yahweh,*
            "those storing up violence and rapine
        in their fortresses."
11 *Therefore, thus my Lord Yahweh has said,*

> *"An adversary, and all about the land;*
> *and it shall bring down your stronghold,*
> *and your fortresses shall be plundered."*

This rhetorical unit contains a general statement about Israel's accountability for its wrongdoings (vv. 1-2), a series of rhetorical questions (vv. 3-6) supporting the contentions that Israel's present adversity is Yahweh's doing and that Yahweh makes known his purpose through prophets (vv. 7-8), a description of Samaria's wrongdoings (vv. 9-10), and a declaration that Israel's adversary which now surrounds the nation shall destroy and plunder it (v. 11). In slightly different terms the unit may be seen as containing the declaration of a general thesis (vv. 1-2) comprising a statement of condition/cause (v. 2a) and consequence/effect (v. 2b), supporting evidence collaborating the relationship of cause and effect (vv. 3-8), a commission to call witnesses to examine evidence (v. 9), a formal charge describing present conditions (v. 10), and a verdict announcing the coming consequences (v. 11). The unit depends upon logical argument to convict and convince its audience.

The unity and integrity of 3:1-11 make it unnecesssary and unwarranted either to consider 3:1-2 as the conclusion to 1:2(3)-2:16 or to subdivide 3:1-11 into a number of small pericopes. In addition, the treatment of 3:1-2 as the conclusion to the speech against the nations (see *THBA* 58-60; *Maag, 9, following Budde) is unwarranted since it pales in comparison with the description of judgment already announced in 2:13-16, utilizes a new term for wrongdoing (*'awon* instead of *pesha'*), does not treat Israel as one among other nations, and contains a wholly new introductory formula ("hear this word" rather than "for three transgressions and for four"). The isolation of three units (vv. 1-2, 3-8, 9-11) by some form critics (see *Wolff; Melugin, 378-79) divides the text into a series of supposedly self-contained sayings or oracles but leaves them without meaningful contexts (see Gitay, 294-95).

[1-2] Verse 1 is extremely awkward. It opens with a call to attention addressed in the plural to the population at large and speaks of Yahweh in the third person. In verse 1b, Yahweh already speaks in the first person prior to the transitional expression "saying." In addition, the terminology in verse 1b is repeated in verse 2 ("the whole family/all the families"). Further, the object of Yahweh's word is identified three times in

verse 1, as "you" (pl.), "people of Israel," and "the whole family which I brought up from the land of Egypt," which appears unusually verbose (compare 3:13; 4:1; 5:1). If verse 1*b* is a gloss, as appears likely, then it can be understood as an attempt by a later editor/copyist to insure that readers understood that Judeans were included in the statements of verse 2. The addition, however, is not evidence for a deuteronomistic redaction of the book; the expression "to bring up from the land of Egypt" is not deuteronomistic (see Hobbs).

The general indirectness of Amos's denunciation of Israel in 2:6-16, where only verses 10-13 contain direct address in second-person speech, is abandoned in 3:1-2. In 1:2-2:16, Israel was fundamentally spoken of as one nation among others but with this unit direct confrontation dominates.

In verse 2, Amos stresses the intimacy which existed between Yahweh and Israel. The semantic range of the verb "to know" covers not only cognitive matters but also the intimacy of personal relationships; the term could be used as a euphemism for sexual relations (see Gen. 4:1). The term in itself, however, does not imply in this context any reference to a special divine election, to the exodus, to the giving of the land, to the revelation of the divine will to Israel (see *Wolff, 176-77), or to a covenant relationship between Israel and Yahweh (so Huffmon). Nor does the term in this text imply that some great task or greater obligation had been placed upon Israel than upon other nations (see *Hammershaimb, 57). All that appears to be implied is that Yahweh was Israel's national God and only Israel's. As such, the two shared a relationship which Yahweh shared with no other people among "all the families of the earth" (for this expression elsewhere, see Gen. 12:3; 28:14).

Because of this unique relationship to the children of Israel, Amos declares, Yahweh could, and was perhaps obligated, to hold them accountable for their iniquities. Again, the term translated "hold accountable" (*paqad*) has a wide semantic usage ranging from "visit" to "take care of" to "muster" to "punish." The context suggests something like "I will call you to account" (so NJPSV). The "iniquities" (a term occurring only here in Amos) are not defined in verse 2, indicating that 3:1-2 should not be treated as an independent, self-contained saying. The iniquities are further defined, however, in verses 9*b*-10.

[3-8] In these verses, Amos employs a series of seven questions (vv. 3-6), all illustrating the principle and inter-

relationship of cause and effect. The questions share three features in common. (1) They all draw upon the world of common everyday knowledge. No special experience or revelatory insight was needed for one to understand the questions or to draw the correct answers. (2) All illustrate the principle of causality in the natural and social realms. (3) The answer to each of these questions is clearly "No." The employment of questions as a teaching device was widely practiced throughout the near east.

The questions and implied answers in verses 3-6 lay the groundwork for Amos's conclusions in verses 7-8. In verse 8, the conclusions are stated in question form. The prophet's argumentation is fundamentally logical in nature utilizing the principle of analogy.

The series of questions opens in verse 3 with an interrogative statement which may be seen as a neutral or rather banal way of getting the series going. Only verse 3 is composed of a single question; the others occur in pairs. Since there are seven questions in verses 3-6, one question had to stand alone.

Various translations have been proposed for verse 3, depending upon how one understands the situation envisioned in the question. The translation offered above is the one most widely found but its straightforward meaning - "Can two people walk together unless they meet?" - appears so simplistic that one wonders how it would have functioned to entice an audience's attention. The verb *hlk* can denote various forms of movement including walking. Similarly, *y'd* can mean "meet" but also "designate", "appoint," in the sense of making arrangements about something (see Exod. 21:8-9). One could thus translate the verse as "Can two people go on a journey together without having made arrangements?" (for other suggestions, see Thomas; *Gordis, 219).

Verse 3 can be seen as alluding back to verse 2, the "two" walking or journeying together being Israel and Yahweh. Throughout Leviticus 26, for example, the relationship between Israel and Yahweh is described as walking, either with or contrary to (see Mic. 6:8). Amos and his audience may also have been familiar with "walk/journey" terminology used in the description of one's relationship to Yahweh and his will.

The matched pair of questions in verse 4 have to do with lions and their hunting. At this point, the questions begin to deal with matters of life and death, destruction and calamity.

The prophet thus begins to interweave emotional and rational appeals. Two phases of the lion's kill are referred to: the roar to frighten away other animals after the prey is downed and the growl from the liar after the victim has been dragged back to feed the young. The references to the lion's roar and giving forth its voice employ terminology identical to that used by the prophet in speaking of Yahweh in 1:2 (see below on v. 8).

Again, verse 5 describes two phases of a hunt, this time with reference to the trapping of birds. The bird swoops down upon the trap on the ground when it spots the bait and the trap springs up from the ground to ensnare the prey.

With verse 6, Amos moves to speak of events associated with the city. People would no doubt have agreed with the affirmation in the first question in this verse. A warning blast on the ram's horn (see 2:2 where the same term occurs) would not have been sounded unless the people were frightened, or when the horn was sounded the people become alarmed.

The second statement of the verse, that misfortune does not befall a city unless Yahweh has brought it about, probably represents the point which Amos wishes his audience to accept and which, unlike the other examples, may not have been self-evident. Interpreters have generally explained Amos's point in 6b in one of two ways. Some assume that all misfortune in ancient Israel would have been automatically attributed to the Deity and thus Amos was simply stating the obvious (for an outline and refutation of this view, see Lindström). The biblical material, however, does not assume that all events were automatically attributed to the Deity as primary cause. Others assume that Amos was refuting a widely held view that because of its special election and status as Yahweh's people, Israel was somehow immune from any misfortune and catastrophe, especially divinely sent calamity (see, for example, Paul, 214). But surely Amos is here not engaging in theological argumentation over Israel's special status and divine causality. His goal was much more modest and must be understood in light of the remainder of this section. Amos's goal would appear to have been to get the audience to agree to the implication of the first six questions where the response was straightforward and commonsensical and then on the basis of such agreement to assent to the final proposition. Acceptance of this proposition would then support his main contention: the present trouble being undergone by Israel, its oppression by neighboring states, was the work of Yahweh, a work already begun and which would culminate in the future devastation of the northern kingdom (see v. 11).

The series of questions in verses 3-6 is followed by three assertions in verses 7-8. The first in verse 7 has been considered a secondary redactional addition by a majority of recent scholars. A number of arguments have been used to support this view. (1) Syntactically, the verse is a declarative assertion throughout, thus differing radically from the preceeding seven questions and from the following two assertions which include interrogative elements. (2) The prose form of the text contrasts with the poetic context in which it occurs. (3) The content of the assertion is considered late and dependent upon deuteronomistic thought and phraseology. The expression, "his servants, the prophets," is found frequently in deuteronomistic and post-Amos literature (see 2 Kings 9:7; 17:13, 23; 21:10; 24:2; Jer. 7:25; 25:4; 26:5; 29:19; 35:15; 44:4). In addition, "to reveal a plan" is a non-prophetic expression (see Prov. 11:13; 20:19; 25:9). (4) The verse is not essential to the train of thought being developed by Amos since verse 8b seems to make the prophet's point just as forcefully.

Verse 7, however, may be viewed not as an extraneous editorial addition but as a significant element in the unit (see Gitay, 298-99). Earlier in the section, Amos had primarily relied on reason and analogical thinking to appeal to and convince his audience. Various elements, such as the affirmation of Israel's special relationship to Yahweh and the consequence of that (v. 2) as well as the imagery employed in the questions in verses 4-6, also contain powerful appeals to the emotions. Verse 7 may be seen as an ethical appeal in which the prophet sought to establish his own authority and credibility in the mind of the audience. If the proposition that Yahweh can stand behind the evil that befalls a city is asserted in verse 6b, then verse 7 can be understood as describing how that can be known, namely, through the revelation of the divine purpose to and by the prophets. On the basis of verse 8b, it is clear that Amos placed his activity in the realm of prophecy, though by professional vocation he was not a prophet (see 7:14). Thus verse 7 serves to substantiate both his activity and what he says.

If one takes verse 7 as an ethical appeal, then the objections to its authenticity may not be so weighty. (1) Syntactically, one would expect a statement about authority to take the form of an assertion rather than a question. (2) Prose is more assertive than poetry; the break from poetry to prose highlights the assertion as assertion. (3) The parallel between this text and deuteronomistic passages does not prove anything more than a shared perspective and vocabulary (see Paul, 215; *Hammershaimb, 60). Although "to reveal a plan" is an expression found elsewhere only in didactic literature, namely in Proverbs, it should be noted that this section of Amos, especially verses 3-6, is highly didactic in nature. In addition, the idea of a divine "secret" or "counsel" (*sôd*) which can be revealed to prophetic figures is found in other prophetic texts (see Jer. 23:18, 22; see Job 15:8). The full statement "unless he reveals his purpose to his servants the prophets" occurs nowhere else in scripture. This uniqueness would hardly suggest that it was copied from elsewhere or added by an editor. (4) Finally, verses 7 and 8*b* are not identical in content. Verse 7 affirms the special revelatory role of the prophet whereas verse 8*b* implies the possibility that anyone may prophesy when Yahweh has spoken.

Verse 8 is the pivotal verse is this unit. The series of questions culminates in 6*b* with the prophet having deftly led his audience to agree that calamity and evil may be the work of Yahweh. Verse 7 then asserts that Yahweh reveals his plan or purpose in everything he does. The first half of verse 8 now picks up and develops the thought of verse 6*b*.

"A lion has roared." What Amos here affirms appears to be the following: the aggression and military action against Israel by the regional/anti-Assyrian coalition is nothing other than the action of Yahweh who, like the lion after downing the prey, has roared to signal a kill and all that remains is for the prey to be dragged away and torn to pieces (see the imagery of Hos. 13:7-8). If the lion has roared who could avoid being frightened. No one!

"My Lord Yahweh has spoken." Amos proclaims that in his actions, Yahweh has spoken. The aggression of neighboring states (see 1:3*b*, 6*b*, 9*b*, 11*b*, 13*b*) is the result of Yahweh's word. Given such speech, "who cannot prophesy?" No one!

[9-11] In verse 9, Amos commands his audience to make proclamation in Ashdod and the land of Egypt inviting the hearers to assemble on the mountains around Samaria to behold the evidence against the capital city. The reason for the invitation to two states is clear. Legal procedures in Israel required two witnesses to provide evidence in a capital case (see Num. 35:30; Deut. 17:6; 19:5). Why these two particular witnesses are chosen remains unclear; probably any two could have performed this function except for a power like Assyria who as Israel's ally would have been prejudiced in favor of Samaria. (Clearly the Greek reading of Assyria instead of Ashdod is not original.)

From the hills around the city, the witnesses are called upon to observe the evidence against Samaria and thus to provide testimony condemning the society of the capital city. The language used by Amos to designate the evidence is the language of oppression. Great outrages and oppressed people (or "oppression" if *'ashuqim* is taken as a collective noun) are found in Samaria's midst. The oppression and outrage referred to in this text are no doubt to be seen as synonymous with the list of wrongdoings denounced in 2:6-8. Governmental officials constituting the ruling class in Samaria were exploiting the native population, the lower classes, and refugees and displaced persons. They sought to preserve the standard of living enjoyed during Israel's higher level of prosperity when Jeroboam II's kingdom was thriving and better international relations flourished. Now under war conditions, in the midst of a shrinking state, with external contacts and trade reduced and displaced persons abounding, wealthier Samarians sought to continue their lifestyles at the expense of their own citizenry.

Verse 10 contains the divine charge against the Samarians. They do not know how to do what is right and just (see 2 Sam. 15:3; Isa. 30:10). The second half of the verse describes those unacquainted with or incapable of doing the right. They are those who store up lawlessness and rapine in their fortresses (for the two terms used together, see Isa. 60:18; Jer. 6:7; 20:8; Hab. 1:3; 2:17). Lawlessness and rapine are opposed to justice and righteousness in Ezek. 45:9. The terms probably refer to acts both against persons and property. The fact that lawlessness and rapine are stored up in their fortresses would indicate that the monarchical administrators and officials are the condemned parties since "fortresses" were previously referred to by Amos as national or royal buildings rather than the homes of the wealthy.

The divine verdict on the situation is rendered in verse 11. An adversary, who already surrounds the land, will overrun the city's fortification and Samaria's fortresses; her storehouses of lawlessness and rapine will be plundered. The verdict is spoken in second-person address directly to the city of Samaria. Here and elsewhere in Amos, the center of Israel's wrongdoing and the object of Yahweh's judgment is Samaria, the capital and administrative center. Although some ancient translations, such as the Targum and Vulgate, and most modern interpreters understand the text as speaking of an adversary who will surround the land sometime in the future (thus reading *yesobeb* for *usebib*), the Hebrew text clearly speaks of the adversary as a present reality (see the NJPSV). The adversary encircling the land is the regional, anti-Assyrian coalition spearheaded in Amos's day by Bit-Adini, Damascus, and Philistia. The prophet envisions a time in the immediate future when this coalition would bring down Samaria and loot the city. The enemy's encirclement of Israel is already a present reality, national defeat and plundering lie ahead.

4. PREPARE TO MEET YOUR GOD (3:12-4:13)

H. M. **Barstad**, *The Religious Polemics of Amos: Studies in the Preaching of Am 2, 7B-8; 4, 13; 5, 1-27; 6, 4-7; 8, 14* (SVT 34; Leiden: E. J. Brill, 1984)37-75; W. **Berg**, *Die sogenannten Hymnenfragmente im Amosbuch* (EHST 45; Bern: Lang, 1974); W. **Brueggemann**, "Amos IV 4-13 and Israel's Covenant Worship," *VT* 15(1965)1-15; P. **Carny**, "Doxologies: A Scientific Myth," *HS* 18(1977)149-59; J. L. **Crenshaw**, "A Liturgy of Wasted Opportunity (Am 4, 6-12; Isa. 9, 7-10, 4; 5, 25-29)," *Semitics* 1(1970)27-37; **Crenshaw**, *Hymnic Affirmation of Divine Justice: The Doxologies of Amos and Related Texts in the Old Testament* (SBLDS 24; Missoula: Scholars Press, 1975); F. C. **Fensham**, "Common Trends in Curses of the Near Eastern Treaties and *Kudurru*-Inscriptions Compared with Maledictions of Amos and Isaiah," *ZAW* 75(1963)155-75; D. N. **Freedman** and F. I. **Andersen**, "Harmon in Amos 4:3," *BASOR* 198(1970)41; H. **Gese**, "Kleine Beiträge zum Verständnis des Amosbuches," *VT* 12(1962)417-38; F. **Horst**, "Die Doxologien im Amosbuch," *ZAW* 47(1929)45-54; P. F. **Jacobs**, "'Cows of Bashan' - A Note on the Interpretation of Amos 4:1," *JBL* 104(1985)109-10; H. **Jagersma**, "The Tithes in the Old Testament," *OTS* 21(1981)116-28; O. **Loretz**, "Vergleich und Kommentar in Amos 3, 12," *BZ* 20(1976)122-25; K. **Koch**, "Die Rolle der hymnischen Abschnitte in der Komposition des Amos-Buches," *ZAW* 86(1974)504-37; S. **Mittmann**, "Amos 3, 12-15 und das Bett der Samarier," *ZDPV* 92(1976)149-67; H. **Moeller**, "Ambiguity at Amos 3:12," *BT* 15(1964)31-34; S. M. **Paul**, "Amos III 15 - Winter and Summer Mansions," *VT* 28(1978)358-60; **Paul**, "Fishing Imagery in Amos 4:2," *JBL* 97(1978)183-90; I. **Rabinowitz**, "The Crux at Amos III 12," *VT* 11(1961)228-31; G. **Ramsey**, "Amos 4:12 - A New Perspective," *JBL* 89(1976)187-91; J. **Reider**, "*dmsq* in Amos 3:12," *JBL* 67(1948)245-48; W. **Rudolph**, "Amos 4, 6-13," *Wort, Gebot, Glaube. Beiträge zur Theologie des Alten Testaments. Walther Eichrodt zum 80. Geburtstag* (ed. H. J. Stoebe et al.; ATANT 59; Zurich: Zwingli Verlag, 1970)27-38; S. J. **Schwantes**, "Note on Amos 4, 2b," *ZAW* 79(1967)82-83; S. **Speier**, "Bemerkungen zu Amos," *VT* 3(1953)305-10; I. K. **Story**, "Amos - Prophet of Praise," *VT* 30(1980)67-80; J. D. W. **Watts**, "An Old Hymn

Preserved in the Book of Amos," *JNES* 15(1956)33-39; **Watts**, "A Critical Analysis of Amos 4:1ff.," *SBLSP* (1972)489-500; A. J. **Williams**, "A Further Suggestion about Amos IV 1-3," *VT* 29(1979)206-11.

3:12 *Thus Yahweh has said,*
> *"Just as the shepherd salvages from the mouth of a lion,*
>> *two legbones or a piece of an ear;*
> *so shall they be salvaged,*
>> *the children of Israel, those ruling in Samaria,*
> *with a corner of a bed,*
>> *and in Damascus bed down."*

13 *"Hear and warn the house of Jacob,"*
> *declares my Lord, Yahweh, God of hosts,*

14 *"Surely on the day I visit the transgressions of Israel upon it,*
> *then I will wreak judgment on the altars of Bethel;*
> *and the horns of the altar shall be cut off*
> *and they shall fall to the ground.*

15 *And I will attack the winter house,*
> *along with the summer house;*
> *and the houses of ivory shall perish,*
> *and the great houses shall be destroyed,"*
>> *declares Yahweh.*

4:1 *Hear this word, you cows of Bashan*
> *who are in Samaria, who are oppressing the poor,*
> *robbing the needy,*
> *saying to their lords, "Bring, and let us drink."*

2 *My Lord Yahweh has sworn by his holiness,*
> *"Surely, the days are coming upon you,*
> *when one will pick you up in baskets,*
> *and your offspring with fish nets.*

3 *And bloated bodies you shall go out,*
> *one woman after another;*
> *and you shall be cast out on the garbage dump,"*
>> *declares Yahweh.*

4 *"Come to Bethel and transgress;*
> *sin much in Gilgal;*
> *and bring your sacrifices in the morning,*
> on the third day your tithes.

5 *And offer up from leavened bread a thanksgiving offering,*
> *and proclaim free will offerings, make them known,*
> *because thus you love to do, O children of Israel,"*

> > *declares my Lord Yahweh.*
> 6 *"And even though I gave to you*
> > *cleanness of teeth in all your cities,*
> > *and lack of food in all your settlements;*
> > *yet you did not return to me,"*
> > > *declares Yahweh.*
> 7 *"And even though I withheld from you the rain,*
> > *with still three months to harvest time;*
> > *and I made it rain upon one city,*
> > *and upon another city I sent no rain;*
> > *one field was rained upon,*
> > *and a field on which it did not rain withered;*
> 8 *and two or three cities staggered to another city*
> > *to drink water but without being satisfied;*
> > *yet you did not return to me,"*
> > > *declares Yahweh.*
> 9 *"I smote you with blight and mildew;*
> > *the increase of your gardens and your vineyards*
> > *and your fig trees and your olive trees,*
> > > *the locust devoured;*
> > *yet you did not return to me,"*
> > > *declares Yahweh.*
> 10 *"I sent against you a plague after the manner of Egpyt;*
> > *I slew your young men with the sword,*
> > > *together with the captivity of your horses;*
> > *and I made the stench of your military camps rise up,*
> > *and into your nostrils;*
> > *yet you did not return to me,"*
> > > *declares Yahweh.*
> 11 *"I wrought destruction among you,*
> > *like the divine destruction of Sodom and Gomorrah;*
> > *and you were like a brand plucked from the burning;*
> > *yet you did not return to me,"*
> > > *declares Yahweh.*
> 12 *"Therefore, thus will I do to you, O Israel;*
> > *surely this will I do to you,*
> > *prepare to meet your God, O Israel."*
> 13 *Surely, the one forming the mountains,*
> > *and creating the wind,*
> > *and making known to humanity his thought;*
> > *the one turning dawn into darkness,*
> > *and treading upon the heights of the earth;*

Yahweh the God of hosts in his name.

This section begins with a divine word announcing the general fate of the Israelite leaders in Samaria (3:12). This description of the coming judgment is then elaborated with reference to the destruction of the altars at Bethel and the homes of the king and his officials (3:13-15) and to the females of Samaria (4:1-3). The worship of the Israelites is denounced as ineffective, even sinful (4:4-5). To illustrate the unwillingness and incapacity of the people to change in spite of calamity, Amos engages in a recital of disastrous events which have befallen the Israelites but have produced no genuine repentance (4:6-11). The section concludes with a divine declaration of a forthcoming calamity analogous to those of the past (4:12) and with a prophetic description of Yahweh in hymnic form highlighting the divine omnipotence (4:13).

[3:12] This verse is a major *crux interpretum* in Old Testament studies. Although the first part of the verse is clear and straightforward, the latter portion has baffled translators ancient and modern. The initial part of the verse refers to the fact that shepherds could not claim the loss of an animal to a predator without supplying proof of the animal's death in the form of the carcass or uneaten scraps from the carcass. Exod. 22:10-13 describes the responsibility of one to whom animals were entrusted. One possible way to lose an animal was for it to be eaten by a wild beast. Thus the law states "if it (the animal) is torn by beasts, let one (the responsible party) bring it as evidence; one shall not make restitution for what is torn" (Exod. 22:13; see Gen. 31:39; 1 Sam. 17:34-35). That such a requirement was characteristic of near eastern culture is indicated by the following stipulation from the code of Hammurabi:

> If a visitation of god has occurred in a sheepfold or a lion has made a kill, the shepherd shall prove himself innocent in the presence of god, but the owner of the sheepfold shall receive from him the animal stricken. (*ANET* 177 § 266)

Obviously, on occasion, only some scraps of the consumed animal would be recoverable. This is the condition presupposed by Amos.

This salvage of scraps from the killed animals is compared to the manner in which some Israelites will be salvaged in the calamity to come. The statement, "thus shall they be salvaged, the children of Israel," is followed by the expression "the ones sitting in Samaria." Although this latter expression is generally taken to refer to the inhabitants of Samaria (RSV and NJPSV: "who dwell in Samaria"; NEB: "who live in Samaria"), it more likely refers to the rulers of Samaria, that is, "those who sit (in power) in Samaria" (see the discussion on *yosheb* in 1:5 above). Thus "rulers of Samaria" defines those Israelites who will be snatched away and survive only as "scraps" after Samaria is attacked. (Note that Amos has already compared Yahweh to a lion, the primary beast of prey in the region; see 1:2; 3:8.)

The final four words of the text provide the main problems in interpretation. Literally they read "with (or "on") a corner (or "piece, edge") of a bed (or "couch") and in Damascus a bed." Part of the difficulty in understanding the text is our lack of knowledge about household furniture and its nomenclature in ancient Israel. Apparently the terms *miṭṭah* and *'eresh*, both translated "bed" above and used in parallel in 6:4, referred to furniture or furnishings used for sleeping. The widespread use of *ershu* in Akkadian (see *CAD* 4.315-18) would indicate that it was the more general term and was used to refer to the item of furniture itself. (The poorer classes may have slept on the floor with no actual bed but only bedding garments or clothes.) The term *'eresh* is used to denote King Og's iron bedstead in Deut. 3:11 and items of furniture taken from King Hezekiah as tribute by the Assyrian ruler Sennacherib in 701 (Oriental Institute Prism III 43; see *ANET* 288 which gives the translation as "couches").

Most modern translations and commentators treat the last four words of the verse along similar general lines marked by two characteristics. (1) It is assumed that reference to the two parts of an animal in the first half of the verse ("two legbones and a piece of an ear") are paralleled by two pieces of furniture in the last part. (2) "Damascus" is assumed to be a mistakenly written word or else denotes some type of material. (Our word "damask" probably does not derive from the term "Damascus"; see *Hammershaimb, 62.) Historical considerations, primarily the assumption that Assyria is the ultimate enemy of Israel in the book of Amos, have led to a downplaying of the importance of Damascus and the regional coalition as the oppressor of the Israelites. On these bases, the following are representative translations:

> with the leg of a bed or the head of a couch (NJPSV).

> like a corner of a couch or a chip from the leg of a bed (NEB).

> with the corner of a couch and part of a bed (RSV).

> at the footboard of a couch and at the headboard of the bed (*Wolff).

Both assumptions on which such translations are made are wrong. First, the statements in the verse are not structured so that the last four words are parallel to "two legbones or a piece of an ear." The latter are joined by the particle 'ô whereas the last two pairs of words in the verse are joined by a waw (û). The last pair of terms is thus not to be taken as paralleling anything else; they develop the thought rather than repeat something already said. Second, one should read Damascus here as the place name even though the spelling is a bit peculiar, using a śin instead of a shin. There is no reason to consider the word as either a mistake or as needing redivision of its letters to read some other terms or needing to be reversed to follow the next word (for a description of the various proposals, see Reider; Rabinowitz; Gese, 427-32; Moeller).

Amos's statement in verse 12 should be understood as follows. Just as a few scraps may be snatched from the mouth of a lion and saved for evidence, so some scraps of the leadership in Samaria will be salvaged along with some fragments of bedding but their place of sleeping will be in Damascus; that is, they will be exiled from the land. The assertion of this verse is therefore clearly not optimistic in spite of the use of the expression "snatch away, salvage, or rescue" (nṣl).

[3:13-15] If verse 12 functions as a thesis sentence referring to the general conditions to come, then what follows both expands on and particularizes the nature of the coming calamities and simultaneously makes it clear that the disasters are the work of Yahweh.

In verse 13, Amos does not specify who is to hear and warn the house of Jacob. Usually this is done as in 3:1 ("chil-

dren of Israel"), 4:1 ("cows of Bashan"), and 8:4 ("the ones panting after the poor"). The indefiniteness of this verse may be
due to the simultaneous call both to hear and to warn or testify
against the Israelites themselves. Who could be singled out to
perform such a task unless it were those among the general
population like Amos himself who felt the necessity to prophesy
(see 3:8b) or the foreigners previously called to observe the
wrongdoings in Samaria (3:9). Perhaps the verb should be
understood as meaning "and be a witness against the house of
Jacob" that God has sufficiently warned the people of the coming calamity (see Isa. 8:2), that is, people are called upon to
note Amos's warning so they could testify to its reality after the
calamity had struck (see Isa. 8:1-4, 16-20).

Verse 14 has Yahweh declare that the altars of Bethel
will be the object of Yahweh's action. The occurrence of both
the plural form "altars" and the single form "altar" is probably
not some later scribal error. If the temple in Bethel shared features in common with the Jerusalem temple, then there was an
altar for burning sacrifices in the courtyard and an incense altar
inside the sanctuary. The horns of the altar to be toppled to
the ground were part of the courtyard altar. Horns or pro-
jections at the corners of the altar served to hold the burning
wood and sacrifices upon the top of the altar.

Since the sanctuary at Bethel was the primary state cult
place for the northern kingdom (see 7:13), Yahweh's attack on
this sanctuary would represent a direct attack on the monarchical institutions of Israel. Throughout the book, Amos's denunciations are primarily addressed against the ruling powers in
the north, the institutions associated with the monarchy and the
monarchy itself, and the capital city of Samaria rather than the
population at large.

Verse 15 announces the destruction of the royal palaces
and perhaps the homes of the governmental officials as well.
The reference to summer and winter houses or palaces probably reflects the fact that the Israelite king possessed two royal
living quarters. It was possible for the winter and summer
quarters to be part of the same building complex. Under such
conditions, part of the palace would be constructed to pick up
the cooling breezes from the Mediterranean in the summer and
another part constructed to take advantage of the sun's rays in
the winter. Jer. 36:22 refers to King Jehoiakim in Jerusalem
sitting in the winter house in the ninth month which may have

simply been part of the royal complex in Jerusalem rather than a separate palace.

For a king to have two separate palaces was a sign of some opulence. Barrakab, king of Sam'al, for example, bragged that he was able to construct himself a second palace whereas his ancestors had possessed only one palace which served as both their summer and winter house (*ANET* 655). King Cyrus of Persia utilized three different palaces:

> Cyrus himself made his home in the centre of his domain, and in the winter season he spent seven months in Babylon, for there the climate is warm; in the spring he spent three months in Susa, and in the height of summer two months in Ecbatana. By so doing, they say, he enjoyed the warmth and coolness of perpetual springtime. (Xenophon, *Cyropaedia* VIII vi. 22)

King Ahab of Israel apparently possessed two palaces, one in the Jezreel Valley for the winter and one in Samaria for the summer (see 1 Kings 21:1, 18). His successors continued to use the winter palace in Jezreel (see 2 Kings 8:29; 9:15) and this may have been the case under Jeroboam II.

The "houses of ivory" probably refer to these royal palaces although they might also be government buildings. Houses or palaces were not constructed of ivory but only decorated with ivory inlay. According to 1 Kings 22:39, Ahab built a "house of ivory" but its location is not given.

It is uncertain whether *battîm rabbîm* in verse 15b should be translated as "many houses" or "great houses." If all the references in verse 15 are to royal palaces then one should translate "great houses." In ancient Egyptian, the title "pharaoh" really meant "great house." Some scholars, however, think that Amos is referring not only to the two royal palace complexes but also to summer and winter mansions owned by wealthy Samarians (see Paul). Ancient Jewish rabbis argued that all seventy of Ahab's descendants (2 Kings 10:1) had both summer and winter houses (see *Eccl. Rabbah* VI. 3 § 2). Probably Amos is here concerned only with the two royal complexes just as he is concerned with the royal sanctuary in verse 14.

[4:1-3] With 4:1, Amos turns his attention to a group he designates as "the cows of Bashan who are in Samaria." Bashan was a geographical region in Transjordan, a fertile elevated plain spanning both sides of the Yarmuk River. The area was noted for its fine pastureland from which came highly valued cattle (see Deut. 32:14; Ps. 22:12; Jer. 50:19; Ezek. 39:18). But what group in Samaria is Amos describing with this title and how is the designation to be understood? Opinions have varied (see Barstad, 37-44). The following are some of the interpretations proposed: (1) "the noble princesses" of the northern kingdom (*Harper, 86), (2) "the women of quality in Samaria, the pampered darlings of society in Israel's royalist culture" (*Mays, 72), (3) "the elite social stratum of the capital city" (*Wolff, 205), (4) a double-entendre for "voluptuously endowed maidens" (Speier, 306-7); (5) "not simply as a reference to indolent, calloused women, but to those who fancy themselves imitators/partakers of the feminine counterpart of Yahweh, bull of Samaria" (Jacobs, 110); and (6) "a paraphrase for the whole of the Israelite people/inhabitants of Samaria" who were engaging in non-Yahwistic, Canaanite cults (Barstad, 40).

The general tenor of verse 1 suggests that the expression "cows of Bashan" refers to an indulged opulent class of women in the capital city. The wording of the verse seems to imply that they were women closely associated with the royal court and monarchical administration. The charges Amos leveled against them indicate economic and governmental exploitation (see above on 2:6b-8). In addition, the women are said to address "their lords." The term "lord" ('dn) implies a special status and should not be translated as "husband." The only Old Testament text where 'dn appears to mean "husband" is Gen. 18:12, but this passage presupposes a condition in which the normal word for husband would have been infelicitious. Abraham is beyond the age when he could "husband" a wife.

The "cows of Bashan" are probably to be understood as the women associated with the royal court in Samaria. These would have included the daughters, wives, and concubines of the king and his sons and perhaps their social circle including women of some government officials who may not have been the king's kin. Whether the expression "cows of Bashan," given a neutral context, was a term of compliment or not remains uncertain. It certainly could have been as ambigious as our word "thoroughbred."

Three accusations are made against the cows of Bashan, all stated in participial form. Thus what began as second-person speech shifts within the first verse to third-person speech. Clearly the use of such speech patterns was common so that participial constructions could be heard as direct address. The women are denounced for exploitation of the poor and powerless. "Oppression" and "robbery" (or "harassment, crushing") occur as verbs in parallel elsewhere in scripture (see Deut. 28:33; 1 Sam. 12:3-4; Hos. 5:11). The poor and needy were already mentioned in 2:6b-7a and the oppressed population of Samaria noted in 3:9. Amos accuses the women of participation in the characteristic wrongdoings of Israelite upperclass society. The third accusation concerns the demands made upon the lords. "Bring, and let us drink" ("let's carouse!" NJPSV) points to conspicious consumption (leading to obesity and bovine fatness?) and an indulgent lifestyle, a lifestyle characteristic of the royal court and so uncharacteristic of the oppressed. The women are depicted as a major stimulus for the extravagant and hence oppressive court lifestyle which Amos condemns. The women are clearly depicted as demanding a lifestyle leading to oppression.

The charges against the women of the court in Samaria (in v. 1) are followed by a description of the women's future condition (vv. 2b-3) introduced as an oath sworn by God (v. 2a). The claim that God had sworn that something will happen is a means to affirm the events' inevitability in stronger terms than merely to declare that God has spoken about them (see 6:8; 8:7; Isa. 14:24). The use of such an expression, however, no more implies that the prophet has witnessed some divine oath-taking ceremony than the expression "thus Yahweh has said" implies that the prophet has received actual auditory communciations or stood in some heavenly audience and listened to divine directives. That Yahweh swore by his holiness probably means no more than that God swore in his own name (see Ps. 89:35-37). Nothing special is implied by the expression. Since an oath was sworn by an appeal to something else, even God is made to appeal in this case to his holiness (see 8:7).

Like 3:12, verses 2b-3 are an interpreter's nightmare. Of the six Hebrew words in verse 2b, four appear nowhere else in the Old Testament in the forms found here. Needless to say, a variety of translations are proposed for verses 2b-3 (for a collection of suggested readings, see Paul; *THBA*, 79-80, 233-34 notes 59-71). The following translations are offered by widely read versions:

when they will take you away with hooks,
　　　　even the last of you with fishhooks.
And you shall go out through the breaches,
　　　　every one straight before her;
　　　　and you shall be cast forth into Harmon (RSV).

when men shall carry you away on their shields
and your children in fish-baskets.
You shall each be carried straight out
　　　　through the breaches in the walls
　　　　and pitched on a dunghill (NEB).

When you will be carried off in baskets,
And, to the last one, in fish baskets,
And taken out [of the city]—
Each one through a breach straight ahead—
And flung on the refuse heap (NJPSV).

when you will be dragged out with hooks,
the very last of you with prongs.
Out you will go, each by the nearest breach in the wall,
to be driven all the way to Hermon (JB).

Commentators have been almost unanimous in seeing in these verses a reference to the deportation of exiles from Samaria. This however hardly seems the case, for a number of reasons. First of all, the instruments noted in verse 2b do not suggest deportation. This is the case whether one reads shields, hooks, baskets, or even ropes. Occasionally an Assyrian king does refer to the use of ropes or nose-rings when speaking of deporting exiles (see *ARI* II § 69), but this is rare and "ropes" does not seem to be the best translation for any of the terms in verse 2b (see Schwantes; Paul, 184-85). Secondly, the term "lift/raise up" (*nś'*) is not a term one would normally associate with exile. Thirdly, the idea of people going out through the breaches straight ahead might suggest escape but not exile where people were rounded up and systematically deported. Fourthly, the expression "cast out" more frequently suggests disposal (see 8:3) but only rarely deportation (see Jer. 22:28). Fifthly, since Amos was thoroughly acquainted with the practice of exile and deportation and speaks of this in places (see 1:5, 6, 9; 5:27; 6:7) utilizing the normal vocabulary, it seems quite peculiar that he should avoid such terminology in this passage if that is the point being made.

What Amos is apparently depicting in verses 2b-3 is the disposal of human corpses after a siege and battle are over. In other words, this text describes a situation parallel to that in 6:8-10. The bodies of the "cows of Bashan" will be lifted up in some type of container or with hooks since the decaying and stinking flesh would make direct handling impossible. Something of what is envisioned here can be illuminated by the story of the death of Nadab and Abihu in Leviticus 10. After these two sons of Aaron were struck dead, their corpses were lifted up or carried away (*ns'*) by their brothers who used their tunics to carry the bodies (v. 5). In addition to the women, their *'hryt* will also be carried out. *'hryt* is here not to be understood as "the last" or "the remnant" but either as "the remains," what will be left of the bodies, or else as those which come after "the posterity/children/descendants" (for the latter usage, see Num. 24:20; Ps. 109:13; Jer. 31:17; Ezek. 23:25; see below on 9:1).

In verse 3, the term *peraṣim* which occurs with the meaning of a bulge or break/breach in a wall is here to be understood as referring to swollen, bloated things (corpses). A *pereṣ* could be a swelling or bulge as well as an opening (see Isa. 30:13; Ps. 144:14; Prov. 3:10). Thus the initial two words in this verse are to be understood as "bloated ones, you/they shall go out" (or "be brought out" if one reads a passive verb form as did some ancient translators). The fact that "bloated ones" is a plural masculine noun does not mean that the term does not refer to the cows/women of Samaria since throughout 4:1-3 there is a mixture of masculine and feminine forms.

The terms *'ishshah negdah* at the end of verse 3a are generally interpreted as meaning something like "everyone straight before her" which makes little sense. The image conveyed by the expression suggests a translation "one woman after another" (see Josh. 6:5, 20: Neh. 12:37) or "one woman against the other" (see Gen. 2:18), that is, in a straight line. Thus verse 3a can be translated "and bloated bodies you shall go out (or "be taken out"), one woman after another."

Verse 3b describes the final disposition of the corpses (see 8:3b; 1 Kings 13:24-25; Jer. 14:16; 36:30). Although the present form of the text was pointed by the Masoretes to be read as an active verb ("you will cast out"), the text makes better sense if one reads a passive sense ("you shall be cast out") as was done in some ancient translations. The place to which the bodies are said to be cast is given in Hebrew as "the Harmon." Ancient translations and modern interpreters have suggested a number of possibilities for this word although many ancient translations merely have transliterations of the Hebrew: Armenia, Harmon, Hermon, on the mountain of Remman, and so on. A likely assumption is that the original read the rare word *hmdmnh* "the dung-pit, garbage heap" found only in Isa. 25:10 (see NEB; NJPSV). When the text was understood in terms of the Assyrian exile, the word was read and understood as "toward Hermon," the mountain range to the northeast in the direction of Assyria.

Amos thus proclaimed a radical form of judgment upon the ladies of the Samarian court. Those who were presently living in luxury and opulence at the court through oppression of the poor would soon become, along with their offspring, corpses to be gathered and discarded on the garbage dump.

[4:4-5] In these verses, Amos condemns aspects of Israelite worship, although the condemnation is made primarily through implication. There are no outright statements of denunciation supplying the rationale for condemnation; participation in the worship at Bethel and Gilgal is simply declared to be transgression or rebellion. The sacrifices implicated in this text are those primarily consumed by the worshipers. The worship was thus treated by the prophet as constituting another example of extravagant self-indulgence. Thus, this pericope is a natural continuation of the material in 3:13-4:3 especially 3:15 and 4:1.

The opening "call to worship" may be seen as the prophet's satirical caricature of official priestly calls to worship. "Come" (or "enter") carries the implication of "going on pilgrimage to." Amos left no doubt about his opinion on the matter; such worship was transgression and wrongdoing.

The two places of worship mentioned, Bethel and Gilgal, had been important shrines throughout Israelite history (on the two sites, see Barstad, 49-54). Numerous stories about their cultic importance were told of both Bethel (see Gen. 12:8; 28:10-22; 35:1-8) and Gilgal (Josh. 4:19-20; 5:2-12; 1 Sam. 7:15-17; 11:14-15). With the breakup of the Solomonic state, Bethel was set aside as one of the major national sanctuaries by Jeroboam I when the north declared its independence from Jerusalem and the Davidic family (1 Kings 12:26-33).

At the time of Amos, Bethel was the primary national sanctuary in Jeroboam's kingdom (see 7;13). Bethel was located about twenty-five miles south of Samaria and about eleven miles north of Jerusalem. The other royally designated national shrine in Israel was at Dan far to the north at the headwaters of the Jordan River. In Amos's day, Dan was probably already in Syrian hands.

According to our historical reconstruction, when Amos appeared on the scene the region just west of the Jordan River where Gilgal was located was already in the hands of Pekah, a rival to Jeroboam II (see above on 1:5). If so, then Gilgal was probably the religious center of Pekah's realm. Amos may have seen the worship at Bethel and Gilgal as fostering national strife. Support for Jeroboam II was expressed at Bethel and for Pekah at Gilgal. This divisiveness and civil strife was considered contrary to the will of God (see below on 5:4-7, 14-15) and thus condemned as criminal. If any value judgment is made between the two cult places, Gilgal seems to be judged more harshly.

In verse 4b, Amos, as if giving priestly instruction, commands the people to bring their sacrifices in the morning and their tithes on the third day. Although Amos was providing a parody on the worship at these shrines, he certainly was not suggesting the extreme conditions reflected in some translations: a sacrifice *every morning* and tithes *every three days* (see RSV). The expression *labboqer* means in "the morning"; "every morning" is expressed by *labbeqarim* (see Isa. 33:2; Pss. 73:14; 101:8; Lam. 3:23).

Was Amos speaking of religious activity in general or some special occasion? One cannot know with certainty. A few texts, however, indicate that the major fall festival in Israel was a three-day affair. (Note that the oldest reference to the festivals in Exod. 23:14-17 does not stipulate the length of the fall festival.) Exod. 19:10-16 and Hos. 6:1-2 suggest a three-day festival. If this major festival was three days long then the prophet would here be referring to the feast of Asiph/Succoth which in Israel was observed at the middle of the eighth month culminating on the fifteenth day of the month (1 Kings 12:32-33). Amos may have had this day in mind in his "cultic proclamation." If so, he would have been referring to the fall festival of 750. His preaching mission would then probably have been carried out just before the festival or perhaps during the two days preparatory to the great celebration of the third day. The fall festival was the time when royal coronations and their anniversaries were celebrated. The fifteenth of the month, the third day of the festival, was the "day of the king" and the beginning of a new regnal year (see 1 Kings 12:32-33; Hos. 7:5). Worship at Bethel and Gilgal at this particular time would have had strong political implications in a country bordering on civil war.

The sacrifices Amos mentions were sacrifices primarily consumed by the worshipers and had no connection with sin and repentance. The *zebahim* (or *zebah hashshelamim*) were sacrifices of well-being. According to the levitical laws concerning these sacrifices, they could be cattle, sheep, or goats (Leviticus 3); the officiating priest received the breast and right thigh and only the fat was burned on the altar (Lev. 7:28-36); the remainder of the sacrifice was returned to the worshiper to be consumed. This type of sacrifice was made as an act of thanksgiving, in fulfillment of a vow, or as a freewill offering (Lev. 7:11-18). The occasion of such sacrifice was a time of conspicuous consumption, expressive of a sense of well-being. The meat returned to the worshiper had to be consumed on the day it was slaughtered if a thanksgiving offering (Lev. 7:15), or within two days, if a freewill offering or in fulfillment of a vow (Lev. 7:16-18).

The thanksgiving sacrifice included the presentation and eating of leavened bread, one loaf of which went to the officiating priest (Lev. 7:13-14). If one takes the verb *qatter* ("burn") in verse 5*a* literally, it would suggest that leavened bread was burned on the altar, an act prohibited by Lev. 2:11. The term may here be used in a generic sense, "offer a sacrifice" or "make an offering."

The publicizing of free-will offerings refers to making known such offerings and inviting others to participate in the affair which should be understood as a gala barbecue. (Perhaps it was on such occasions that wine taken as exaction was drunk in the sanctuaries and poor people's garments were spread out to lounge upon; see 2:8.) Something of the occasion can be seen in the description of feasting at the annual festival at Shiloh found in 1 Sam. 1:1-9*a*.

The reference to bringing the tithe on the third day could imply that this was the special day designated for their presentation. A legend about Jacob was told to justify the giving of tithes at Bethel (see Gen. 28:18-22). Nothing is said in this story however about the time for bringing or the disposition of the tithe. First Sam. 8:15, 17 refers to a tenth of the grain, vineyards, and flocks taken by the king and redistributed to the royal officials but this appears to have been a royal tax of some sort. According to Deut. 14:22-29, the tithe was consumed by the worshipers except in the third year when it went to the Levites and the poor. Num. 18:21-23 assigns the tithe to the Levites while Lev. 27:30-33 simply declares it to belong to Yahweh, that is, it went to the sanctuary and priestly establishment (see Jagersma).

The context of Amos's reference to the tithe does not indicate that it was considered a burden since, like the sacrifices, it was something the people loved to do or were set on doing. This would imply that, like the types of sacrifices mentioned, the title was primarily utilized and enjoyed by the contributors. The situation suggested seems to agree more with the description of the tithe's disposition in Deut. 14:22-29, but since Amos is engaged in caricature and overstatement one cannot be certain.

Several things should be noted about the content and implications of this text since it has played a significant role in attempts to understand the prophetic evaluation of the cult (see further, on 5:21-24). (1) Amos is certainly not condemning cultic worship in its totality and advocating some cultless form of religion or propounding morality as the essence and only criterion of religion. (2) Not all forms of sacrifice are even mentioned much less condemned outright. No reference is made to the purgation sacrifice (*ḥaṭṭat*) or the reparation offering (*'asham*), all mandatory under certain circumstances. (3) The sacrifices parodied by the prophet were all voluntary offerings, made at the instigation of the worshipers. (4) None of the sacrifices mentioned was related to sin and repentance. (5) The meat of such sacrifices was consumed by the worshipers. (6) The context indicates that the sacrifices were condemned as another example of the self-indulgence of the ruling establishment (see 3:15; 4:1). (7) The lower classes of Israelite society were probably incapable of such sacrificial extravagance because of the expense involved, particularly if they were under heavy taxation burdens. (8) If Bethel and Gilgal were cult centers for rival political groups, this would have contributed to Amos's negative evaluation of sacrifices offered there.

[4:6-11] In these verses, Amos alludes to a number of calamities (a *catalogus calamitus*) which had struck the Israelites, relates these to divine activity, and accuses the people of not repenting in light of these destructions. All these events are described as troubles already past but as harbingers of a great catastrophe to come. Seven calamities may be isolated although the refrain "yet you did not return to me" and the expression *ne'um yhwh* are repeated only five times. The seven calamities were hunger and shortage of food (v. 6), drought (vv. 7-8), crop diseases (v. 9) locusts (v. 9), plague (v. 10), war (v. 10), and earthquake (v. 11).

The reiteration of the refrain would indicate that the prophet felt that the people had not associated these events with the judgment of Yahweh (see 3:6b) or that the calamities had made no significant impact on Israelite society. The troubles are described in general categories and, without doubt, many were part of recurring patterns of life in the area. Whether the prophet's audience would have clearly associated the calamities with particular episodes in their recent history remains uncertain since few specifics are noted.

The famine noted in verse 6, where "cleanness of teeth" indicates not having eaten, appears to have been widespread. The lack of food does not appear to have been related to the troubles noted in verses 7-9 since these are depicted as local affairs.

Drought was common to the Palestinian area. The region lies between the desert and the sea, and if the western winds in winter do not bring adequate moisture from the sea, rainfall can be sporadic and sparse. Although the territory occupied by the Israelites and Judeans was small, about one hundred fifty miles north-south and about fifty miles east-west, the area has an enormous diversity in climate. Some sections receive less than ten inches of rain per year, others over fifty inches. The region has basically two seasons, a rainy cool season from October to April and a rainless summer from May to September. The rainfall is greater in the areas closest to the sea, highest in elevation, and farthest to the north.

Grain is harvested in May and June so lack of rainfall in February and March ("three months before harvest") would have been disastrous for crops. The spottiness of the rainfall and the shortage of water in the towns are simply noted as Yahweh's doing, without any association of the climatic conditions with the social or moral status of the people involved. Crop diseases and locusts affected not only the grain crops harvested in late spring but also the grapes, figs, and olives harvested primarily in late summer.

In verse 10, Amos refers to "a plague after the manner of Egypt." There seems to be no reason to understand this as a reference to the plagues associated with the exodus (Exodus 7-11). It is simply a general statement about a plague like those for which Egypt was famous. Interestingly, the Assyrian eponym lists note that plagues struck Assyria in the years 803, 765, and 759. These must have been significant or they would not have made the lists as one of the years' most important phenomena. Whether the latter plague only a few years before Amos's appearance also struck Israel is uncertain but possible.

After a reference to the plague, Amos alludes to calamities in war. Elite troops ("young men") were slain, chariot steeds were captured, and the smell of unburied bodies emanating from the army camps filled the people's nostrils. In spite of such specific allusions, which must have been clear to the audience, the identity of the military campaign involved remains a mystery. Two things appear to be clearly presupposed. (1) Israel had not only been engaged in a major battle but also had suffered a serious defeat in war. (2) For Amos's point to have had any relevance, this rout on the battlefield must have been a recent occurrence. The only option for such a military calamity would appear to be a battle between Israel and the regional coalition. Possibly one should think of a military encounter with Damascus during Israel's loss of much of the Transjordan (see 1:3).

The imagery of verse 11 appears to suggest an earthquake disaster. The verb "to overthrow, destroy" (hpk) is used in the story of the destruction of Sodom and Gomorrah (Gen. 19:21, 25, 29) although this event is never explicitly referred to as an earthquake. A short time after Amos, and following the earthquake noted in 1:1, the prophet Isaiah compared the consequences of an earthquake to the destruction of Sodom and Gomorrah, the archetype of total calamity (Isa. 1:9-10; see also Deut. 29:23; Isa. 13:19; Jer. 49:18; 50:40). Those who escaped the earthquake are described as a brand plucked from the fire (see Isa. 7:4). Fire and earthquake are associated since fires were frequently kept burning in homes and with the collapse of houses, conflagration resulted (see Isa. 1:7).

Verses 6-11 contain frequent parallels to other biblical passages which pronounce various curses on the people (see Lev. 26:14-45; Deut. 28:15-68; 1 Kings 8:33-37; *Wolff, 213-14 for comparisons). These parallels are not sufficient to argue that Amos 4:6-13 are additions to the book serving "to remind the audience of the final destruction of the northern kingdom as an independent political entity by the Assyrians in 721" (*Wolff, 221). Neither does this material indicate that Amos was a cultic functionary in a covenant renewal ritual (*Reventlow, 75-90) or a prophetic spokesperson issuing a challenge for covenant renewal between Yahweh and Israel (Brueggemann). On this issue, three factors should be noted. (1) Amos in 4:6-11 describes events already past (as in Isa. 9:8-21) not curses to befall Israel at some future time. (2) The parallels with the imagery in other biblical texts are not so close as to indicate either the use of a standard sequence of curses or redactional copying. (3) There is no evidence in the book indicating that Amos was familiar with or preached on the basis of a covenant between Israel and Yahweh.

[4:12-13] With verse 12, the prophet shifts his focus to coming events and picks up the theme of Yahweh's judgment already announced in 3:12. The coming disaster, the people's confrontation with their God, will be analogous to the calamities of the past.

The opening of verse 12 contains two parallel statements that appear redundant: "thus will I do to you" and "this will I do to you." One way to explain this feature, other than to see it as a mistake requiring emendation, is to view it as repetition for emphasis. Another approach sees the repetition as a result of conflation. A copyist, according to this theory, was confronted with slightly variant readings in two manuscripts of Amos. Instead of choosing between them, the scribe incorporated both readings thus preserving the two variant readings with their practically complete similarity (so *Gordis, 222-24).

At any rate, Amos has Yahweh tell Israel to prepare to meet their God, not in the sense of calling the nation to repentance, but alerting them that doom in the form of a direct confrontation with God was at hand. A greater calamity than those previously noted was about to strike. The Israel that would not return to Yahweh even after having experienced one divinely sent calamity after another must now confront Yahweh in yet another disaster.

The language of the warning is highly military in character. The terms "prepare/get ready" (*hikkôn*) and "to meet" (*liqra't*) appear primarily in military contexts. For the former, see Josh. 8:4; Ps. 7:13; Prov. 21:31; Isa. 14:21; Jer. 51:12; Ezek. 7:14; 38:7; and for the latter, see Num. 21:23; Josh. 8:14; 11:20; Judg. 7:24; 20:31; 1 Sam. 4:1-2; 17:21, 48, 55; 23:28; 2 Sam. 10:9-10; 18:6; Ps. 35:3; Job 39:21). Preparation to encounter God is referred to in Exod. 19:11, 15; 34:2.

Verse 13 is a hymnic section containing five descriptive assertions about Yahweh, all introduced with participles. Three issues have occupied commentators in interpreting this verse: its relationship to the other two hymnic sections in Amos (5:8-9 and 9:5-6), the authenticity of this hymnic material, and the relationship and function of the material in its contexts.

Practically all interpreters agree that all three hymnic texts have features in common and share some type of relationship. Beyond this recognition of a common content and style, opinions vary (see the histories of research in Berg, Crenshaw, 5-46, 147-58; * Wolff, 215-17). Scholars have viewed the sections as three separate hymns (*Cripps; *Weiser) or as two (so Horst), three (Watts), or four (Gaster) stanzas or fragments of a single composition. Arguments in favor of a common composition or common origin for the material are based on the similarity of theme, the use of participial constructions throughout, and the presence of a common refrain "Yahweh is his name."

Most scholars deny that this hymnic material was part of the oral presentation of Amos, but differ over whether it was included in the original editing of the Amos material or was inserted secondarily, perhaps as late as post-exilic times. Those who view the material as redactional additions to the words of Amos assume that later editors inserted these sections for particular reasons though these reasons may no longer be discoverable.

The function of the hymnic material is variously assessed. Most interpreters consider the material, whether ascribed to Amos or not, to be doxological, that is, intended to offer praise to the Deity (see Story) although the texts are frequently referred to as doxologies of judgment (see Horst; Crenshaw). A doxology of judgment combines both praise and confession in a context of judgment (see Josh. 2:19). Carny has rightly challenged the interpretation of verse 13 as a doxology whether utilized simply to express praise, to confess guilt, or to call to repentance and renewal of covenant. He understands the verse as a prophecy of destruction stipulating the punishment proclaimed in verse 12 and to come on the day of judgment. Both of these approaches seem to read more into the text than is there.

The content of verse 13 explicates the nature of the God whom Israel had been warned it would directly confront in an adversary situation. The participial phrases describe God in terms of divine activity. Two speak of divine creativity (*yṣr* and *br'*; forming and creating), one notes God's revelation of divine thought to humanity (*mgd*; making known, see 3:7), and two speak of terrifying actions of God(*'śh* and *drk*; turning and treading).

The description of God focuses on the Deity as creator, revealer, and performer of awesome events. This is the Deity Israel must face in judgment. Verse 13 thus clearly fits its context and brings the thought of verse 12 to a logical conclusion.

Did Amos compose verse 13 and the other hymnic verses, utilize an existing hymn which he subdivided into three segments, or borrow sections from various existing hymns? Such a question cannot be answered with any certainty. A number of factors would suggest that Amos drew upon an existing hymn or hymns and incorporated the material into his speeches. (1) The subject matter of the hymnic passages differs radically from the rest of the book. The material in 4:6-11 overlaps some of the hymnic material in theme but any real similarity in content is rather remote. (2) Series of participles describing God are unique to this material in Amos. (3) The repetitive refrain "Yahweh (God of hosts) is his name" suggests that the hymnic material was probably employed in some form of communal worship (see below on 5:26). (4) Parallels to this hymnic material occur elsewhere in the Old Testament (see Ps. 95; Job 9:5-10).

5. FALLEN IS THE VIRGIN OF ISRAEL (5:1-17)

S. **Amsler**, "Amos, prophète de la onzième heure," *TZ* 21(1965)318-28; H. M. **Barstad**, *The Religious Polemics of Amos: Studies in the Preaching of Am 2, 7B-8; 4, 1-13; 5:1-27; 6, 4-7; 8, 14* (SVT 34; Leiden: E. J. Brill, 1984)76-88; J. **Berridge**, "Zur Intention der Botschaft des Propheten Amos. Exegetische Überlegungen zu Am 5," *TZ* 32(1976)321-40; O. **Eissfeldt**, "Der Gott Bethel," *ARW* 28(1930)1-30 = his *Kleine Schriften* (Tübingen: J. C. B. Mohr [Paul Siebeck], 1962)1.206-33; A. **Fitzgerald**, "*BTWLT* and *BT* as Titles for Capital Cities," *CBQ* 37(1975)167-83; M. J. **Hauan**, "The Background and Meaning of Amos 5:17B," *HTR* 79(1986)337-48; F. **Hesse**, "Amos 5, 4-6. 14f.," *ZAW* 68(1956)1-17; A. V. **Hunter**, *Seek the Lord! A Study of the Meaning and Function of the Exhortations in Amos, Hosea, Isaiah, Micah, and Zephaniah* (Baltimore: St. Mary's Seminary & University, 1982)56-105; J. P. **Hyatt**, "The Deity Bethel and the Old Testament," *JAOS* 59(1939)81-98; J. **Jackson**, "Amos 5, 13 Contextually Understood," *ZAW* 98(1986)434-35; J. **Lust**, "Remarks on the Redaction of Amos V 4-6, 14-15," *OTS* 21(1981)129-54; K. **Neubauer**, "Erwägungen zu Amos 5, 4-15," *ZAW* 78(1966)292-316; T. M. **Raitt**, "The Prophetic Summons to Repentance," *ZAW* 83(1971)30-49; L. J. **Rector**, "Israel's Rejected Worship: An Exegesis of Amos 5," *ResQ* 21(1978)161-75; J. J. **Schmitt**, "The Gender of Ancient Israel," *JSOT* 26(1983)115-25; **Schmitt**, "The Virgin of Israel: Meaning and Use of the Phrase in Amos and Jeremiah," *Program and Abstracts of the XII Congress of the International Organization for the Study of the Old Testament (IOSOT*, (Jerusalem: IOSOT, 1986) 122; C. S. **Shaw**, "Micah 1:10-16 Reconsidered," *JBL* 106(1987)223-29; G. V. **Smith**, "Amos 5:13 - The Deadly Silence of the Prosperous," *JBL* 107(1988)289-91; N. J. **Tromp**, "Amos V 1-17. Towards a Stylistic and Rhetorical Analysis," *OTS* 33(1984)56-84; J. **de Waard**, "The Chiastic Structure of Amos V 1-17," *VT* 27(1977)170-77; D. **Wicke**, "Two Perspectives (Amos 5:1-17)," *CurTM* 13(1986)86-96; L. **Zalcman**, "Astronomical Allusions in Amos," *JBL* 100(1981)53-58.

5:1 *Hear this word which I am lifting up over you as a*
    dirge, O house of Israel,
 2 *She has fallen no more to rise,*

the virgin of Israel;
abandoned upon her soil,
with no one to raise her up.

3   For thus my Lord Yahweh has said,
"The city that goes forth a thousand,
shall spare a hundred;
and the one that goes forth a hundred,
shall spare ten, for the house of Israel."

4   Surely, thus Yahweh has said to the house of Israel,
"Seek me and survive,

5   and do not seek Bethel;
and do not go to Gilgal,
and do not cross over to Beer-sheba;
surely, Gilgal shall go into exile
and Bethel shall become nothing."

6   Seek Yahweh and survive;
lest the house of Joseph flare up like fire,
and devour and without anyone to extinguish it for
Bethel.

7   O those who turn justice to wormwood,
and cast righteousness to the ground.

8   The one making the Pleiades and Orion,
and turning to dawn deep darkness,
and darkening day into night;
the one who summons the waters of the sea,
and pours them out upon the face of the ground;
Yahweh is his name;

9   the one who flashes forth destruction against the
stronghold so that destruction comes against the
fortified city.

10   They hate the one putting matters right in the gate
and the one speaking honestly they abhor.

11   "Therefore because you levy taxes on the poor
and take exactions of grain from them;
houses of hewn stone you have built,
but you shall not dwell in them;
splendid vineyards you have planted,
but you shall not drink their wine.

12   Surely I know how many are your transgressions,
and how numerous are your sins;
you who oppress the innocent, who take a bribe,
and turn aside the needy ones in the gate.

13   *Therefore the one who understands that time*
     will be silent,
     because an evil time that will be."
14   *Seek good and not evil,*
     that you may survive;
     and it may be that Yahweh the God of hosts will be with
     you, just as you say.
15   *Hate evil and love good,*
     and establish justice in the gate;
     perhaps Yahweh the God of hosts will be merciful,
     to what remains of Joseph.
16   *Therefore thus Yahweh the God of hosts my Lord has*
     said,
     "In all the open places there shall be wailing;
     and in all the streets they shall say; 'alas, alas!'
     and they will call the farmer to mourn,
     and to wailing those skilled in lamenting;
17   *and in every vineyard there shall be wailing,*
     when I pass through your midst,"
                              said Yahweh.

This rhetorical unit has three basic internal characteristics. In the first place, it interweaves statements on calamities present and to come (vv. 2-3, 5b, 11ab-b; 13, 16-17), accusations against the people for wrongdoing (vv. 7, 10, 11aa, 12), and admonitions exhorting particular types of action (vv. 4-5a, 6, 14-15). Second, it interweaves statements presented as the words of Amos (vv. 1-2, 6-9, 14-15) with statements presented as divine speech (vv. 3-5, 10-13, 16-17). Third, the hymnic, participial matter in verses 8-9 occupies a central position in the unit.

An overarching pattern gives structure to the unit. The prophet begins with lamentation (vv. 1-3), moves to exhortation and admonition (vv. 4-6), pronounces accusations and judgment (vv. 7-13), returns to exhortation and admonition (vv. 14-15), and repeats the theme of lamentation (vv. 16-17). The unit is thus a tightly woven presentation with chiastic features (see de Waard; Hunter, 102-4; Tromp).

[1-2] The prophet calls his audience to hear a word which he is lifting up over them but a word which turned out to be like a funeral dirge. In Hebrew, the funeral dirge or lament was called a *qinah* and consisted of lines with five beats

(generally 3 + 2 but apparently sometimes 2 + 3). Presumably, the *qinah* was intoned over the corpse or at the grave at the time of the deceased's burial. In 2 Sam. 1:17-27, David intones a *qinah* at the time of the death of Saul and Jonathan although their bodies are elsewhere. When Abner was killed at Hebron, David led the people in mourning and recited a *qinah* at his grave (2 Sam. 3:31-34). "To raise up a lament" or "to lift up a *qinah*" refers specifically to the reciting of the elegy over the deceased (see 2 Chron. 35:25). Prophets could use the imagery of the funeral and recitation of the *qinah* to symbolize the future fate of those over whom the *qinah* was spoken (see Jer. 7:29; 9:10; Ezek. 19:1; 26:17; 27:2, 32: 28:12; 32:2). Although women were closely associated with lamenting and mourning rites (see Jer. 9:17-22), this was clearly not their exclusive domain as the cases of David and Jeremiah illustrate.

Verse 2 contains Amos's *qinah*. He employs the expression "fallen," characteristically used of one who had died tragically or unnecessarily rather than from disease or age (2 Sam. 1:19; 3:34). The fallen one is spoken of in feminine terms. She has fallen and lies abandoned upon her own land. The terminology is such that the hearer might not have assumed her to be dead since this is not explicitly stated. The reference to the absence of anyone to raise her, to stand her on her feet, could imply a state other than death. The verb used (*qum*, even in the hiphil) does not suggest the idea of someone picking up a corpse and carrying it away. The prophet may have been deliberately ambiguous. The *qinah* reference and form would suggest a funeral lament but the description of the female, and her condition, helpless and unhelped, could suggest a potentially fatal condition, but one in which the victim is not yet dead. Amos certainly does not present "a brief, bitter report of the death, a report which emphasizes repeatedly the finality of that death" (*Wolff, 237). The victim is described as fallen, unable to stand up on her own, and with no one to place her on her feet.

Who is this female to whom Amos refers? Almost without exception, interpreters ancient and modern have understood the female to be Israel, "the virgin Israel." They have assumed that the construct relationship reflected in the wording, "the virgin of Israel," is to be read as an appositional relationship, "the virgin Israel." Ancient Greek translations did preserve the Hebrew construct relationship (*parthenos tou*

Israel) and the Targum translated "one of the daughters of the congregation of Israel." Modern English translations reflect the reading, "the virgin Israel." Contrary to traditional interpretation, the expression probably does not refer to the state of Israel as a whole but only to the capital city of Samaria (see Fitzgerald; Schmitt, 1986). The use of feminine imagery with reference to cities is common in the Old Testament as the recurring expression "daughter Zion" testifies. (See Ezek. 16; 23 where Samaria and Jerusalem are personified as females.) Feminine images are not used to refer to Israel as a people (see Schmitt, 1983). Thus the syntax of the expression and the use of feminine imagery in the Old Testament support the reading "the virgin of Israel," its referent being "Samaria, 'the virgin of Israel'" (see Jer. 18:13; 31:4, 21). (See on 3:9-11, 12; 4:1 and below on 6:8 where "the pride of Jacob" is used to denote Samaria.)

Amos intoned his dirge over Samaria to symbolize her coming prostration in her own land. Such a symbolic prediction against the capital city of Jeroboam II constituted a prediction of disaster against the reigning family and its supporters throughout the north as well as against the city of Samaria. In this light, the reference to the house of Israel in verse 1 should not be taken simply as a reference to the Israelite population as a whole. In verse 1 and elsewhere in Amos (5:3, 4, 25; 6:1, 14: 9:9), "house of Israel" seems to have a more restricted reference than "house of Jacob" (3:13; 9:8) or "house of Joseph" (5:6, 15). The house of Israel probably referred to the monarchy and to partisans of the reigning house of Jehu.

The depiction of a fallen Samaria "abandoned upon her soil" and "with no one to raise her up" (literally "there is no one who causes her to rise") suggests a deteriorating situation for the capital city and the reigning monarchy. The one who might have raised her up could have been either the Israelite population or a foreign ally. Internally, however, Jeroboam was confronted with a greatly disaffected population many of whom favored cooperation with the regional coalition. Israel's major ally, Assyria, was ruled by the ineffective King Assur-nirari V (754-745) and the Assyrian army remained in the homeland.

[3] Amos followed his dirge with a statement presented as a word of Yahweh predicting future events and conditions. Such predictions could have been intended and understood as advocacy of a particular policy. By predicting a future condi-

tion, prophets were implicitly advocating those policies that
would lead to that condition (see below on 7:10-11).

But what is declared in verse 3? The verse clearly refers
to the mustering of troops by cities in time of military need.
Such troops were raised in the cities and then sent to join the
national army. The verb employed (*ys'*), described the sending
of troops to battle (see 1 Sam. 17:20; 2 Sam. 18:2-6). Thus the
city that sent forth a thousand was a city that could muster a
thousand troops when the need demanded. The prophet
speaks of a ratio of 1000 to 100 and 100 to 10 (the numbers
reflect the size of military units). The first number in each case
represents the figure mustered by the city. What does the second figure represent and what is said about these figures?
Generally it is assumed that one should translate "it (the city)
shall have a hundred (ten) left." That is, the city that sends to
battle a thousand shall have only a hundred survive and return.
Such a reading is understood in one of two ways. (1) The figures emphasize the enormity of the destruction that will overtake the Israelite forces, destruction so great that only ten percent of the troops will survive. This interprets the statement as
an expression of pessimism (see *Wolff, 237). (2) The fact that
ten percent will survive is indicative of hope for the future and
is thus Amos's affirmation of a redemptive remnant. This
interprets the statement as an expression of optimism (see Berridge, 322-24).

The traditional translation and the two interpretations
based on this translation appear to be faulty. The following
expanded translation provides the sense of the text:

> Thus my Lord Yahweh has said,
>   "The city accustomed to sending a thousand soldiers to
>   battle, shall supply only a hundred,
>   and the city accustomed to sending a hundred soldiers
>   to battle, shall supply only ten,
>   for the army of the house of Israel."

This translation is based on four considerations. (1) The hiphil
form of the verb *sh'r* should be read in an active not a passive
sense as is done in modern translations. A passive sense would
have required the niphal. (2) "The city" is the subject of the
verb *tash'ir*, so it is the city which has to do with the hundred
and the ten. Thus the reading "shall supply/spare." (3) The

expression "for the house of Israel" instead of being a senseless phrase to be deleted (so *Wolff, 227) or a misplaced phrase to be transferred to follow "thus my Lord Yahweh has said" (see *BHS* notes) is of strategic importance. (4) Although Amos does use the noun *she'erit* "remnant, what is left" (1:8; 5:15; 9:12), when he uses a verb to express "being left over" he employs the term *ytr* (6:9).

Clearly, verses 2 and 3 should be read together, with verse 2 stating a condition and verse 3 giving a reason for that condition. Samaria (although the city may not realize it) is or will be in dire straits because of the disaffection of the Israelite cities which shall give only token support to Jeroboam II.

Within three years of Amos's preaching, the family of Jeroboam was exterminated in a bloody uprising led by Shallum (2 Kings 15:8-10) so his support must have been waning already in the prophet's day.

[4-5] The divine exhortations in verses 4b-5a posit two alternatives to the house of Israel. On the one hand was Yahweh. On the other hand were the religious centers of Bethel, Gilgal, and Beer-sheba. The motivation offered for seeking Yahweh was survival. The motivation for not seeking the noted cultic centers was a warning about what would overtake these places.

Several interpretations of these two verses must be ruled out of consideration. (1) The choice here is not between worship of Yahweh and the worship of other gods. Nowhere in the book does Amos give any hint that apostasy or syncretism was an issue in the culture of his day. While it is true that a god Bethel was known in the eastern Mediterranean world (see *ANET* 534; Eissfeldt; Hyatt), this does not appear to be a reference to such a deity. If it were, it would still leave unexplained the references to Gilgal and Beer-sheba. (2) The exhortation to follow certain actions and to eschew others should not be understood as prophetic irony (Hunter, 70-75, 96-98). (3) The proclamation of exhortation in this passage does not represent some schism within the prophet himself by which the prophet's proclamation "is noticeably unsettled by another word of Yahweh which comes upon the prophet, a word so strange as to seem an intrusion from another world" (Hesse, 9; see *Wolff, 237-38). (4) The statements themselves are not a condemnation of certain sanctuaries and, by implication, an advocacy of Jerusalem as the only legitimate place of worship (*Kapelrud, 37). (5) The tendency to find a deep theological thrust in the material is uncalled for: "This exhortation is not tinged by any irony; Yahweh's freedom to stand by his life-giving word, even in the hour of death, asserts itself" (*Wolff, 239).

The reference to "seeking Yahweh/Bethel" probably alludes to no special activity whether inquiring of God through a prophet (see 1 Kings 22:5; 2 Kings 22:13; Jer. 21:2) or some other religious activity. The imperative ("seek") and prohibitive ("do not seek") are parallel to "do not go" and "do not cross over to" which suggests that "seek" should be similiarly translated: "be concerned with" or "go after."

As noted earlier (see on 4:4), Bethel and Gilgal were probably the religious centers involved in the struggle between the house of Jeroboam and the rival to the throne, Pekah son of Remaliah. Pekah's reign of twenty years, which ended shortly after the beginning of his twentieth regnal year at the fall festival in 731, was calculated beginning with the fall festival of 750. If Amos's ministry is to be dated to the year 750-749, he may have been preaching near the time of Pekah's coronation at the fall festival of 750 (see Chapter 1, section 6). The admonition not to seek Bethel and Gilgal would thus be an appeal not to participate in the party strife and budding civil war (see below on v. 6).

But why the admonition not to cross over to Beer-sheba? This question is a bit complicated because it is uncertain to which Beer-sheba Amos refers. According to the Jewish historian Josephus, there was a Beer-sheba in lower Galilee (*War* II 573, III 39). According to 1 Sam. 8:1-3, Samuel set up his sons as judges in Beer-sheba, which would make better sense if the Beer-sheba referred to was in the north, in the region of Ephraim and Benjamin. Samuel's activity and influence were located in this area and primarily connected with the cities of Bethel, Gilgal, Mizpah, and Ramah. The best known Beer-sheba was located in the Negeb of Judah, and was the traditional southernmost city in Israel and Judah (see 1 Sam. 3:20; 2 Sam. 3:10). The city was especially associated with the patriarchs Abraham and Isaac (on Beer-sheba, see Gen. 21:14-33; 22:19; 26:23-33; 28:1-10; 46:1, 5).

In all probability, the reference here is to the southern Judean Beer-sheba. The expression "cross over to" implies that the city was outside of traditional Israelite territory. But why is

Beer-sheba placed in the same category with Bethel and Gil-gal? In all likelihood, there was a group of Judean towns, espe-cially in southwest Judah, which were disaffected with the pro-Assyrian policies of Samaria and Jerusalem. By the time the prophet Micah began his career, the opposition of Judean towns to Jerusalem was strong (see Shaw). Micah 1-2 which date from a time shortly before the takeover of Samaria by Menahem in 747 (2 Kings 15:13-16) already reflects this strong anti-Jerusalem, pro-coalition sentiment. (Micah 2:13 probably alludes to Menahem's march to Samaria.) Beer-sheba may have been one of the religious centers where Judean dissidence found expression supported by Edomite, Philistine, and Meunite backers of the regional coalition (see below on 9:11).

If the exhortation not to go to Bethel, Gilgal, and Beer-sheba now takes on some clarity, "seeking Yahweh" denotes non-participation in the civil strife that soon tore Israelite society apart. Amos may have meant no more than this. Non-participation in the struggle left matters open, offering the pos-sibility of avoiding civil war and thus survival (see on 5:15).

Amos has Yahweh announce that Gilgal would surely go into exile. Pekah's policy was strongly pro-Syrian and anti-Assyrian. Amos no doubt sensed that the regional coalition in the west would eventually be suppressed by the Assyrians, but not before the coalition wreaked havoc in Israel (see on 6:14), destroyed Samaria (see on 4:1-3; 6:8-10), and brought Bethel to nought (see on 3:12; 9:1). The lack of any reference to the fate of Beer-sheba in verse 5 is probably due to the fact that the Judean pro-coalition movement was not yet very well coor-dinated (but see below on 7:9,16).

[6] In verse 6, Amos continues the exhortation but this time in a statement unattributed to Yahweh. Two problems beset the first stich of verse 6b, namely, the identity of the sub-ject and the meaning of the verb *slh*. Most translations and commentators assume that Yahweh is the subject and that the verb means something like "break out." Ancient Greek trans-lators read the line as "lest the house of Joseph flame up like fire" which probably represents the sense of the passage. Although an Akkadian verb *salu/selu* occurs with the meaning "light a fire," the verb *slh* does not appear with this meaning in the Old Testament. The absence of any preposition or direct accusative marker before "house of Joseph" would lead one to see this expression as the subject.

Seeking Yahweh is proposed in this verse as an alternative to the house of Joseph being engulfed by flames, that is, aflame with civil strife and war. The house of Joseph here appears as a larger entity than the house of Israel and would have included the non-Judean Israelites, that is, the supporters of both Jeroboam II and Pekah, and whatever other factions there may have been. Shallum, who brought the house of Jeroboam to an end, seems not to have belonged to the same faction as Pekah although he was probably pro-coalition (2 Kings 15:8-10).

Amos warns his audience, the house of Israel, that once the fire of civil war is ignited, it will consume and there will be no one to put out the flames on behalf of Bethel. (Although Greek manuscripts read house of Israel rather than Bethel, the latter is probably the better reading.) In the warfare attendant upon civil strife, Bethel will be destroyed. According to our interpretation of 1:5, Pekah already controlled territory in the Valley of Aven only a few miles south of Bethel. Interestingly, Amos here appears to show real concern for the cultic center of Bethel.

[7-9] In these verses the prophet, using primarily participial forms, first characterizes his audience or a component thereof (v. 7) and then characterizes the Deity (vv. 8-9). The two characterizations thus contrast with and thereby define one another.

The content of verse 7 sounds so strongly like a statement of lament or disgust that many scholars have supplied a "woe" at the beginning (*Wolff, 229). The sense of the text is not so much "woe to those who turn" but "O those who turn." Regardless, the verse both accuses and expresses disgust with the factions at the point of igniting civil war.

The prophet characterizes the troublemakers as those who turn "justice" (*mishpat*) to wormwood. The latter is a bush-like plant of the Artemisia genus whose pulp has a sharply bitter taste (see 6:12). The plant yields a slightly aromatic dark green oil used in absinthe liqueur. (The term "wormwood" apparently lies behind our word "vermouth.") The term wormwood is used in the Old Testament together with "gall/poison" (Deut. 29:18; Jer. 9:15; 23:15; Lam. 3:19) to denote bitterness and sorrow (see Prov. 5:4; Lam. 3:15).

Verse 7b repeats the idea of verse 7a in different terms and with a different metaphor. "Righteousness" (*ṣedaqah*) they have cast down upon the ground like some discarded object. The word pair "justice and righteousness" occurs elsewhere in Amos (5:24; 6:12) and rather frequently in the Old Testament (see Gen. 18:19; 2 Sam. 8:15; 1 Kings 10:9; 1 Chron. 18:14; 2 Chron 9:8; Isa. 1:21; 5:7; 9:7; 28:17; Jer. 22:15; Ps. 72:1-2; 89:14; 119:121; Prov. 1:3; 2:9; 8:20; 16:8; 21:3). In many of these texts, the terms and their referents are a special concern and responsibility of God and the king, who establish and uphold justice and righteousness. The terms do not appear together in legal texts in the Pentateuch. "Justice" and "righteousness" in this text probably refer to right and proper order in society. It was the opposite of the civil strife brewing in the land which threatened to set the house of Joseph aflame. To define justice and righteousness in this text merely in terms of the legal and juridical system of Israel is to take far too narrow a view of Amos's concerns. Certainly, lack of justice in the legal system was one of his concerns (see 2:6b-7), but justice and order in the larger political and social realm were even greater matters for him (see below on 5:15, 24).

In contrast to those condemned in verse 7 for disregard of law and order in society, Amos presents a hymnic description of Yahweh, highlighting the fidelity of the divine both in regulating the natural order and in executing destruction. The one who made Pleiades and Orion, turns (the same verb as in 7a!) night into morning and day into darkness, who gathers the waters of the sea and douses the land, is one who upholds proper order in creation. Yahweh's fidelity is also manifest in the power to destroy (v. 9). When Yahweh flashes forth (or indicates) destruction against the stronghold (see 3:11b), destruction comes. Since this straightforward reading of the text makes sense, there is no need to force the text to provide a further astral reference: "who makes Taurus rise after Capella and Taurus set hard on the rising of the Vintager" (so NEB). The fidelity and faithfulness of God and the incongruity of the Israelites' behavior make destruction inevitable.

[10-13] These verses pick up and continue the theme of accusation and judgment begun in verse 7. The implied speaker in verse 10 is uncertain. The "I" in verse 12 could indicate Yahweh as the speaker of verses 11-13 but no such clue exists for verse 10. This ambiguity in the identity of the speaker is fairly common in prophetic speech and indicates that the prophets were not engrossed with the matter of distinguishing

what was attributed to the divine and what not (unlike their modern interpreters!). The prophet, of course, was the actual speaker; God as the implied speaker was called upon to give a sense of authority and omniscience to the words spoken.

The two parallel statements in verse 11 seem to spell out the implications of the indirect participial construction in verse 7. It has become an axiom in Old Testament studies that Amos's references to "(justice) in the gate" (5:7a, 12b, 15a) concern the hearing of court cases and the administration of civil suits. The following quotes from *Wolff provide an illustration:

> For Amos the exercising of "justice" - i.e., the proper functioning of judicial procedures - takes place "in the gate" . . . . Thus by "justice" Amos means that order which establishes and preserves peace under the law; this order is realized in practice through the legal decisions made in the gate, where matters of local jurisdiction were settled. (p. 245)

> The expression "in the gate" shows that . . . it is the local judiciary proceeding which is in view . . . . (p. 248)

The assumptions underlying such a theory are primarily established on the basis of Amos 5:10, 12, 15. The theory then becomes the basis on which these same texts from Amos are interpreted.

It is highly unlikely that ancient Israelites, when they heard the expressions "in the gate" or "justice in the gate" thought of local judicial and court processes. This is indicated by a number of factors. (1) The main gate of a town was utilized for all manner of activities. It was a place of public lounging, especially by the elderly (Job 29:7; Ps. 69:12), a place to meet one's clients, acquaintances, and associates (2 Sam. 15:2; Ruth 4:1), a place to secure witnesses (Deut. 22:15; 25:7), a place to conduct negotiations (Gen. 34:20), and so on. In other words, it was a place of public activity, but activity of all sorts, including public assemblies and forums, marketing, socializing, negotiating, and no doubt on occasion the hearing of court cases. (2) Old Testament legal texts never stipulate "in the gate" as the place for court cases and judicial proceedings nor use the expression as a synonym for legal process. The gate was a place for stoning after conviction (Deut. 17:2-7; 21:18-21; 22:23-24) and probably served as the scene of some legal proceedings (see Deut. 25:5-10). (3) The expression "in your gate(s)" is frequently used in a broad sense meaning "in your towns/villages" or "in your midst." Deuteronomy, for example, speaks of eating flesh in all your gates (= within any of your towns), of the Levite within your gates, and so on (see Deut. 12:12, 17, 18, 27).

If the expression "in the gate" cannot be taken as prima facie evidence that Amos is speaking about cases in a court of law, then other options for understanding this material should be examined. That judicial process is not involved is suggested by two further factors. (1) The vocabulary of the text is completely devoid of legal terminology. Terms signifying judging, witnessing, and so on do not appear. The terms that are used "to hate", "to reprove/set matters straight" and "to speak truthfully/completely" are not legal terms. They are the language of argumentation and dialogue. There is certainly nothing in this text or elsewhere in the Old Testament that indicates that the *môkîah* referred to in verse 10a "was the one in the circle of the elders who determined which party was in the right" and "wielded the authority of decision (*Wolff, 246). The terminology suggests a situation of hotly debated issues, the choosing of sides, and extreme hostility but not a formal court process. (2) The preceding material, in 5:1-6, indicates reference to party factions and political groupings which threatened to drag the people into civil war. Pro- and anti-Jeroboam, pro- and anti-Pekah, pro- and anti-Assyrian, and pro- and anti-coalition groups must have been straining the fabric of Israelite life. Those attempting to bring some sense to the situation, to speak the truth in public debate and argumentation in the gate, were hated and despised. (Note that Isaiah [28:6] had a good word to say about those turning back the battle at the gate, that is, opposing warfare in public forums, probably a situation similar to that in Amos.)

Verse 11 contains both a condemnation and a sentence of judgment. Both are stated in direct address. Those condemned in verses 7 and 10 in indirect address and those with direct address in verses 11-12 are the same group. As we have noted, the movement from indirect to direct address does not imply a different audience or addressee. Such shifts are frequent, especially in "woe" speeches (see on 5:1 and 6:1-2). The nature of the wrongdoing condemned is somewhat uncertain.

The verb *bshs* (in participial form with second masculine plural suffix) only occurs here in the Old Testament. It is commonly related to the Akkadian term *shabasu* with a transposition of letters being assumed. The Akkadian word refers to imposing levies or taxation in kind (see *Soggin, 89; *Wolff, 247). The second colon in the verse condemns the exaction or confiscation of wheat (*bar* was threshed, clean grain; see Gen. 41:35). The poor upon whom the burdens were placed (see 2:7) were probably landowners but members of the lowest order of free peasants (see Lev. 19:15). The judgment to come upon the oppressors was the loss of property; someone else would live in their hewn-stone houses and drink the wine from their excellent vineyards (see Isa. 5:8-10). Clearly Amos is here condemning the leaders of society. Whether those collecting levies and exactions were members of the royal establishment, that is, part of Jeroboam's administration, or leaders of the anti-Jeroboam factions is unclear but the latter is more likely. Taxation and levies by the central government might have been disliked but they could hardly be called illegal or "sins" (see v. 12*a*). In 5:2-3, Amos laments the "fall" of Samaria but does so without blaming the city and its leadership directly. This suggests that factors other than the wrongdoings of the Samarian leadership are being condemned. There are, however, some parallels between the charges in verse 12*b* and those in 2:6*b*-7*ab* and 4:1*ab* which are clearly aimed against the establishment in Samaria. Nonetheless, pro- and anti-Samarian groups could certainly have followed similar practices to raise means for their programs. The wealthy too may have been subjected to such levies and impositions but it would have been the poor that were especially hurt by such moves.

In verse 12*a*, Amos declares that the sins and crimes of the wrongdoers are innumerable. He then, in verse 12*b*, enumerates three classes of such behavior, the first two using participial phrases and the second a finite verbal form. (1) "Those oppressing the innocent/righteous" does not apparently refer to legal wrongs. The verb *ṣrr* generally denotes acts involving violence/aggression (see the noun in 3:11) or confinement/restraint (see 2 Sam. 20:3). Legal injustices could be included here although political and military wrongdoings seem more likely. In this case, the innocent would be persons unaligned in the internal political struggle but persecuted for neutrality and perhaps even incarcerated (see on 5:13).

(2) "Those taking a bribe/ransom" is not an expression normally associated with legal contexts (see Exod. 23:8). The term *koper* ordinarily refers to a ransom or expiation paid to forfeit loss of life (see Exod. 21:30; Num. 35:31; Prov. 6:32-35). Only in 1 Sam. 12:3 does the term appear to mean bribery. One should perhaps again understand the reference against the background of the civil strife current at the time (note how Isa. 9:20 describes the later but similar strife that plagued Israel). (3) Turning aside the needy ones in the gate may refer to legal injustices but in light of our earlier discussion of "in the gate" the statement could have a very general application. In times of social conflict the rights and needs of the underprivileged get "turned aside."

The conclusion to this subsection in verse 13 seems to offer a piece of advice inappropriate to Amos's preaching; many scholars consider it a late addition (see *Wolff, 233, 249-50). However, if one understands it as a warning comparable to verses 4-6 and 14-15, interpreting it in light of the political strife and party factions presupposed elsewhere in 5:1-17 makes good sense. The expression *śkl b* should be interpreted as governing the word "time" and as meaning "to understand, take heed" (see Pss. 32:8; 101:2 and *Gordis, 232-33). Thus the prophet declares that the one who understands that time coming will remain silent for it will be a miserable time. "That time" would refer to the time when the struggle between factions in Israel culminates in civil war and the house of Joseph bursts into flame (see v. 6*b*). To speak out and join sides would show lack of understanding; better to remain quiet and uncommitted to any side because ultimately no faction will succeed. "To remain quiet/neutral" would be to seek the good and hate the evil (see vv. 14-15).

[14-15] In these verses (see Hunter, 79-95), Amos returns to exhortation. The material is clearly formulated as words of the prophet and the tentative optimism expressed in verses 14*b* and 15*b* is presented as a highly conditional speculation of the prophet. Amos was apparently unwilling to formulate these optimistic statements either in unconditional form or as a divine word.

The two verses consist of imperative exhortations followed by consequence clauses. The exhortations plead with the audience to "seek good and not evil" and "hate evil and love good." Although these exhortations appear highly general and sound like clichés admonishing one to love "the good, the true, and the beautiful," this probably was not the case. The imperatives in these verses "seek/love good" should be understood in political terms. This is indicated by two factors. (1) The word "good" was used in ancient near eastern texts and in the Old Testament with political connotations (see *TDOT* 5. 310-2, 311-13). The expression was employed to denote proper relationships and loyalty to treaty and political arrangements, often in parallel to "brotherhood." In vassal treaties, it refers to the faithful obedience of the vassal to the overlord. In the Old Testament, "good" (*ṭob*/*ṭobah*) is used in combination with "peace" (*shalom*; see Gen. 26:29; Deut. 23:7; Isa. 52:7; Jer. 8:15) or as a synonym for treaty/covenant relationships (Gen. 26:29; 2 Sam. 7:28). (2) The context of Amos's exhortation suggests that "good" is not some ethical or moral ideal but rather a political matter. The political strife and potential civil war alluded to in 5:1-17 allows one to see the call to seek good as a call to political order and tranquility, a call to end the political dissension.

"Evil" in the context represents the opposite of "good." If the latter denotes harmony and order in society then the former refers to strife and discontent. Amos thus issues an appeal for an end to the inner Israelite political dissension and party struggles of the time.

The first consequence clause in verse 14*a* reaffirms the statement attributed directly to God in verse 4*b*. "Seeking good/Yahweh" is the precondition for the people's survival. In verse 14*a*, it is uncertain whether one should translate "seek good and not evil so that you may (or "might") survive." That is, it is uncertain whether Amos held out an assurance or merely a possibility. The second consequence clause in verse 14*b* supports the latter. The jussive verb form (*wihi*) indicates possibility or a wish but not an assurance and parallels the "perhaps" in verse 15*b*. If "Yahweh will be with you" is synonymous in meaning to "you may survive," then Amos only holds open a possibility that the nation will continue, not an assurance that it will even if the civil strife is ended. Israel at the time faced not only the threat of internal disintegration, but also the threat of the regional coalition already encircling the land (see 3:11).

The assertion that Yahweh was/would be with them was obviously a claim made by the people, perhaps by all factions involved, as the "just as you have said" indicates. Even the possibility that Yahweh might be with them, the prophet made conditional upon a radical change in society, an end to the political dissension.

In verse 15a, Amos reverses the order of the terms "good" and "evil" and substitutes the word "to love" for the word "to seek." This interchange indicates that "to seek" does not denote cultic activity in either verse 4b or 14a. It is uncertain whether the final clause in verse 15a should be read as a purpose clause ("in order to establish justice in the gate") or as a parallel exhortation ("and establish justice in the gate"). In either circumstance, "justice in the gate" would imply order in society and thus denote political more than juridical concerns.

In verse 15b, Amos holds out his great "perhaps." Even a major change in internal politics could only produce possibility of divine favor. For "Yahweh to be gracious" should be understood as parallel to "so that you may survive." For God to be gracious would mean that the people would survive, but Amos offers no assurance, since the end of internal dissension would not remove the external threat of the coalition against Israel. The reference to "what remains/the remnant of Joseph" suggests that northern territory had already been lost to various members of the coalition. Lost territory included major portions of Transjordan, Galilee, and the coastal plain which had been taken by Damascus, Philistia, Tyre, and Ammon (see 1:3, 6, 9, 13). The fact that Amos refers to what remains "of Joseph" rather than "of (the house of) Israel" could indicate that he included territory held by Pekah and other anti-Samarian factions. Joseph was the father of Ephraim and Manasseh (see Gen. 41:50-52; 48; Deut. 33:13-17), that is "Joseph" or "the house of Joseph" was made up of the tribes/regions of Manasseh and Ephraim. Isa. 9:21 preserves a reference to the conflict between Ephraim and Manasseh, though probably in this case referring to the struggle between Pekah and Menahem after the latter had seized the throne in Samaria (see 2 Kings 15:13-16), but a struggle paralleling that between Pekah and the house of Jeroboam.

[16-17] Amos concludes this rhetorical unit with the same theme with which he began, namely, lamentation. Although Amos had held open a window of hope for the house of Israel and the remnant of Joseph (vv. 4, 14-15), it was only a hope of survival not of good times or even of avoiding coming calamities (see 4:12). In verses 16-17 he reaffirms, in words

attributed to the Deity, that massive calamity lies ahead. Bypassing any description of the nature of that calamity, he focuses on its consequences. Wailing and mourning will pervade the land, in the open places (squares) where people normally assemble (the city gates, the sanctuary courtyards, and threshing areas), in the city streets, and even in the vineyards which were often the scene of jubliation and joy (see Judg. 9:37; 21:19-21; Isa. 16:10; Jer. 48:33). City and countryside shall both be involved. From professional mourners to the farmers (or farmhands), all shall share in the wailing and weeping. The calamity and the mourning to come are attributed to a work of Yahweh who will pass through (*'br b*) their midst (see Exod. 12:12).

6. THE DAY OF YAHWEH IS DARKNESS
AND NOT LIGHT (5:18-27)

H. M. **Barstad**, *The Religious Polemics of Amos: Studies in the Preaching of Am 2, 7B-8; 4, 1-13; 5, 1-27; 4-7; 8, 14* (VTS 34; Leiden: E. J. Brill, 1984)89-126; R. **Borger**, "Amos 5, 26, Apostelgeschichte 7, 43 and Surpu II, 180," *ZAW* 100(1988)70-81; S. **Erlandsson**, "Amos 5, 25-27, ett crux interpretum," *SEÅ* 33(1968)76-82; A. J. **Everson**, "The Days of Yahweh," *JBL* 93(1974)329-37; S. **Gevirtz**, "A New Look at an Old Crux: Amos 5:26," *JBL* 87(1968)267-76; D. R. **Hillers**, "*Hôy* and *Hôy*-Oracles: A Neglected Syntactic Aspect," *The Word of the Lord Shall Go Forth: Essays in Honor of David Noel Freedman in Celebration of His Sixtieth Birthday* (ed. C. L. Meyers and M. O'Connor; Winona Lake: Eisenbrauns/American Schools of Oriental Research, 1983)185-88; Y. **Hoffmann**, "The Day of the Lord as a Concept and a Term in the Prophetic Literature," *ZAW* 93(1981)37-50; J. P. **Hyatt**, "The Translation and Meaning of Amos 5, 23-24," *ZAW* 68(1956)17-24; C. D. **Isbell**, "Another Look at Amos 5:26," *JBL* 97(1978)97-99; H. **Junker**, "Amos und die 'opferlos Mosezeit,'" *TG* 27(1935)686-95; C. **van Leeuwen**, "The Prophecy of the *yom yhwh* in Amos V 18-20," *OTS* 19(1974)113-34; J. **Milgrom**, "Concerning Jeremiah's Repudiation of Sacrifice," *ZAW* 89(1977)273-75 = his *Studies in Cultic Theology and Terminology* (SJLA 36; Leiden: E. J. Brill, 1983)119-21; W. **Muss-Arnolt**, "Amos V 26(21-27)," *Expositor* 6th Series 2(1900)414-28; J. M. **Sasson**, "The Worship of the Golden Calf," *Orient and Occident* (Festschrift C. H. Gordon; ed. H. A. Hoffner, Jr.; AOAT 22; Kevelaer/Neurkirchen-Vluyn: Butzon & Bercker/Neukirchener Verlag, 1973)151-59; N. **Schmidt**, "On the Text and Interpretation of Amos 5:25-27," *JBL* (1894)1-15; K. **Schunck**, "Strukturlinien in der Entwicklung der Vorstellung vom 'Tag Jahwes,'" *VT* 14(1964)319-30; K. A. D. **Smelik**, "The Meaning of Amos V 18-20," *VT* 36(1986)246-48; E. A. **Speiser**, "Note on Amos 5:26," *BASOR* 108(1947)5-6; M. **Weiss**, "The Origin of the 'Day of the Lord' - Reconsidered," *HUCA* 37(1966)29-72; E. **Würthwein**, "Amos 5, 21-27," *TLZ* 72(1947)143-52.

5:18 *Ah, those desiring the day of Yahweh;*
what will the day of Yahweh be for you?
It will be darkness and not light,
19 *as if a person were fleeing from a lion,*
and met a bear;
and went into a house and leaned a hand against the
wall, and was bitten by a snake.
20 *Will the day of Yahweh not be darkness and not light,*
and gloom with no brightness to it.
21 *"I hate, I despise your pilgrimage festivals,*
and I take no delight in your solemn assemblies.
22 *Surely if you offer up to me burnt offerings*
and your cereal offerings, I will not respond
favorably;
and the well-being sacrifices of your fattened animals
I will not look upon.
23 *Take away from me the sound of your songs,*
and to the music of your flutes I will not listen;
24 *but let justice flow like waters,*
and righteousness like an ever-flowing stream.
25 *Did you bear to me sacrifices and meal offering*
in the wilderness forty years, O house of Israel?
26 *And did you bear the canopy of your king,*
and the palanquin of your images,
the star-standard of your God,
which you have made for yourselves?
27 *But I will carry you into exile beyond Damascus,"*
has said Yahweh, whose name is the God of hosts.

This rhetorical section is composed of three subunits (vv. 18-20, 21-24, 25-27). The first is presented as the words of the prophet while the second and third are ascribed to the Deity. The unity of the material is indicated by three factors. (1) No special introductory formulas indicating a new beginning appear in the section. (2) A central theme, the topic of cultic services, ties the subunits together. (3) No climax or definitive concluding statement (see 2:13-16; 3:11; 4:12-13; 5:16-17) appears before verse 27.

[18-20] The unit begins with the attention-getting particle *hôy* followed by a plural participle. Although the origin and function of *hôy* are widely discussed and debated (see *TDOT* 3.

359-64; Hillers), it probably served as nothing more than a special device for attracting attention and introducing material formulated in an impersonal manner. To this extent, the *hôy* + participle as an introduction varied little from a simple participial form. *Hôy* is generally translated as "woe," "ah," "o", or even left unnoted in translation.

The ones impersonally addressed in verse 18*a* are those desiring the day of Yahweh. Amos here offers no definition of the day of Yahweh but only a description of its character. His depiction of the day as one of darkness and calamity is obviously presented as the opposite of what was attributed to the day by his audience.

Scholars have hotly debated the origin, nature, and denotation of the day of Yahweh in early Israel (see van Leeuwen; Everson; Barstad, 89-108). Five theories have been most commonly advocated and defended. (1) The day refers to a final eschatological time associated with the ideas of a cosmic catastrophe and judgment and had its origin in a widely shared near eastern eschatology. (2) The day referred to a particular day and event in Israel's cultic calendar, namely, the time of Yahweh's reenthronement on the climactic day of the fall festival. (3) The designation developed out of military life and referred to the day of battle when Yahweh granted victory to the Israelite troops and defeated the enemies. (4) The day was especially associated with the covenant and covenant renewal between Yahweh and Israel. (5) Any occasion associated especially with Yahweh and considered a time of special divine activity could be considered a day of Yahweh.

In all probability, the expression "day of Yahweh" was not such a technical term as to be applicable to only one type of occasion or activity especially associated with the Deity. The complex of topics in 5:18-27 suggests that the day of Yahweh referred to by Amos was a cultic occasion. References to festival occasions, extensive offerings, songs and music making, and religious procession suggest a particular day in the fall celebration, probably the third day of the Feast of Ingathering (Booths/Tabernacles) which celebrated Yahweh's kingship and was the occasion of the royal coronation and its anniversary celebrations (see on 4:4-5).

As the festival marking the end of the old and the beginning of a new year (see Exod. 23:16*b*; 34:22), a feature of the celebration was the belief that the next year's destiny and

character were determined by the Deity. Like all new year festivals, it provided the occasion to bid farewell to the recent past
and to look with hope and expectation to the coming year.

Amos, having shifted to direct address in verse 18*b*, con-
fronts his audience with the conclusion that the day will be a
time of gloom and darkness without light and brightness. To
illustrate his evaluation he compares the day and what Yahweh
has in store for the people to a person fleeing a lion, encounter-
ing a bear, and eventually gaining what one would consider
safety only to be bitten by a snake (note Gen. 3:15; Num. 21:6;
Jer. 8:17 and the bronze cultic snake symbol destroyed by
Hezekiah in 2 Kings 18:4). Only a dismal future could lie
ahead of those whom such a day of Yahweh awaited.

[21-24] Although without the use of a signifier, Amos
shifts to divine speech in verse 21 and continues this through
verse 27. In this section, Amos has the Deity condemn a wide
array of cultic activities and then offer one exhortatory command. Some of the terminology of rejection in these texts was
employed in the cult and therefore would have been normal
and "diplomatic" in speaking of the divine attitude toward cultic
acts. The expressions, "take delight in, smell" (*ruḥ*), "respond
favorably, accept" (*rṣh*), and perhaps "look upon" (*nbṭ*) belong
in this category. The harsh declarations of renunciation at the
beginning ("hate, despise"), however, are caustic. The combination of "hate" and "despise" occurs nowhere else in scripture.

Amos, first of all, has Yahweh pronounce a harshly
negative judgment on festivals and assemblies in verse 21. The
continuity between this verse and verses 18-20 on the day of
Yahweh is evident in the theme: the day of Yahweh as calamity
and divine reaction to Israel's worship as negative. In fact, verse
21 could be understood as the reason offered to support the
disastrous view of the day of Yahweh. The day will be darkness
because Yahweh hates their religious observances. The term
translated festival is the plural of the Hebrew *ḥag*. When *ḥag*
appears without further definition, it refers to the great fall pilgrimage festival (see Judg. 21:19) which was the major festival
in the cultic calendar (see 1 Sam. 3:1, 7, 21). It was also the festival connected with royal coronations and thus the royal festival par excellence (see 1 Kings 8:2; 12:32-33) involving assemblies at the royal sanctuaries. If Amos has Yahweh hate their
fall festivals, what did he mean by this? Two possibilities suggest themselves. (1) Yahweh hates all their observances of the

fall festival, past and present. (2) The fall festival/pilgrimage and assembly were being held at two major royal sanctuaries simultaneously. (*hagge*, used here, before a suffix could be either a plural or a dual form.) If so, then Amos is probably condemning the observance of the fall festival and its associated assembly at the two shrines, Bethel and Gilgal (see 4:4; 5:5). The former was, of course, associated with the house of Jeroboam II and monarchical rule in Samaria. The latter, as we have argued, was associated with a rival claimant to the throne, Pekah. (On the fall festival at Bethel, see 1 Kings 12:32-33.) Amos condemns what constituted two competitive observances of the same festival, contributing to the further polarization and disintegration of Israelite society.

Verse 22, in which Amos has Yahweh condemn various sacrifices, should be read as a divine oath. The particles *ki 'im* introduce the matter sworn (see 2 Sam. 3:35; 1 Kings 17:12). Thus the verse could be translated as "when you offer up to me burnt offerings and your cereal offerings, I have sworn that I will not respond favorably, and the well-being sacrifices of your fattened animals, I have sworn that I will not look upon them favorably." The fact that the entire section beginning with v. 21 was stated as divine speech led to the omission of any statement such as "Yahweh has sworn" (see 4:2; 6:8; 8:7).

Even if Amos had been discussing the issue theoretically rather than addressing a specific case with all its particularities (see above on 4:4-5), he does not declare all forms of sacrifice unacceptable. Three different sacrifices are noted. These are the burnt offering (*'olah*), the cereal offering (*minhah*), and the well-being offering (here called *shelem* rather than the normal *shelamim*). These sacrifices fell into the category of voluntary offerings. They were sacrifices brought at the initiative of the worshiper, except when they accompanied mandatory offerings. Voluntary offerings are discussed in Lev. 1-3; 6:8-18; 7:11-36. Voluntary offerings on their own had no direct connection with sin, guilt, or transgression. Mandatory offerings, those required by God to remedy and restore the situation created by sinful offenses (discussed in Lev. 4:1-6:7; 7:1-10), were the purgation offering (*hattat*) and reparation offering (*'asham*). Amos does not mention, and therefore certainly does not condemn, mandatory offerings in either 5:21-23 or 4:4-5.

The celebration of the fall festival involved extensive sacrifice, celebration, and various types of activity. Several Old

Testament texts shed light on the festivities. At the festival in
the seventh month, the time of the celebration in Jerusalem,
Solomon and "all the people of Israel" sacrificed more sheep
and oxen than could be counted (1 Kings 8:5). The king himself presided at the rituals and offered the sacrifices. 1 Kings
9:25 reports that Solomon, at all three major festivals, offered
up burnt offerings and well-being offerings (*'olot* and
shelamim).

Exodus 32 and 2 Samuel 6 suggest something of the
activity at such celebrations (see Sasson). In addition to
sacrifices and feasting, these texts refer to drinking, game playing or sporting, singing, dancing, shouting, blowing of the ram's
horn, and other matters (Exod. 32:6, 17-19; 2 Sam. 6:5, 12:19;
see Judg. 9:26-27; 21:19-24; 1 Sam. 1:9; 1 Kings 1:9). Such
activities as these are what Amos has Yahweh express disgust
over (v. 23).

In verse 24, Amos confronted his audience with the
demand of Yahweh for justice and righteousness, for proper
order in society. Over against the festivities of the autumn
celebrations that contributed to the divisiveness of society,
Amos places the topic that is the constant theme of the
exhortations in the book (see 5:4-5, 14-15). Like his younger
contemporary, Isaiah, Amos declared that what the hour
required was not expressions of devotion in the form of self-
serving religious activity but a new state of social order (see Isa.
1:11-17). For worshipers to attend either Bethel or Gilgal at
this time and to participate in these royal festivals was only to
add to the solidification of party factions and thus to contribute
to the turmoil of the time (see 4:4*a*). To throng to Bethel and
Gilgal was not to resort to Yahweh (5:4-5) nor to seek good
(5:14-15) nor to create justice and righteousness (5:24). No
wonder Amos declared that the one who understands the time
should remain silent and sit tight, not choose sides and march
to royal assemblies (see 5:13).

The two metaphors used to speak about justice and
righteousness draw on imagery associated with water. This was
no accident since a central motif of the fall festival was the
coming of the autumn rains and the renewal of streams. "Let
roll along (*weyiggal*) justice like waters and righteousness like a
perennial stream" draw on the imagery of cascading waters and
flowing streams that never ran dry, thus stressing both suf-
ficiency and permanence. Amos's audience here surely must

have heard a pun on Gilgal in *weyiggal*. Nowhere else in Scripture is the verb *gll* used of waters. The play on words here parallels Amos's earlier *haggilgal galoh yigleh* "Gilgal shall surely go into exile." (5:5*b*).

[25-27] The last sub-unit in this section begins with a question which apparently assumes a negative response: "No, the house of Israel did not bring well-being sacrifices and cereal offerings to Yahweh during their forty years in the wilderness." Again, Amos does not argue that no sacrifices were brought, but only that these two particular kinds were not. Cereal offerings (which included breads of all kinds; see Lev. 2:4-10) and well-being offerings (consumed by the worshipers except for the suet and the officiating priest's share) would have constituted the main food items consumed at the autumn festival. To distinguish between these and other sacrifices (burnt, purgation, and reparation offerings) may seem quibbling to the contemporary reader, but that is because moderns tend to lump the multiple types of offerings into one category and thereby obscure the differentiation made by the ancients. For example, *Wolff concludes, "here a tradition lives on according to which the first generation of Israel abided only under God's law, free from the demand to sacrifice" (p. 265).

The prophet Jeremiah seems to have shared the view that certain sacrifices were not offered in the wilderness (see Milgrom). In Jer. 7:21-23, the prophet chides his contemporaries, suggesting that they treat their burnt offerings (*'olot*) as well-being offerings (*zebaḥim*) and consume the flesh of both. He then has Yahweh swear that these two types of sacrifice were not commanded at the time of the exodus. Rather, there people were commanded to heed Yahweh's voice and walk in the way Yahweh commanded them. Amos is arguing that practices observed in the fall festivals at royal shrines were not known in the wilderness.

The reference to conditions in the wilderness indicates that the prophet and his audience were familiar with the idea of such a period in the people's version of their history (see 2:10*b*) and that the prophet could appeal to the conditions which he at least assumed to have existed at that time in order to contrast them with those of his own time. One could not assume, on this basis, that Amos and his contemporaries were familiar with what came to be the full biblical account of the wilderness period.

A second question follows in verse 26 which, like that in verse 25, implies a negative response. Two preliminary remarks are necessary before examining the content of this verse. (1) Early in the history of the interpretation of this text, the items mentioned in the verse (*skt* and *kyn*) were understood as references to pagan deities; the passage was then interpreted as Amos's condemnation of Israelite apostasy. This interpretation is probably already represented in the Masoretic vocalization of the text. The Masoretes vocalized *skt* and *kyn* to give a reading *sikkut* and *kiyyun*. This vocalization was used to imitate the vowels in the words *şiqquş* and/or *gillul* meaning "detestable, impure thing" and "idol." This vocalization was a way of ridiculing what were assumed to be the names of non-Israelite gods (see 2 Kings 17:30). (2) The meaning of a third term in the verse (*kokab*), a term appearing in its singular form only one other time in the Old Testament (Num. 24:17), was misunderstood and interpreted simply as "star." (The plural form *kokabim* is clearly used in the Old Testament to mean "stars, heavenly bodies.") A particular meaning of *kokab* (a term used with various significations in Arabic), which probably elucidates biblical usage, has been preserved in Persian.

The translation given above is based on the following considerations. (1) The expression *sikkut malkekem*, generally assumed to refer to an Assyrian god (but see Borger) and often translated "Sakkuth your king" (but see NEB), is to be read *sukkat malkekem* and translated as "the canopy (or "booth") of your king" (see the Greek which read "the tent of Moloch").

(2) The expression *kiyyum şalmekem*, generally translated something like "Kaiwan, your images" and related to an Assyrian astral deity, is to be understood as a noun form of the verb *kun* in construct to the expression "your images." The verb *kun* meaning "be firm, set" would suggest a noun referring to something solid or substantial. When related to "images, statues," the term would probably refer to the place where these were stood (and thus "pedestal"; see NEB) or the means used to carry them (and thus a portable "palanquin"). The context suggests the latter meaning since it was borne about or lifted up (see the verb *nś'* at the beginning of the verse).

(3) The expression *kokab 'elohekim* is not to be deleted (see NEB) or read in an appositional manner ("the star, your god," or "your star-god"; see RSV), but understood as a construct phrase and elucidated on the basis of later Persian.

Although resorting to the Persian language to understand the referent of the term may seem farfetched, this appears to offer the best interpretation and since the word *kokab* was probably a technical term, earlier usage and meaning may have been preserved even in a later language. In Persian, a *kaukaba* was part of the regalia carried in royal processions. F. Steingass gives one of the uses of the term as "a polished steel ball suspended to a long pole and carried as an ensign before the king" (*A Comprehensive Persian-English Dictionary* [London: Routledge & Kegan Paul, 1892] 1063). In addition to this meaning, the Persian term could refer to a star worn as a sign of rank or to a royal train, retinue or cavalcade. The utilization of evidence drawn from Persian to read the Hebrew term as "standard/ensign/emblem" can be justified on three grounds. (a) In Persian, the feminine *kaukaba* and masculine *kaukab* forms have retained a connection with "star." The Arabic term *kaukab* means "star," but can also be used to refer to something considered superior or outstanding as well as a company or group. Thus the semantic fields in Persian, Arabic, and Hebrew are close. (b) The Hebrew spelling of the word with a long vowel in the first syllable even in the construct state shows a parallel to the spelling in both Persian and Arabic. (c) The understanding of the word as a standard or ensign is borne out by Num. 24:17. In this text, the word stands in parallel with *šebeṭ* "scepter."

Thus all three items mentioned in verse 26 refer to paraphernalia carried in processions. Amos's second question therefore asks, "Did you carry these items in the wilderness?" The assumed answer would of course be negative.

The term *sukkah* generally refers to a temporary shelter or covering which could be used for animals (Gen. 33:17), by farmers living temporarily in the field (Isa. 1:8; Job 27:18), by soldiers (2 Sam. 11:11), and by celebrants at festival time (Lev. 23:42-43; Neh. 8:14-17). The fall festival eventually became known as the Feast of Booths (Deut. 16:13, 16; 31:10; Lev. 23:34). Metaphorically, Yahweh had a *sukkah* (Pss. 27:5; 76:2). The ark, while outside the temple, was apparently covered by a *sukkah* (2 Sam. 11:11). In referring to the "*sukkah* of your king," Amos was probably referring to a temporary canopy carried over the king in a religious/royal procession. This seems more feasible than either to understand the reference to "the king" as a reference to Yahweh or to take *sukkah* as a festival booth temporarily resided in by the monarch since there would seem to be no reason why the latter was then carried.

The "palanquin for your images" refers to the litter used to carry religious objects in processions (see *ANEP* no. 538). Although the word "image" *ṣelem* would seem to imply statues or representations of the Deity, it is uncertain what these were. Hosea (in 3:4) speaks of "pillar, ephod, and teraphim" as components in Israelite worship without any censure of their presence and use. There is no evidence either to support or refute the idea that the "calf" of Bethel (see 1 Kings 12:28) was carried in religious processions, but the calf may have been just as portable as the ark in Jerusalem.

The "star-standard of your God" was perhaps carried as a sign of divine presence or authority. In ancient near eastern iconography, such standards are common in depictions of deities (see *ANEP* nos. 305, 488, 598, 625). Frequently these symbols of divinity are star shaped, often in the form of a star within a circle. The stars vary from four to eight points, sometimes attached to a standard but often not, and almost always depicted within a circle (see *ANEP* nos. 355, 529, 533, 535, 577, 698, 700, 701, 837). On occasion the star is depicted winged as well (*ANEP* no. 493).

The assertion "which you have made for yourselves" at the end of verse 26 may be a scribal addition. Two factors suggest this. The words overload an already lengthy line. This type of addition and value judgment, also reflected in the Masoretic pointing of the preceding part of the verse, would represent another example of the tendency of later editors to deprecate the religious practices of earlier generations. (The deuteronomistic editors of the Kings material, like many modern commentators, are distinguished in this regard.) If genuine, it would express a negative opinion on Israelite religion by Amos.

Three general conclusions may be drawn about the content of verse 26. (1) Amos is here not depicting and condemning pagan deities nor criticizing Israel for apostasy. The items noted should be seen as traditional elements of the Yahwistic cult. (2) The imagery involved is that of a procession, perhaps led by the king and bearing the representations of royal and divine authority. (3) The most likely occasion reflected in such imagery was a procession made on the climactic day of the fall festival celebrating the reenthronement of Yahweh and the anniversary and reaffirmation of the royal coronation. If Pekah's coronation in Gilgal was carried out at the same time as the reaffirmation at Bethel of Jeroboam's rule, it is no wonder Amos saw in such acts the blossoming disintegration of Israelite society.

The divine declaration of coming exile in verse 27 concludes the rhetorical unit begun in verse 18 and provides an illustration of Yahweh's action that is darkness and not light. There is an artistic and dramatic development of expression in verses 25-27. Although different verbs are employed, Amos uses a sequence of ideas: to carry offerings to God, to carry processional artifacts, and to carry into exile.

The destination of the exiles is spoken of in general terms as "beyond Damascus." Most interpreters have agreed that the statement shows "clearly that Amos has the Assyrians in mind" (*Wellhausen, 84). Such a verdict may be only partially true. Pekah's association with Rezin of Damascus and his support of the regional coalition placed him and his followers on a collision course with Assyria. But that lay some time in the future. For Jeroboam and his supporters, relying on and hoping for Assyrian intervention, the more immediate danger was the regional coalition at the time supported by Shamshi-ilu of Bit-Adini (see 1:5) which lay "beyond Damascus."

7. THOSE UNDISTURBED IN ZION
AND SAMARIA (6:1-14)

G. W. **Ahlström**, "King Josiah and the *dwd* of Amos 6.10," *JSS* 26(1981)7-9; N. **Avigad** and J. C. **Greenfield**, "A Bronxe *phiale* with a Phoenician Dedicatory Inscription," *IEJ* 32(1982)118-28; H. M. **Barstad**, *The Religious Polemics of Amos: Studies in the Preaching of Amos 2, 7B-8; 4, 1-13; 5, 1-27; 6, 4-7; 8, 14* (SVT 34; Leiden: E. J. Brill, 1984)127-42; M. **Dahood**, "Can One Plow Without Oxen? (Amos 6:12): A Study of *ba-* and *'al*," *The Bible World: Essays in Honor of Cyrus H. Gordon* (ed. G. Rendsburg et al.; New York: Ktav, 1980) 13-23; U. **Dahmen**, "Zur Text- und Literarkritik von Am 6, 6a," *BN* 31(1986)7-10; S. **Daiches**, "Amos VI.5," *ET* 26(1914-15)521-22; G. R. **Driver**, "A Hebrew Burial Custom," *ZAW* 66(1955)314-15; H. J. **Elhorst**, "Amos 6.5," *ZAW* 35(1915)62-63; D. N. **Freedman**, "But Did King David Invent Musical Instruments?" *BRev* 1(1985)48-51; H. **Gottlieb**, "Amos und Jerusalem," *VT* 17(1967)430-63; J. C. **Greenfield**, "The *Mazeah* as a Social Institution," *AA* 22(1974)451-55; J. D. **Hawkins**, "Hamath," *RLA* 4.67-70; D. R. **Hillers**, "*Hôy* and *Hôy*-Oracles: A Neglected Syntactic Aspect," *The Word of the Lord Shall Go Forth: Essays in Honor of David Noel Freedman in Celebration of his Sixtieth Birthday* (ed. C. L. Myers and M. O'Connor; Winona Lake: Eisenbrauns/American Schools of Oriental Study, 1983)185-88; W. L. **Holladay**, "Amos VI 1Bb: A Suggested Solution," *VT* 22(1972)107-10; J. J. M. **Roberts**, "Amos 6.1-7," *Understanding the Word: Essays in Honor of Bernhard W. Anderson* (ed. J. T. Bulter et al.; JSOTSS 37; Sheffield: JSOT Press, 1985)155-66; J. A. **Soggin**, "Amos VI:13-14 und I:3 auf dem Hintergrund der Beziehungen zwischen Israel und Damascus im 9. und 8. Jahrhundert," *Near Eastern Studies in Honor of William Foxwell Albright* (ed. H. Goedicke; Baltimore: Johns Hopkins Press, 1971)433-41; L. E. **Stager**, "The Finest Olive Oil in Samaria," *JSS* 28(1983)241-45.

6:1 *Ah, those who are undisturbed in Zion,*
> *and who are confident in Mount Samaria,*
> *the notables of the first of the nations,*
> *and the house of Israel that pins their hope on them.*

2 *Pass over to Calneh and observe,*
  and go from there to Hamath the Great,
    and go down to Gath of the Philistines.
  Were they not greater than these kingdoms?
    Was not their territory larger than your territory?—
3 *those who are flippant about the evil day,*
  yet you bring near the reign of terror.
4 *Those who are reclining upon couches of ivory*
    and lolling upon their beds,
  and eating lambs from the flock
    and calves from the stall;
5 *those who are improvising to the sound of the harp,*
    they prize for themselves musical instruments
      as though they were David;
6 *those who are drinking from wine basons,*
    and they rub themselves with the choicest of oil,
      but are not sickened over the breakup of Joseph;
7 *therefore, now they shall go into exile at the head of the exiles,*
    and the banqueting of the lollers shall cease.
8 *Yahweh my Lord has sworn by his life,*
    declares Yahweh God of hosts,
  "I loathe the pride of Jacob,
    and its fortresses I detest;
  and city and everything in it I will deliver up."
9 *And it will be such that if [a unit] of ten men were left in one*
  house, then they will die. 10 *While gathering it up [the*
  unit], carrying it, and burning it to bring out the bones
  from the house, then one will say to whomever is in the
  recesses of the house, "Is there still any with you?" And he
  shall reply, "None." And he shall say, "Hush!" in order
  that their be no mention made of the name of Yahweh.
11 *Surely Yahweh is giving his order,*
    and one will smash the great house into rubble
    and the small house into fragments.
12 *"Do horses run on a cliff?*
    Does one plow [a cliff] with oxen?
  Do you turn justice into poison
    and the fruits of righteousness into wormwood?
13 *Those who are rejoicing over Lo-debar,*
    those who say, 'Have we not with our own strength
    taken for ourselves Karnaim?'
14 *Surely I am rousing up against you, O house of Israel,"*

> *declares Yahweh God of hosts,*
> *"a people and they shall oppress you*
>   *from the entrance of Hamath to the Wadi of the*
>   *Arabah."*

These verses form a well structured and integrated whole. In words unattributed to the Deity (vv. 1-7), Amos first characterizes the behavior of the citizens and leaders of Samaria. The characterizations themselves serve as denunciations and accusations against the people. The use of participial forms dominates verses 1-6, interrupted only occasionally by finite verbs and by the aside in verse 2 which offers evidence that the people have no reason for their unperturbed attitude. The announcement of coming exile concludes the prophetic comments.

The oath of Yahweh in verse 8 is offered as both a confirmation of the prophet's prediction that the leaders will be exiled and as an extension of the judgment to include the whole of Samaria and its population. In a second aside (vv. 9-10), Amos describes the consequences of the city's destruction and then reiterates the decision of Yahweh in terms of the destruction of the royal governmental buildings (v. 11).

Verses 12-14 contain an oracle attributed to Yahweh which in the form of three interrogatives accuses the people of unbelievable behavior (v. 12), ridicules them for their lack of any sense of reality (v. 13), and assures them that the enemy at their gate will oppress them throughout the length and breadth of their land (v. 14).

[1-7] Amos begins this section with a denunciation of the complacency and lack of any sense of emergency which characterized the leadership in both Jerusalem and Samaria (v. 1). The attitude condemned is not so much one of complete and arrogant self-confidence as it is one of unawareness of and failure to admit the gravity of the situation at hand, as v. 2 illustrates. (See the use of *bṭḥ* in Judg. 18:10 and *sh'n* in Jer. 30:10.)

The reference to Zion in verse 1 does not "present grave interpretive problems" (*Wolff, 269). First of all, it illustrates the prophet's rhetorical skill. Beginning with reference to someone other than his immediate audience, it functions to engage and disarm the hearers. Second, it reflects the political reality of the time. Jerusalem, as a satellite to Samaria (see

Chapter 1, section 4), was of one mind and policy with its northern partner. It had been a Samarian subordinate for years and would continue to be so until King Ahaz and the city "saw a great light" and asserted independence from Israelite dominance (see Isa. 9:2). The policy and attitude of Samaria was mirrored by Jerusalem at the time. As the rest of 6:1-14 illustrates, Samaria set the policy for the house of Israel, both Israel and Judah.

Three groups are called to account in verse 7. The references to Jerusalem and Samaria are clear, but who are "the notables of the first of the nations"? It cannot be the Israelites themselves or "the self-acknowledged 'choicest' stratum of society," "the elite class of Samaria" (so *Wolff, 274) since the house of Israel "goes to them" or better "pins their hopes" (NJPSV) on them. (*bw' l* here has the same meaning as *bw' 'd*; see Isa. 45:24; Ps. 65:2; Job 6:20.) Those to whom the house of Israel went (see Hos. 5:13) and those in whom they sought security were the Assyrians. In spite of the temporary diminution of Assyrian power and influence, the house of Jeroboam continued its pro-Assyrian policy and its refusal to cooperate with the western coalition (see Chapter 1, section 1). The Israelite subordination to and dependence on Assyria, begun by Jehu, never faltered throughout the reign of his dynasty and was continued by King Menahem and his son (see 2 Kings 15:19-20). It was this stance of the house of Israel that lay at the root of the regional hostility to Israel. The expression "the first of the nations" was a term as apropos for Assyria as it was inappropriate for Israel. Not even Israel itself, much less the prophet Amos, would have had the gall to speak of Israel as the world's premier power! Amos makes it clear that at the moment, he evaluated Assyrian might as offering Israel no hope. He held the Assyrian notables, perhaps in Israel to shore up the waning authority of Jeroboam at the anniversary of his coronation, as representative of a power which at the moment could promise no salvation to the house of Israel. (Apparently Amos was not so negative about the long-range potential of Assyria since he probably saw Assyria as the eventual suppressor of the western powers denounced in 1:3-2:3.)

To substantiate his case that there was no basis for the complacency of the house of Israel, Amos invited his audience to look at the cases of Calneh, Hamath, and Gath (v. 2). Unfortunately, we know practically nothing about the fate and state of these three kingdoms at the time of Amos. Calneh (Kullani in Assyrian texts and Calno in Isa. 10:9) was the principle city of the region of Unqi in northern Syria. Nothing is known of the city during the mid-eighth century. Tiglath-pileser III conquered the town in 738 and annexed the region to Assyria as a directly governed province. That Calneh was in opposition to Assyria in 738 does not imply that the same was the situation in 750. Hamath on the middle Orontes River, on the other hand, was probably pro-Assyrian from the beginning of the century until after 738. Zakkur, king of Hamath, was opposed by a Syrian coalition headed by Benhadad of Damascus late in the ninth or early in the eighth century. He was rescued from the coalition's siege, probably by Assyria (see *ANET* 655-56). In 738, nineteen districts of Hamath rebelled against Assyria, although Hamath itself remained loyal (see *ANET* 283). That Hamath was in control of extensive territory by 738 does not imply that the state was strong in 750. In 743-740, Tiglath-pileser had suppressed a major north Syrian coalition. Hamath may have been rewarded at the time for its loyalty with an increase of territory. Gath at the time of Amos was probably dominated by Ashdod, as it was in 713-711 when Sargon subdued an anti-Assyrian revolt in Ashdod and took Gath in the process (see *ANET* 286; and above on 1:6-8). Gath had apparently followed a policy of being anti-Damascus (see 2 Kings 12:17) and thus a policy in line with Israel and Judah. (The Gath captured by the Judean king Uzziah noted in 2 Chron. 26:6 was probably not the main Philistine city of Gath but another Gath of which there were several.)

Amos's challenge to Zion and Samaria to take to heart the cases of Calneh, Hamath, and Gath of Philistia indicates, first of all, that these kingdoms had followed a policy of pro-Assyrianism just as had the house of Israel. Second, it implies that these kingdoms were now under the dominance of the powers of the regional coalition, just as Amos argued that Israel would very shortly be (see vv. 7, 14).

The subordination of Calneh, Hamath, and Gath to the coalition is implied in the two questions in verse 2. At this point some comments about the translation proposed are necessary. (1) A negative particle is implied but not present in both of the questions. That is, in normal interrogatives one would use a negative like "not" if one expects an affirmative response. ("Is it not so?") Interrogative statements in the scriptures in which an affirmative response is anticipated, however, sometimes dispense with the negative particle (see *Gordis, 239-42). Examples of this phenomenon are found in Gen. 3:1; 1 Sam. 2:27; 1 Kings 22:3; Jer. 31:19; and Job 20:4-5. (2) The absence of any finite verb in both forms of the question leaves the tense open. Reading the conditions described as characteristic of the past best suits the context. (3) The almost universal tendency to exchange some of the pronominal suffixes should be avoided.

The following is an expanded and supplemented form of the half verse which expresses the prophet's questions and anticipates an affirmative answer:

> Were not Calneh, Hamath, and Gath of Philistia once greater kingdoms than Israel and Judah and was not their combined territory larger than the territory of Israel and Judah?

The presupposition is that earlier these kingdoms were larger and more powerful but this was no longer the case. Their territory and power had been broken by the western regional coalition. If these kingdoms suffered such a fate, surely Israel and Judah must expect the same. Just as their pro-Assyrian posture did not aid them, so neither will it aid Israel and Judah.

With verse 3a, Amos reverts to descriptions formulated in participial form although verse 3b employs a second-person plural, finite verb. Verse 3 should be seen as identifying those to whom the imperatives and questions of verse 2 are directed. In verse 2, Amos challenges the people to learn a lesson from the history of their neighbors. Amos describes his audience as excluding or pushing away the thought of any day of calamity that might overtake them and therefore as refusing to learn from history. They are flippant about what the prophet understood as a grave and dangerous time. In fact, in their behavior, their pretense, and attitude, they bring near the reign of terror (understandig *shbt* as the infinitive construct of *yshb*). Whether Amos is here saying that their attitude encourages an invasion and further harassment by the coalition or whether it prompts the divine wrath or both cannot be determined. Certainly if the leaders felt that they had nothing really to fear and that Assyria would eventually come to the rescue, then they were not taking seriously the reality of the situation. The fact that Amos does not highlight the internal strife in the house of Joseph in this unit (but see vv. 6b and 12b), strife that undoubtedly weakened Israel militarily and invited conquest, would imply that he saw the indulgent and lackadaisical behavior of the people (see vv. 4-6a) as angering God and thus as bringing near the day of evil. In other words, in their actions depicted in verses 4-6a the people bring near the reign of terror (an invasion by the coalition) which will result in exile (v. 7) which is in reality a judgment of God (v. 8).

Two attitudes are condemned by the prophet in verses 4-6. The first, in verses 4-6a, is the indulgent and extravagant lifestyle of the rich and infamous in Samaria. In the long list of activities nothing illegal is condemned. Thus the prophet is not concerned with the issue of illegality but with the issue of immorality. Under other historical and ecomonic circumstances, some of these activities would have been characterized as normal and indeed as evidence of divine blessing (see the depiction of feasting and frivolity in the good time to come in Isa. 25:6; 30:29). The regulations concerning the well-being offerings encouraged the periodic interruption of the normal flow of life with conspicious consumption (see Lev. 7:11-18).

The images depicting the indulgence and extravagance of the Samarian citizenry derided by Amos no doubt exaggerate reality beyond the level of credulity, but prophets were never noted for understatement. The activities noted are so described as to portray a people totally obsessed with luxury, self-indulgence, and narcissism. Couches and beds decorated, like the royal quarters (see 3:15), with ivory inlay were a sign of economic well-being. (On the fragments of ivory inlay excavated in the ruins of ancient Samaria, see *King, 142-50.) Young lambs from the flock and stall-fed calves provided prime meat. Music was apparently performed rather ineptly by the people who considered themselves musicians and connoisseurs in a class with David (see *Gordis, 242-43). Wine was consumed in huge quantities and the body rubbed with only the choicest, "most virgin," of oil (see *Mishnah Menahoth* 8:4-5 on the methods of producing grades of oil; see also Steger). Amos probably did not ridicule the use of oil on the body but the grade of oil used since in a dry climate with infrequent bathing, oiling the body was almost a necessity.

Verse 6b, rather than being a secondary addition inserted into the text by some hypothesized disciple of Amos (so *Wolff, 277), represents the pivotal element in Amos's denunciations in verses 4-6. Instead of being sickened to their stomachs over the breakup of Joseph, the members of the establishment were continuing their ordinary lifestyle as if normalcy prevailed. The "breakup/ruin" of Joseph refers to the political strife in the north attendant upon Pekah's move against Jeroboam. In 5:15, Amos had spoken about "what remains of Joseph," that is, the territory still held by the Israelites after major encroachment across its borders by members of the coalition. The fact that Joseph was now only a remnant of its former self was the result of external factors. The "breakup of Joseph" noted in 6:6*b* alludes to the internal civil strife already underway and which eventually threw Israel into a state of civil war just as Amos had warned (5:6).

The declaration of the consequences to come in verse 7 reiterate the theme of approaching exile. Two elaborations of the theme appear here. First, the leaders of the people, those described in verses 4-6, shall be the first to go into exile or shall march at the head of the exiles as they depart. At any rate, they will still have the distinction of being "first." Secondly, the partying of the people will come to an end.

In verse 7*b*, Amos uses the term *mrzḥ* which occurs elsewhere in the Old Testament only in Jer. 16:5, in the context of lamentation for the dead. The term occurs in several Semitic languages, used of a social/religious association and the feasting occasions held by such a group (see Barstad; Greenfield). Both Amos 6:7 and Jer. 16:5-9 connect the *mrzḥ* with feasting. Although the Jeremiah text mentions the house of *mrzḥ* in a context of funerary laments, this certainly does not indicate that worship of the dead or of pagan gods was involved (so Barstad). The term may have been used generally to refer to any special occasion or group meeting where feasting was the primary activity.

[8] The oath of Yahweh in verse 8 is offered as confirmation of Yahweh's attitude toward the people's behavior and attitude and of the coming judgment. (The expression "declares Yahweh God of hosts" should be deleted or more likely read at the end of the verse and *mt'b* read as *mt'b*.)

Three times Amos notes that Yahweh swore (4:2; 6:8; 8:7) and once uses an oath formula to introduce a divine declaration (see on 5:22). In these texts, God swears by "his holiness" (4:2), "his life" (6:8), and "the pride of Jacob" (8:7).

The oath in verse 8 contains two parts, one stating the divine sentiment and the other a declaration about coming divine action. The verbs of emotion, "abhor" and "hate," are strong terms, which Amos had earlier used to denote the people's attitude toward those trying to bring sense and rationality to the political situation (5:10). The objects of Yahweh's feelings are "the pride of Jacob" (= Samaria) and "its fortresses." Just as he had earlier used the designation "virgin of Israel" to speak of Samaria so here he uses the expression "pride of Jacob." That Amos is not here speaking of an attribute of the people, "the arrogance of Jacob" (so *Wolff, 282), is indicated by several factors. (1) In this verse, the pride of Jacob possesses fortresses, a term elsewhere used by Amos with regard to cities and particularly capital cities (see 1:4, 7, 10, 12, 14; 2:2, 5 and especially 3:9-10). (2) Elsewhere such expressions are used to designate cities. Isa. 4:2 speaks of the time when the "branch of Yahweh" (= the Davidic ruler) will be beautiful and glorious and "the fruit of the land" (= Jerusalem) will become "the pride and glory" of Israel's fugitives. (3) In 8:7, Yahweh swears by "the pride of Jacob," hardly to be understood as "the arrogance of Jacob," but quite understandable if reference is to the city of Samaria.

The emphasis on Samaria which such a reading would suggest is perfectly understandable. At the time, Jerusalem, referred to in the opening verse of this unit (6:1), was subordinate to Samaria and policy of state for the two kingdoms was set in Samaria. Throughout the book, Samaria and its rulers are a primary focus of the prophet's denunciation (see 3:9-11, 12; 4:1).

Yahweh's oath about the future declares that the city will be delivered up along with everything or everyone in it. The city will be taken and looted by an enemy (see 6:14).

[9-10] In a prose digression, Amos proposes a hypothetical situation to describe how pathetic matters shall be after Samaria is overrun by its opponents (v. 8) and its people exiled (v. 7). The scene Amos portrays for his audience parallels the depictions in 4:2b-3 and 8:3, namely, the collection and burial of the remains of rotting corpses. In 4:3, the assumption appears to be that the corpses will not be buried; in 8:3, the final disposition of the bodies remains uncertain.

The prophet's background scenario in verse 9 assumes that if ten men were left or escaped alive in a house, then they would die. No reason is given for their death nor is anything said about how they died. There is nothing in the text to suggest Amos was talking about a plague as is assumed by most commentators. The verse should be taken in context, namely, the depiction of the capture of Samaria (v. 8) and the destruction wrought by the enemy (v. 11). Probably Amos is here alluding to the survival of a squad of ten soldiers. The reference to "one house" would then be to one of the palaces or government buildings (see v. 11) where a group of ten men might escape apprehension in the recesses of the building (hardly possible in a normal family home). In a captured town, they would end up dying (starving?) because of the military situation. Israelite military forces were apparently divided into units of ten, fifty, a hundred, and a thousand (see Exod. 18:21-25; Deut. 1:15; 2 Kings 1:9-14). In 5:3, Amos mentions three of these constituencies.

Once conditions permitted, the remains would be collected so the bones could be brought out of the city ruins and buried (v. 10). The translation of this verse offered above is based on the following considerations. (1) The first three terms in the verse are to be read as verbal forms denoting actions taken to remove the remains and make them handlable rather than as terms describing the person or persons who performed this service. Therefore one should not translate any of the terms as "kinsman, he who burns him" (RSV), "paternal and maternal uncle" (so medieval Jewish interpreters; see *Gordis, 246), "a man's uncle and the embalmer" (so NEB; see Driver), and so on. (2) The roots $n\acute{s}$ and srp ($= \acute{s}rp$) have their normal meaning, "to pick/lift up" and "to burn." The term *dod* is not the noun meaning "uncle, caretaker, lover" but a denominative form from the word *dud* denoting a container used for carrying items or material (see 2 Kings 10:7; Jer. 24:1-2; Ps. 81:6). (3) The masculine singular pronominal suffix refers back to the unit of ten men. Although the term ten here is feminine, it is used with the masculine noun "men" and elsewhere takes masculine verb forms (see Gen. 18:32). The suffix thus refers back to the bodies of the collective ten-men unit and is to be translated "it." Thus the first part of the verse is to be rendered: "While gathering it up, carrying it, and burning it to bring out the bones from the house, then one will say. . . . "

The burning of the corpses is to be understood on the analogy of 1 Sam. 31:8-13 rather than in light of 2 Chron. 16:14;

21:19; and Jer. 34:5. The latter texts refer to honorific fires burned at the time of the deceased's funeral and suggest something like "to burn incense for" (see the NJPSV's rendering of Amos 5:10). In 1 Sam. 31:8-13, the men of Jabesh-gilead snatch the bodies of Saul and their sons from the wall of Beth-shan, flee with these to Jabesh, and once in safe territory burn the bodies and then bury the bones. The burning in this situation, as in Amos 5:10, was to stifle the stench and render the remains into a form that could be handled. Cremation is clearly not indicated in either case.

The reason for the silence and for abstaining from saying the name of Yahweh remains uncertain. Was the situation so ominous that it would appear irreligious to say something like "praise/thank Yahweh" when no more corpses remained? Was the point to emphasize that since Yahweh's intention was to slaughter everyone in Samaria (see v. 8) then to mention Yahweh's name would call to divine attention the presence of those living in the ruins of the city and thus bring their lives into jeopardy as well? We simply cannot be certain.

[11] After the short digression, Amos returns to the topic of Yahweh's destruction of Samaria. Having already stated the divine decision in the form of an oath (see v. 8), the prophet now refers to Yahweh's issuing of a command. The use of a participial form of the verb "to order/command" implies a present condition; Yahweh is already giving the order.

The verb *wehikkah* should be translated in an active sense as "it/he/one shall smash" rather than in a passive sense "shall be smitten." The active sense leaves open the question of who is to do the destruction. Four possibilities exist: Yahweh's order, Yahweh (see 3:15), some calamity like an earthquake (see on 9:1), or an outside oppressor. The latter seems most likely since Amos speaks of the people who shall oppress the entire country in the concluding summation in verse 14.

The "great house" and the "small house" probably refer to palaces or government buildings in Samaria rather than to the summer and winter palaces noted in 3:15 or to Israelite houses in general. Perhaps Amos intended his audience to understand "the one house" in verse 9 to refer to one of these.

[12-14] The divine speech which concludes this unit opens with three questions. This triple series is indicated by the particles *h . . . 'im . . . ki . . .* (for other such examples, see Num. 11:12; Isa. 66:8; Jer. 18:14-15; 31:20; Mic. 4:9; Hab. 3:8;

Job 7:12; 10:5-6). All three of the questions assume a negative response.

The first question and answer are clear. Horses do not run on a rocky cliff. That would be out of the question because of the danger involved.

The second question is a bit more uncertain since there are two ways to read the text. One way assumes that "a cliff" in the first question is also to be understood as implied in the second question although it is not actually written. In this case, the implied answer would be, "No, one does not plow a cliff with oxen." Another way to read the text is to adopt a word division first proposed in 1772 by J. D. Michaelis. This involves reading *bbqrym* as *bbqr ym* and translating, "Does one plow a sea with oxen?" Although the first suggestion seems the most likely, either posits an impossibility.

The third question implies that justice and the fruits of righteousness cannot be turned into poison and wormwood. Yet that is what Israel has attempted. By "justice" (*mishpat*) and "righteousness" (*sedaqah*) Amos seems to be speaking in political and military rather than legal categories. Elsewhere "justice and righteousness" or "justice" appear in contexts concerned with the civil strife current in Israel which threatened the country with civil war (see 5:7, 24; 5:15). Where Amos speaks of the abuse of the poor and perversion of the legal system, these terms do not appear (see 2:6b-8; 3:9-10; 4:1; 8:4-6). The state of normalcy in the country had been disrupted, but such divinely established order could not be disturbed without divine displeasure and punishment. Civil war and military action (v. 13) which turned justice into poison and the fruits of righteousness into wormwood would be punished by divinely sent oppression (v. 14) as horses and oxen on a cliff invited disaster (v. 12a).

In verse 13, Amos has Yahweh define those to whom the questions of verse 12 were addressed. They were those rejoicing over military victories at Lo-debar and Karnaim. (The Masoretes pointed the name Lo-debar to read *lo' dabar*, "a thing of nought." The name Karnaim means "double horns.") Lo-debar (see Josh. 13:26 [corrected]; 2 Sam. 9:4-5; 17:27) and Karnaim (see Gen. 14:5) were towns in Transjordan southeast and east of the Sea of Galilee. These towns had no doubt been part of Jeroboam II's kingdom, at least in its earlier days. Amos's contemporaries were bragging about taking these places, as the formulation of the attributed quotation makes clear: "Have we not taken Karnaim with our own strength for ourselves?"

If the forces of Jeroboam II took these towns, from whom had they been seized? Apparently Jeroboam II had inherited control of the two from his father (see 2 Kings 13:25). Two candidates seem possible. (1) The troops of Damascus had moved into the Transjordan in force and had humiliated Israel in the area (see 1:3). (2) The territory claimed and ruled by Pekah with Syrian aid could have included these towns. At any rate, Jeroboam's forces would have been retaking territory previously theirs. Thus the irony of Amos's comment. If the region was claimed by Pekah even jointly with Syria, which seems most likely, then Israelites were taking towns from other Israelites. Political order had been poisoned and turned to wormwood.

In verse 14, Amos has Yahweh declare a response to the situation. The use of the participial form (*meqim*) indicates the present reality of the threat to Jeroboam's state. The people Yahweh is raising up to bring an end to the civil strife in Israel and punish the people for their wrongdoings are the coalition forces headed by Damascus.

The oppression to come on Israel is to extend from the entrance of Hamath to the Wadi of Arabah. The entrance of Hamath, the region between the Lebanon and anti-Lebanon mountains, marked the northern border of the region ruled by Jeroboam II at its largest extent (see 2 Kings 14:25). The other border noted in the Kings text is the Sea of the Arabah, that is, the Dead Sea. The expression, "the Wadi of the Arabah," occurs only here, thus no certainty is possible about what Amos meant. Various proposals have been made or are possible. (1) Since Arabah was a term that could refer to the Jordan Valley both north and south of the Dead Sea (for the former see Deut. 11:30; Josh. 8:14; 2 Sam. 2:29), the Wadi of the Arabah could designate the Jordan River. (2) Assuming a mistake in the Hebrew, some scholars have identified the stream with the Brook of Willows in Transjordan (see Isa. 15:7) or the Brook of Egypt south of Gaza (see Gen. 15:18; Isa. 27:12). (3) The most likely candidate would appear to be the Wadi es-Suweinit and el-Qelt valley, perhaps the lower reaches of el-Qelt (see on 1:5). Located in this area was the town of Beth-arabah (see Josh. 15:6; 18:22). At any rate, the territory demarcated by

Amos as destined for oppression was the territory of Jeroboam west of the Jordan River. The oppressor was no doubt Syrian forces headed by Rezin and backed by the coalition.

The leaders in Jerusalem and Samaria, who at the time were acting as if no immediate threat lay at hand and were pursuing their indulgent lifestyles, were soon to feel the wrath of divinely wrought oppression. Perhaps these leaders believed that Assyria would move decisively to squelch the western coalition or else assumed that the coalition itself would not be strong enough to bring the kingdom of Jeroboam to its knees. Amos proclaimed otherwise.

8. VISIONS AND THE FUTURE (7:1-9; 8:1-9:15)

P. R. **Ackroyd**, "The Meaning of Hebrew *dôr* Considered," *JSS* 13(1968)3-10; H. M. **Barstad**, *The Religious Polemics of Amos: Studies in the Preaching of Am 2, 7B-8; 4, 1-13; 5, 1-27; 6, 4-7; 8, 14* (SVT 34; Leiden: E. J. Brill, 1984)143-201; G. **Bartczek**, *Prophetie und Vermittlung. Zur literarischen Analyse und theologischen Interpretation der Visionberichte des Amos* (EHS XX111/120; Frankfurt/Bern/Cirencester: Lang, 1980); J. M. **Bracke**, "*sûb sebût*: A Reappraisal," *ZAW* 97(1985)233-44; W. **Brueggeman**, "Amos' Intercessory Formula," *VT* 19(1969)385-99; G. **Brunet**, "La vision de l'étain. Reinterpretation d'Amos VII 7-9," *VT* 16(1966)387-95; A. **Carlson**, "Profeten Amos och Davidsriket," *RelBib* 25(1966)57-78; G. H. **Davies**, "Amos - The Prophet of Re-Union," *ET* 92(1980-81)196-99; M. **DeRoche**, "Yahweh's *rîb* Against Israel: A Reassessment of the So-Called 'Prophetic Lawsuit' in the Preexilic Prophets," *JBL* 102(1983)563-74; K. **Galling**, "Die Ausrufung des Namens als Rechtsakt in Israel," *TLZ* 81(1956)65-70; H. **Gese**, "Das Problem von Amos 9, 7," *Textgemäss. Aufsätze und Beiträge zur Hermeneutik des Alten Testament. Festschrift für Ernst Würthwein* (ed. A. H. J. Gunneweg and O. Kaiser; Göttingen: Vandenhoeck & Ruprecht, 1979)33-38; **Gese**, "Komposition bei Amos," *SVT* 32(1981)74-95; M. **Greenberg** "The Hebrew Oath Particle *hay/he*," *JBL* 76(1957)34-39; D. R. **Hillers**, "Amos 7, 4 and Ancient Parallels," *CBQ* 26(1964)221-25; H. W. **Hoffmann**, "Zur Echtheitsfrage von Amos 9,9f.," *ZAW* 82(1970)121-22; W. L. **Holladay**, "Once More, *'anak* = 'Tin', Amos VII 7-8," *VT* 20(1970)492-94; H. **Junker**, "Text und Bedeutung der Vision Amos 7, 7-9," *Bib* 17(1936)359-64; U. **Kellermann**, "Der Amosschluss als Stimme deuteronomistischer Heilshoffnung," *EvTh* 29(1969)169-83; B. **Landsberger**, "Tin and Lead: The Adventure of Two Vocables," *JNES* 24(1965)285-96; C. **van Leeuwen**, "Quelques problemes de traduction dans les visions d'Amos, chapitre 7," *Übersetzung und Deutung* (Nijkerk: Callenbach, 1977)103-12; J. **Limburg**, "Amos 7:4: A Judgment with Fire?," *CBQ* 35(1973)346-49; B. O. **Long**, "Reports of Visions Among the Prophets," *JBL* 95(1976)353-65; J. **Mauchline**, "Implicit Signs of a Persistent Belief in the Davidic Empire," *VT* 20(1970)287-303; W. A. G. **Nel**, "Amos 9:11-15: An Unconditional Prophecy of Salvation during the Period of the Exile,"

OTE 2(1984)81-97; F. J. **Neuberg**, "An Unrecognized Meaning of Hebrew *dwr*," *JNES* 9(1950)215-17; J. **Ouellette**, "The Shaking of the Thresholds in Amos 9:1," *HUCA* 43(1972)23-27; **Ouellete**, "Le mur d'étain dans Amos VII, 7-9," *RB* 80(1973)321-31; G. **von Rad**, *Old Testament Theology*. Volume II: *The Theology of Israel's Prophetic Traditions* (Edinburgh/New York: Oliver and Boyd/Harper & Row, 1965); B. D. **Rahtjen**, "A Critical Note on Amos 8:1-2," *JBL* 83(1964)416-17; H. N. **Richardson**, "*SKT* (Amos 9:11): 'Booth' or 'Succoth'?," *JBL* 92(1973)375-81; A. **van Selms**, "Isaac in Amos," *OTWSA* 7-8(1964-65)157-65; K. **Seybold**, *Das davidische Königtum im Zeugnis der Propheten* (FRLANT 107; Göttingen: Vandenhoeck & Ruprecht, 1972); F. R. **Stephenson**, "Astronomical Verification and Dating of Old Testament Passages Referring to Solar Eclipses," *PEQ* 107(1975)107-20; J. **Strange**, *Caphtor/Keftiu. A New Investigation* (ATD 14; Leiden: E. J. Brill, 1980); S. **Talmon**, "The Gezer Calendar and the Seasonal Cycle of Ancient Canaan," *JAOS* 83(1963)177-87 = his *King, Cult and Calendar in Ancient Israel: Collected Essays* (Jerusalem: Magnes Press, 1986)89-112; S. **Wagner**, "Überlegungen zur Frage nach den Beziehungen des Propheten Amos zum Südreich," *TLZ* 96(1971)653-70; P. **Weimar**, "Der Schluss des Amos-Buches. Ein Beitrag zur Redaktionsgeschichte des Amos-Buches," *BN* 16(1981)60-100; M. **Weinfeld**, "The Extend of the Promised Land - the Status of Transjordan," *Das Land Israel in biblischer Zeit* (ed. G. Strecker; Göttingen: Vandenhoeck & Ruprecht, 1983)59-75.

7:1 *Thus my Lord Yahweh showed me, and, behold, one was creating [a swarm of] locusts as the late-planted crops were beginning to sprout, namely, the late-planted crops after [the time of] the king's mowing.* **2** *And when it had finished devouring the green plants of the land, then I said, "O my Lord, Yahweh, please show forbearance. How can Jacob stand, because he is so small?"* **3** *Yahweh relented concerning this. "It shall not come to pass," said Yahweh.*

  4 *Thus my Lord Yahweh showed me, and, behold, my Lord Yahweh was summoning for a disputation with fire and it devoured the great deep and was consuming the land.* **5** *And I said, "O my Lord Yahweh, please refrain. How can Jacob stand, because he is so small?"* **6** *Yahweh relented concerning this also. "It shall not come to pass," said my Lord Yahweh.*

7 *Thus he showed me, and, behold, my Lord was stand-ing upon a wall of tin and in his hand was tin.* **8** *And Yahweh said to me, "What do you see, Amos?" And I said, "Tin." And my Lord said, "Behold, I am setting tin in the midst of my people Israel. I will not pass him by again.* **9** *And the cult places of Isaac shall be laid waste, and the sanctuaries of Israel shall be made desolate; and I will rise up against the house of Jeroboam with the sword."*

8:1 *Thus my Lord Yahweh showed me, and, behold, a basket of late summer fruit.* **2** *And he said to me, "What do you see, Amos?" And I said, "A basket of late summer fruit." And Yah-weh said to me, "Late summer has come upon my people Israel. I will not pass him by again.* **3** *And the walls of the palace shall wail in that day," declares my Lord Yahweh, "many will be the corpses, in every place one will dump (them). Hush."*

4 *Hear this, those who pant after the needy*
 so as to destroy the afflicted of the land,
5 *saying, "When will the new moon be past,*
 so that we may sell grain;
and the sabbath so we may open to sell wheat,
 making small the ephah and making great the shekel,
 defrauding with deceitful weights,
6 *buying the poor for silver,*
 and the needy for a pair of sandals,
 and selling the refuse of the wheat?"
7 *Yahweh has sworn by the pride of Jacob,*
 "I will never forget any of their deeds!
8 *And because of this should not the land be in turmoil,*
 and every inhabitant in it mourn;
and all of it rise up like the Nile,
 and be agitated and subside like the River of Egypt"
9 *"And it shall come to pass on that day,"*
     declares my Lord Yahweh,
 "that I will make the sun set at noon,
 and I will darken the earth in broad daylight;
10 *and I will turn your festivals into mourning,*
 and all your songs into dirges;
and I will put sackcloth upon all loins,
 and baldness upon every head;
and I will make it like the mourning for an only child,
 and the end of it like a bitter day."
11 *"Behold the days are coming," declares my Lord Yahweh,*

"when I will send a famine on the land,
not a famine for bread and not a thirst for water,
but rather for hearing the words of Yahweh.
12   *And they shall wander from sea to sea,*
and from the north and unto the south;
they shall roam seeking the word of Yahweh
but they shall not find it.
13   *In that day, the fair maidens and young lads*
shall faint from thirst;
14   *the ones swearing because of the guilt of Samaria,*
and saying, 'By the life of your God, O Dan,'
and, 'By the life of the way of Beer-sheba,'
but they shall fall and not stand up again."
9:1   *I saw my Lord standing by the altar, and he said,*
"Smite the capitals so that the thresholds shall shake,
and shatter them on the heads of all of them;
and what is left of them I will slay with the sword;
not one of them shall flee away,
and not one of them shall escape as a fugitive.
2   *If they burrow down to Sheol,*
from there my hand shall take them;
and if they ascend to the heavens,
from there I will bring them down.
3   *If they hide in the height of the woodlands,*
from there I will search out and take them;
and if they conceal themselves from my sight at the
bottom of the sea
from there I will command the serpent and it
shall bite them.
4   *And if they go into captivity before their enemies,*
from there I will command the sword
and it will slay them;
because I will set my eyes upon them,
for evil and not for good."
5   *And my Lord, Yahweh of hosts,*
the one who touches the earth and it trembles,
so that all its inhabitants mourn,
and all of it rise up like the Nile,
and sink like the River of Egypt;
6   *the one who builds in the heavens his chambers,*
and his vault over the earth he sets;
the one who gathers the waters of the sea,

and pours them out upon the face of the ground,
              Yahweh is his name.
7 "Are you not like the children of the Cushites to me,
     O children of Israel?" declares Yahweh.
    "Did I not bring up Israel from the land of Egypt,
     and the Philistines from Caphtor,
     and Aram from Kir?"
8 Behold the eyes of my Lord Yahweh
     are upon the sinful kingdom.
    "And I will destroy it from upon the face of ground,
     except that I will not destroy
        the house of Jacob," declares Yahweh.
9 "Surely I am giving my order,
      and by all the nations I will make the house of
        Israel shake,
      like something is shaken in a sieve;
      and not a bonded joint shall fall to the ground.
10 By the sword they shall die,
      all the sinners of my people,
      the ones who say, 'The evil shall not come near and
        overtake us.'
11 In that day, I will stand upright the tottering canopy
        of David,
     and I will wall up their breaches,
     and his repudiators I will restore,
     and I will rebuild it as in the days of old;
12 so that they shall possess what remains of Edom and all
        the nations
     over which my name was called,"
      declares Yahweh, the one doing this.
13 "Behold the days are coming," declares Yahweh,
    "when the plowman shall meet the reaper,
     and the treader of grapes the one who carries the seed;
     and the mountains shall drip sweet wine,
     and all the hills shall wave [with grain].
14 And I will reverse the fate of my people Israel,
     and they shall rebuild the ruined cities
       and inhabit them,
     and they shall plant vineyards and drink their wine,
     and they shall till gardens and eat their produce.
15 And I will plant them upon their land,
      and they shall not be uprooted again from their land

> *which I have given them"*
> *says Yahweh your God.*

The first six rhetorical units in the book of Amos concludes with proclamations of severe coming disasters, all presented in the form of divine speech directed to the audience in second-person address (see 2:13-16; 3:11; 4:12-13; 5:16-17; 5:27; 6:14). Only in this final rhetorical unit does the prophet conclude with an optimistic word about the future (9:11-15) and then only after a final declaration of coming disaster upon the kingdom and house of Israel (9:8-10).

In all the units, reasons are offered for the coming disasters so that the troubles can be understood as justifiable acts of Yahweh's judgment (see 2:6-8; 3:10; 4:1, 4-5; 5:10-12; 5:21-23; 6:4-6; 8:4-6). The rationale offered for the judgment and disaster is therefore an integral part of each of the units.

The four visions in 7:1-9 and 8:1-3, even though the last two contain proclamations of judgment, do not constitute an independent unit. They offer no rationale nor basis for the disasters announced in 7:8*b*-9 and 8:2*b*-3. Similarily, the descriptions of coming disaster in 8:7-9:10 contain no rationale for the acts of judgment. The accusations in 8:4-6 offer the rationale for the disasters announced in both the preceding and following material. This indicates that the final rhetorical unit is composed of 7:1-9 + 8:1-9:15. (Note that even the judgment on Amaziah [7:17] in the Amos narrative [7:10-17] contains the reason for the announcement of disaster in v. 16*b*.)

The visions of the prophet are to be interpreted in light of their rhetorical use and thus as basic elements in his proclamation. This means that certain forms of interpretation and speculation about the visions, while interesting, are not germane to an understanding of either their use or their content. (1) The visions are sometimes seen as constituting Amos's call to a prophetic ministry and are then used to fill out the terse comment that Amos makes in 7:14-15 explaining his appearance in Bethel (see *Harper, cviii, cxxiv-cxxv for discussion of this view). None of the vision material, however, contains any reference to a call or a commission. (2) The vision accounts have been used as a means to comment on the inner life and to psychologize about the experiences of the prophet. One recent interpreter has written:

Thus the hard road along which Amos was led in the visions, unbroken till at least the third or fourth vision, must be considered the decisive preparation for his appearance in the northern kingdom. He must have been trembling still from the shattering impact of these insights, experienced in profound isolation, when at the time of his public appearance, he likened his compulsion to speak with the terror induced by a lion's roar (3:8), and when he announced to Amaziah that Yahweh had summoned him away from the flock to prophesy against Israel (7:15). . . . That Amos' deadly certainty must have ripened in him gradually can perhaps be concluded from the fact that some visions point to different seasons of the year. (*Wolff, 296)

Obviously such conclusions have to be read into the material and rest on hypothesized deductions. (3) It has been argued that Amos actually functioned in worship services as an official part of the cultic activity at Bethel where he performed an intercessory role (*Reventlow, 30-56; Brueggemann). Although Amos preached at Bethel where the royal sanctuary was located, it is highly unlikely that he did so in an official capacity and with an established office as his treatment by the priest Amaziah indicates. (4) The distinctions between visions one to three and four (or five if 9:1-4 is considered a vision report) have formed the basis for seeing two phases in Amos's career: one carried out at Bethel which ended after the third vision report and the intervention of Amaziah, and a later activity in Judah to which 8:1-9:15 belong (*Gordis, 249-53; *Watts, 27-50). Such a position assumes too sharp a distinction between visions three and four, assigns the placement of 7:10-17 to an actual chronological course of events rather than to thematic considerations, and hypothesizes a Judean phase for the prophet which has no basis in the text.

The vision accounts should be viewed from a rhetorical perspective without regard to the personal experiences that may have lain behind them or to the chronological framework within which such experiences might possibly have occurred. The prophet's use of the vision reports in his proclamation not only added a level of dramatic appeal but also served what

Aristotle called *ethos* or the ethical dimension of persuasion which depends on the character of the speaker as it comes through the speech to the audience (*Rhetoric* I. 2. 1356a). The autobiographical and narrative form of the vision reports serves four important persuasive functions. (1) They establish a type of speaker-audience relationship that is impossible with purely declaratory material. In the reporting of "personal experience," the speaker and audience share a rapport with each other as joint hearers of a "story." Audience and speaker together share the vision report. (2) The "eye-witness" dimension given the material adds an authoritative aspect to both the speaker and to what is said. In ancient Israel, as in all cultures, evidence based on or presented as first-hand experience had a greater claim to a response, even if negative, than mere assertion. (3) The vision report involves a greater emotional power of persuasion than mere declaratory assertions. The narrative quality of the material allows the audience the occasion to identify with what is reported and to become a participant in the report. In addition, Amos used the report form, especially in the first two visions, to demonstrate his identification with the audience. The role of intercessor reported by the prophet is one in which the prophet as narrator presented himself as representative of the people, as one standing between the people and God pleading the audience's cause. (4) The genre of a first-person vision report, in spite of its autobiographical form and in apparent contradiction to (2) above, depersonalizes the message. That is, by placing the content of the divine word within a vision context, the genre tends to release the prophet from direct responsibility for what is said; attributing it to the divine simultaneously enhances its claim to authority.

[7:1-3] An identical overall pattern characterizes both of the first two vision accounts. The prophet reports that God showed him something; what was seen is then depicted; Amos intervenes in direct address to the Deity; and Yahweh relents. No indication is given to explain why Amos associated what he saw with divine action against the people or why, upon seeing the locusts and the fire, the prophet should think of judgment against Israel. In the rhetorical context, Amos must have assumed that his audience would accept such an association. If the proclamation of the vision reports followed immediately after the judgment preaching in chapter six, then the association could have surely been more easily made.

Three problems plague the translation of verse 1. First, the statement translated above as "he was creating [a swarm of] locusts" in the Hebrew really reads "one creating locusts." Probably, but not explicitly, the one creating/forming is to be understood as Yahweh. (Amos may here have employed a double entendre. He and the audience may have connected the one fashioning a swarm of locusts with Rezin of Damascus and the coalition forces whom Isaiah [9:11-12] depicted as devouring Israel with open mouth.) The term *yoṣer*, a participle, is used to describe Yahweh in the hymnic material in 4:13. The term for locusts (*gobay*), of which biblical Hebrew has several (see Joel 1:4), only occurs elsewhere in Nahum 3:17 and may imply a meaning like "swarm of locusts."

Second, the green vegetation consumed by locusts is denoted by a Hebrew term (*leqesh*) which does not occur elsewhere in the Bible, although the root is used in the term *malqosh* the "later rains" that fall in March-April and aid in the final growth of the winter grain (see Deut. 11:14). In the so-called Gezer Calendar, a tablet named after the place of its discovery and probably dating from the ninth century, the various seasons/months of the year are noted in an inscribed ditty (see *ANET* 320). The text lists the seasons beginning in the fall. The fifth and sixth months are given as *lqs* (see Talmon; Rahtjen). Whether the growth was from newly planted seed or was second growth after hay harvest remains uncertain.

Third, the expression rendered "after the king's mowing" could just as easily be translated "after the king's sheepshearing." The term *gzz* is generally used of sheepshearing (Gen. 31:19; 38:12-13; 2 Sam. 13:23) or of shorn wool (Deut. 18:4; Job 31:20). Only Ps. 72:6 uses the term of mown grass. Sheepshearing of course took place in the late winter/early spring and was a time of celebration (see 1 Sam. 25:1*b*-11) even among the royal family (see 2 Sam. 13:23-29). As a shepherd, perhaps an employee of the royal or religious establishment, Amos would have been conversant with the special occasion and used this to specify the time implied in his vision. On the other hand, if the term refers to the royal mowing, does this refer to the harvest of hay on royal lands or to a mowing of farmer's land to secure hay? Although the king's claim of one mowing from farmer's lands is not mentioned in the Old Testament (but see 1 Kings 18:5), the king's right to a cutting is known from later Roman practice in Syria (*THBA* 143). If this be the case, then Amos provides another example of the royal administration's encroachment on peasant property.

Amos depicts himself as intervening with Yahweh asking that the Deity show forbearance. The verb *slḥ* has no object here so "to forgive" is probably not the meaning intended. Nothing in the vision indicates divine action against wrongdoing. The parallel verb in the second vision, *ḥdl*, simply carries the connotation of stopping or ceasing something. To argue that "although no guilt is in any way described, forgiveness is nevertheless the decisive presupposition for an effective cessation of the locust plague which is understood as punishment" (*Wolff, 297) is theological eisegesis.

The prophet's intercession argues that Jacob cannot endure such a calamity because he is so small. Amos nowhere depicts Jacob and the house of Israel as self-confident and powerful, at the pinnacle of prosperity and strength, as is assumed by practically all interpreters of the book. As Amos sees the people's condition, Jacob is so small, God should at least have pity on the pitiful.

Yahweh relents (or repents, has a change of mind) and declares that such a disaster shall not come about. This presupposes that Yahweh was the source of, or at least allowed the formation of the locust swarm. If Amos was using the formation and devouring of the locusts as an analogy for the coalition's aggressions against Israel, then he is suggesting that the group's previous actions against Israel had been serious but, because of Yahweh's forbearance, had not completely devastated.

[7:4-6] The nature of the calamity in the second vision has been much discussed. The issue turns on the understanding of the expression *qore' larib ba'esh*. A literal translation gives something like: "(one) calling/summoning to a quarrel/disputation by fire." By dividing the consonants differently, some scholars have proposed an alternative reading, *lrrb 'sh*, and translated "a rain of fire" (see Hillers). Others suggest reading *lhbt* or *lshbyb 'sh* and translate "a flame of fire." The present form of the text should be preserved (see Limburg) and understood as follows. A *rîb* was not a judgment or a formal court case (see De Roche) but a quarrel or controversy. A quarrel by fire would in all likelihood refer to warfare, that is, to the settlement of disputes and conflicts by military means (see Isa. 66:16). It is difficult to avoid the conclusion that Amos is here alluding to the internal civil and political strife in the country represented not only by the rebellion of Pekah and his efforts to establish himself as a claimant to the throne in Samaria but also by the disaffection of much of the population. Earlier, in 5:6, Amos had admonished the people to seek Yahweh lest the house of Joseph flare up like fire and devour, with no one to extinguish the flames.

The fire of the controversy is described in mythological categories by the prophet. (Note that Amos again draws on the terminology of the hymnic material; *qore'* appears in 5:8; 9:6.) The fire devours the great deep, the subterranean waters over which the earth rested and which fed the springs and rivers (Gen. 7:11; 49:25). Having devoured the deep, the fire turns on the land. (The rare word *ḥeleq* [see 4:7] apparently denotes the portion of the world that is not water and is to be regarded as a synonym of *yabbashah*; see Gen. 1:9.)

Amos again intervenes and requests the Deity to halt the destruction, offering the same rationale as in the previous vision report. Yahweh relents and declares that the destruction shall not come to pass. Prior to Amos's day, civil strife and struggle had threatened but not yet engulfed the land. The internal conflict had not yet reached the stage of an all consuming fire. Pekah had yet to be crowned as a rival monarch.

[7:7-9] The third and fourth visions have a different structure from the first two. In these, Amos is shown something, is then asked by the Deity what he sees, and responds. Yahweh then makes a declaration which employs some feature of the vision as part of a pronouncement of coming disaster. In addition, the first two visions are told so as to indicate that their referents are past while those of the third and fourth visions are still future.

The first thing that must be said about the third vision is that the traditional exegesis of this text is probably wrong. The traditional understanding, reflected in most modern translations, originated in medieval Jewish exegesis (see Brunet). It sees the text as describing Yahweh "standing beside a wall built with a plumb line, with a plumb line in his hand" (RSV). This reading is based on assuming (1) that the term *'anak* = lead = plumb bob/line, (2) that the expression "wall of *'anak*" = a wall built with a plumb line, and (3) that the imagery in the vision concerns a determination of Israel's guilt through measuring its perpendicularity apropos of Yahweh's will. This interpretation must be rejected for several reasons (see Holladay). (1) The term *'anak*, which occurs nowhere else in scripture, appears to be a Hebrew borrowing of the Akkadian term *annaku* which means "tin" (see Landsberger; *CAD* 1/II 127-30). The normal Hebrew words for "lead" and "tin" were *'operet* and *bedil*. (2) The expression "wall of *'anak*" cannot be understood as a wall built with the aid of an *'anak* but rather a wall built of or covered with the substance. (3) The context does not indicate an act in which Israel is measured and judged according to some standard. The imagery is military in nature as v. 9 clearly indicates.

Yahweh is presented as positioned upon or beside a tin wall, with tin in his hand, and as setting (reading *śam* as a participle) tin in the midst of the people of Israel. Obviously, this literal reading provides no meaningful sense. The term "tin" must have a second level of reference, that is, the term must signify something to which tin was related. Tin combined with copper produces bronze, an important metal in ancient times used in the manufacture of weapons and other artifacts. The expression "a wall of bronze" in Jer. 1:18; 15:20 is used to describe the prophet's invulnerability. Probably *'anak* is used in these verses to describe an impregnable wall (playing on the image of a siege machine?) and weaponry. Tin, because of its use in alloys like bronze, could have been used like the term "iron" to arouse frightening associations (see above on 1:3). "Tin" could have been used metaphorically for "warfare" or "strife."

The main sources of tin in the eastern Mediterranean world were in Anatolia. In the mid-eighth century trade with this region was controlled by Urartu, Assyria's arch rival. Urartian control of the trade routes from Anatolia had cut off the flow of raw materials into Assyria, perhaps creating a shortage of tin and other metals. As allies of Urartu, the regional coalition may have been supplied with tin from these sources.

The wall of *'anak* in the vision is distinguished from the *'anak* which Yahweh declares he is now placing in the midst of Israel. The wall would seem to symbolize something exterior but terrifying to Israel while the hand-held instrument or material placed in Israel's midst would seem to symbolize some internal terrifying element. Both are related to Yahweh and associated with divine action. The most logical explanation of this imagery sees the wall as a symbol of the coalition enemies of Israel (see 3:11) and the *'anak* in Israel's midst as the growing civil strife within Israel.

Verse 9 has Yahweh spell out the consequences of the vision's imagery. The first half of the verse states one set of consequences without relating them directly to divine activity; the cult places of Isaac and the sanctuaries of Israel shall be destroyed. Reference to Isaac occurs in Amos only in 7:9 and 7:16. The association of Isaac with Beer-sheba in the patriarchal traditions would indicate that the references to Beer-sheba in 5:5 and 8:14 also have to do with Isaac or the house of Isaac. As was noted in the discussion of 5:5, Beer-sheba was probably used by Amos to refer to the disaffected southern and southwestern cities which became disloyal to the Israelite-Judean royal houses over their pro-Assyrian policy and refusal to join the regional coalition (see below on 9:11). In the description of Uzziah's reign (785-760) in 2 Chronicles 26, the Judean king is pictured in control of much of southwestern Palestine where his authority and influence extended to the entrance of Egypt (2 Chron. 26:8). In the reign of his successor Jotham (759-744), matters were completely reversed. He was forced to build fortifications in the hills of Judah itself to protect his domain (2 Chron. 27:4). The most likely explanation for this is that territory was lost not only to the Philistines and Edomites but that even some Judean cities had declared independence from Judah. It is this group of Judeans disaffected with the Davidic-Israelite, pro-Assyrian policy of whom Amos speaks in references to Isaac and Beer-sheba. In describing the coming disasters, Amos speaks of the destruction of the cult/high places of Isaac and the sanctuaries of Israel. (The term *bamot* does not appear to have had a negative insinuation nor to have been used pejoratively in the eighth century. The plural form could apparently be used of a single cultic complex; see Mic. 1:5.) The only sanctuary center mentioned in Amos that could be associated with Isaac is Beer-sheba (see 5:5; 8:14), perhaps the main cultic center for the southern pro-coalition group. The other sanctuaries refered to, other than Jerusalem (1:2), are Bethel (3:14; 4:4; 5:5-6; 7:10, 13), Gilgal (4:4; 5:5), and Dan (8:14). If Gilgal was under Pekah's control, then all of these latter shrines had official and monarchical connections.

In verse 9b, Amos has Yahweh declare hostility toward the house of Jeroboam II (see on 7:11). One would assume that the reference to the sword should be understood in military categories, namely, with reference to a foreign invasion and battle. If that is the case, then Amos must have been referring to the regional coalition (see on 3:11 and 6:14). On the other hand, the reference may have been to the internal strife that eventually would topple the house of Jeroboam six months into the reign of his successor (see 2 Kings 15:8-10). In fact, the prediction that Yahweh would rise up against the house of Jeroboam could have been heard, and even have been intended by the prophet, as a call for the assassination of Jeroboam and his house. Predictions of future conditions and pronouncements of divine action could have functioned as calls to activity by the audience (see above on 5:3). Simultaneous with or shortly before Amos, the prophet Hosea declared that Yahweh was going to visit the blood of Jezreel on the house of Jehu, bring to an end the reign of the house of Israel, and break the bow of Israel in the Valley of Jezreel (Hos. 1:4b-5). All three of these statements appear to refer to the same phenomenon: the defeat and annihilation of Jeroboam's forces and the Israelite royal house in a major military conflict in the Valley of Jezreel. Hosea's announcements of disaster may also have functioned as calls to action and been used to justify the annihilation of the family of Jehu/Jeroboam (see Jeremiah's announcement/appeal in Jer. 22:18-19). At any rate, both Hosea and Amos proclaimed Yahweh's intention to destroy the reigning family.

The Amos narrative in 7:10-17 clearly indicates that at least the official establishment in the north saw the prophet as fomenting conspiracy against Jeroboam, and that accusations, if not charges, were brought against him. The similarity between these accusations and Amos's proclamation in verse 9b led to the placement of 7:10-17 following 7:9.

[8:1-3] In the fourth vision, Amos sees what is apparently a basket of summer fruit ("figs" NJPSV). The term *qayiṣ* is used elsewhere both of the season (Gen. 8:22; Isa. 28:4; Jer. 8:20; Ps. 32:4; Amos 3:15) and the "fruit" of the season (2 Sam. 15:1). In Yahweh's response to the prophet in verse 2b, the word is reused: "the *qeṣ* has come upon my people Israel." This is assumed to be a play on the word *qṣ* meaning "end" (from *qṣṣ* "to cut off"). It is doubtful, however, that this is the case. In the Gezer Calendar, the last month of the year is spelled *qṣ*. This would indicate that the final month of the year

is what is meant here. This would suggest that Amos declared
that Israel was in its last days but not that "the end" had already
come upon the people (see Jer. 8:20; Rahtjen).

Verse 3, paralleling 7:9 in the third vision, spells out
what lies ahead for Israel. The description is one of lamentation and death (see 4:2-3; 5:16-17; 6:9-10). The opening phrase
in verse 3 appears to read "the songs (*shirot*) of the
palace/temple will wail" but this does not make good sense.
"Songs" is thus often corrected to "female singers" (*sharot*) or
"princesses" (*śarot*). The translation offered above assumes
that *shirot* is equivalent to *shurot* "walls" (see *Gordis, 256-57).
When the judgment of Yahweh strikes in the form of military
calamity or civil war, then the walls of the palace will wail, that
is, will reverberate with the sounds of wailing. Corpses shall be
everywhere and left unburied. Silence shall be necessary as a
response to the horrible situation (see 6:9-10).

[8:4-6] These verses offer the rationale for the coming
disasters announced in 7:1-9; 8:1-9:10. They contain the only
charges of wrongdoing in the material. The accusations parallel closely those made in 2:6b-7a and 4:1a. The new element in
8:4-6 is the more elaborate description of the greed and corrup-
tion of the mercantile class used in the exploitation of the poor
and impoverished.

The material is formulated in indirect discourse so the
wrongdoers are never addressed directly. The charges are
given as sarcastic quotations by the wrongdoers themselves.
The merchants are depicted as restlessly and begrudgingly
awaiting the passage of holidays, new moon and sabbath, in
order to return to business. Although no Old Testament text
offers an explanation for the observance of the new moon,
several passages attest to its observance (see Num. 10:10 28:11-
15; 1 Sam. 20:5, 24; 2 Kings 4:23; Isa. 1:13-14; Hos. 2:11). The
new moon marked the first day of the month. The beginning of
the first and seventh months had special importance and
required a definite proclamation since feast days later in the
month were set a specific number of days into the month. The
sabbath referred to may have been the regular observance of
the seventh day or perhaps the middle of the month, thus being
equivalent to the Akkadian *shappatu/shabattu*. On the other
hand, the term "sabbath" may have been used to refer to any
day, in addition to the regular seventh day, when normal
occupational work was prohibited (see Lev. 23:24, 32). At any

rate, the prophet's point is clear: the merchants are so greedy they cannot wait to open shop, thus being even incapable of enjoying the respite from business granted by holidays.

In addition to harboring avarice, the merchants are presented as deceitful, "buying low, selling high," giving "short measure, high prices" (v. 5) and trading in second-class merchandise (v. 6b). The use of deceitful weights and other fraudulent business practices are condemned in numerous places in the scriptures (Lev. 19:35-36; Deut. 25:13-16; Ezek. 45:10-12; Prov. 11:1; 16:11; 20:10, 23). For Amos, mercantile deceit was exceptionally costly for the poor and impoverished since it could lead to indebtedness and eventual debt servitude (v. 6a).

[8:7-8] The words formulated as prophetic speech in verses 4-6 are confirmed by appeal to an oath of Yahweh (see 4:2; 6:8). Here Yahweh swears by "the pride of Jacob," in all likelihood a reference to the city of Samaria (see on 6:8). The "pride of Jacob" hardly refers to Yahweh ("As truly as I am the pride of Jacob . . . ; so *Marti, 217) nor is it used ironically ("Yahweh's oath is just as unalterable as Israel's haughty arrogance is beyond reform"; so *Wolff, 328). Yahweh swears that the deeds committed by the mercantile class will never be forgotten, that is, they shall be punished.

The general statement of punishment for the mercantile wrongdoing (note the "this" at the opening of vv. 4 and 8) describes an upheaval of the country comparable to the rise and fall of the Nile River in Egpyt. Practically all commentators assume that the reference is the prediction of an earthquake since the following verse employs the terminology of an eclipse thus suggesting major natural abnormalities. The rise and fall of the Nile, however, takes several months, which would suggest some disorder and chaos lasting over a period of time. The Nile inundation could on occasion be highly destructive. For example, conditions produced by a devastating inundation in the third year of Pharaoh Osorkon III (787-759) were compared to the chaotic disorder at the time of creation. A hieratic graffito inscribed on the wall of the hypostyle temple wall at Luxor reports that the flood waters "reached the cliffs (on each side of the Nile valley) as at the beginning of the world; the land was in its power as though (in the power of) the sea; there was no dyke made by the hand of man which could resist its force . . . . All the temples of Thebes were like marshes; . . . the people . . . were like swimmers in the water. . ." (CAH 3/1, p.

567). There is no reason why the Israelites and the prophet
Amos should not have been acquainted with such episodes or
even this episode in particular.

In all likelihood, Amos was comparing the state of
Israelite society with its social disorder and civil strife already
present to the pattern and destructiveness of a Nile inundation.
This is suggested by three factors. (1) Verse 8 is more closely
connected with the preceding (vv. 4-7) than with the following
material (vv. 9-10). The activity thus described would appear to
be correlated with the oppressive policies of Jeroboam II, his
administrators, and the mercantile class. (2) The fact that verse
8 is formulated as a question implies that the audience possessed present evidence making possible an affirmative
response. (3) The term *rgz*, meaning "to tremble, be agitated,"
need not refer to the earth's physical trembling and shaking as
in an earthquake. In 1 Sam. 14:15-16, the expression "the land
trembled" is used to describe the panic and turmoil which
seized the people after Jonathan attacked and defeated a
Philistine garrison. In Isa. 14:3, a nominal form of the term is
used to refer to the agitation produced by a foreign invasion.
Thus Amos here seems to be addressing a simple question to
his audience: are not the social oppression and economic
exploitation under Jeroboam II the main reasons for the agitation already present in the land which, like the Nile inundation,
swells, stirs up, and subsides but is certain to repeat itself?
Surely in the rebellions of Pekah and Shallum the leaders must
have appealed to the social and economic conditions of
Jeroboam's reign to justify their uprisings (see below on 8:14).

[8:9-10] Three pronouncements formulated as divine
speech and introduced by "and it shall come to pass on that
day," "behold the days are coming," and "in that day" speak in
more detail of the coming disasters. Although all three units
are presented as divine address, direct attribution to the Deity
occurs only twice (vv. 9*a*, 11*a*). In the first of these descriptions
(vv. 9-10), Amos employs the imagery of a solar eclipse to
illustrate the suddenness of the coming calamity. Amos's contemporaries would probably have been familiar with the awe
and dread produced by eclipses. A total eclipse had been
visible in the region on 9 February 784 and 15 June 763. (The
occurrence of the latter is noted in the Assyrian eponym list.
This reference establishes the date for the year in which it is
noted and thus provides a linchpin for dating backwards and

forwards and thus for dating the years and events mentioned in these texts.) Although Amos seems to be predicting a future solar eclipse, his interest lies in using the imagery to illustrate the point made in verse 10. As an eclipse suddenly transforms things into their opposite, making the sun set before evening and bringing darkness in the middle of broad daylight, so the people's lives shall suddenly be transformed from celebration and joy to lamentation and mourning.

The "festivals" mentioned, as in 5:21, should not be interpreted as the three different pilgrimage festivals (see Exod. 23:14-17) nor as a series of yearly observances of the fall festival, the festival *hag* par excellence. Rather, the plural of *hag* here should probably be understood as denoting the observance of the same festival at the same time at different sanctuaries (see on 4:4-5; 5:21). In fact, the reference is probably to the celebrations of the climactic day (in Amos's time, the third day) of the fall festival at the various shrines mentioned in the book.

According to Amos, festival time would be transformed into its exact opposite. Instead of sacrifices, feasting, celebration, the noise of songs, and the melody of harps (see 5:22-23), there would be mourning, dirges, sackcloth, and baldness. In other words, there would be a complete reversal of normal conditions. References to mourning occur frequently in the book (see 1:2; 5:16*b*; 8:8). On the lament or dirge, see above on 5:1-2. Sackcloth was coarsely woven material worn to illustrate a state of abnormality (see Gen. 37:34; Isa. 20:2; Joel 1:8, 13; Jonah 3:6-9). It was apparently worn around the hips. Wailing and mourning women often lamented bare-breasted with their clothes tied with sackcloth around the waist (see Isa. 32:11; *ANEP* no. 459). Baldness or shaving the head is frequently associated with mourning (see Isa. 15:2; 22:12; Jer. 16:6) and probably reflects the practice of pulling out one's hair as a sign of lamenting. The "it" referred to in verse 10*b* is a feminine singular suffix and probably alludes back to the *hag*. The high feast day, the prophet said, would begin like a day of mourning over the loss of an only child and end like a day of bitterness. That is, it would be mourning from start to finish. The day of the festival as Yahweh's special day when the destiny for the coming year was determined (see on 5:18-20) is here depicted in the gloomiest of hues.

[8:11-12] In these verses, the coming calamity is depicted with imagery drawn from famine (see 4:6-8). The

famine, however, will not be due to lack of food or water but to
a lack of hearing the words of Yahweh or due to even the
absence of the word itself. Amos depicts the people as wander-
ing from sea to sea, from north to east, that is, everywhere,
searching for the word from Yahweh but in vain. The picture
one gets is one of agitated insecurity, that is, the people in
upheaval and anxiety (see 8:8). The presentation of the days to
come, in other words, must have resembled the political
turmoil, uncertainty, and anxiety already characteristic of
Israelite life. The people were seeking answers at various
places (see 5:4-5), but according to Amos they had sought and
would seek in vain.

[8:13-14] This small section, especially verse 14, has
been the subject of much discussion resulting in diverse interpretations (see Barstad for the history and diversity of interpretation). Scholars have widely assumed that the opening
statement in verse 14 refers to swearing in the name of a deity
other than Yahweh, and have thus hypothesized polytheistic
worship in Samaria. (This text is then generally associated with
5:26, also interpreted as reflecting polytheistic worship.) The
deities most widely suggested as mentioned in the verse are the
goddess Ashimah referred to in 2 Kings 17:30 (see RSV and
NEB; Barstad), the goddess Asherah (*Maag, 55-56; on
Asherah, see TDOT I 438-44), and a deity Asham-Bethel or
Ishumbethel supposedly mentioned in texts from a Jewish
colony at Elephantine in Egypt (see *Robinson, 103-4; ANET
491). Others assume the "guilt of Samaria" to be a (sarcastic)
reference to the calf image set up by Jeroboam I (see
*Wellhausen, 93-94; *Harper, 184) or some other image (see
BDB 80; TEV). Some scholars argue that the opening of verse
14 is a later editorial addition inserted to pass judgment on
Samaria and the worship of Ashimah associated with the city
after the Assyrians provincialized the region (see *Mays, 149).
Proper translation and interpretation of the passage will be
shown to render such construals unnecessary.

In verse 13, Amos refers to the maidens and lads who
will faint from thirst. Who were these maidens (betulot) and
lads (bahurim)? First of all, the two terms in singular (Deut.
32:25; 2 Chron. 36:17; Jer. 51:22; Ezek. 9:6) or plural (Ps.
148:12; Isa. 23:4; Zech. 9:17; Lam. 1:18; 2:21) form appear in
combination rather frequently. Used in combination, they thus
tend to represent a class of females and males. Second, in most

of these texts, they appear as a youthful class over against adults and elderly. Third, based on the meaning of the designation *betulah*, the terms, especially when used in combination, would appear to designate prepubescent youths. A *betulah* was a pre-menstruant female: "who is accounted a *betulah*? She that has never suffered a menstrual flow, even though she was married" (*Mishnah Niddah* 1:4). According to the Gemara on this passage, a female could even be a mother and still be a *betulah* (*Niddah* 8b).

According to verse 14, the young maidens and lads were those who were swearing. In practically all cultures, however, oaths sworn by minors have no binding authority. The *Mishnah*, for example, states that "no oath is imposed in a claim by a deaf-mute, an imbecile, or a minor, and no oath is imposed on a minor; but an oath is imposed when a claim is lodged against the [property of a] minor, or against dedicated property" (*Shebuoth* 6:4). Young maidens and lads would certainly have been minors without responsibility. If that be the case, then how could they be swearing?

The terms *betulot* and *bahurim* must have been used metaphorically by the prophet. As was noted in discussing 5:2, *betulah* could be used to denote a city or town. Amos in 8:13, therefore, would appear to be referring to rebel cities as the ones swearing.

The opening words in verse 14 are to be translated, "the ones swearing because of the guilt/iniquity of Samaria." This translation is based on three considerations. (1) The term *'ashmat* is simply the construct form of the noun *'ashmah* which means "wrong, guilt, iniquity." No name or circumlocution for a god or cultic object is involved. (2) The *b* is to be understood as expressing a causal sense and not as part of the normal expression "to swear by" (*shb' b*). (For *b* used in a causal sense, see Gen. 18:28; 29:20; 39:9; 1 Kings 18:18.) (3) The actual oaths given in verse 14 only begin after the expression "and they who say" which in the context could be translated "saying" (see NJPSV).

Because of the wrongdoing and oppressive policies of Jeroboam and the Israelite leaders in Samaria, towns previously loyal to the dynasty and capital were no longer giving their allegiance to the dynasty. They were now in rebellion against the house of Jeroboam and thus covenanting together in opposition to the reigning houses of Israel and Judah. Perhaps they are designated by the terms for young minors since they are functioning as new recruits and in a context of pressure, not quite responsible for their actions.

Amos mentions two places in verse 14, namely, Dan and Beer-sheba. Elsewhere he refers to Bethel, which was the cultic center under the control of Jeroboam (see 7:13), to Gilgal and Beer-sheba (4:4; 5:5), and to the sanctuaries of Isaac and Israel (7:7). As was noted in discussing 4:4; 5:5; and 7:7, Gilgal was probably the major shrine of the group supporting Pekah, and Beer-sheba the shrine for a group of southern/southwestern towns, primarily Judean, that were in defiance of Jerusalem and thus of Jeroboam's pro-Assyrian dominance over Israel and Judah. How does Dan fit into this situation? Dan, which lay at the foot of Mt. Hermon near one of the sources of the Jordan River, had been declared a royal shrine by Jeroboam I when Israel broke away from Judah at the death of Solomon (see 1 Kings 12:28-30). At the time of Amos, Dan was probably in the hands of Rezin of Damascus. When Syria invaded Israel, Dan was one of the first cities to be taken (see 1 Kings 15:16-20). Amos 1:3 indicates that by the mid-eighth century Damascus had regained control of much of Transjordan, although according to 6:13 the Israelites had carried out some counteroffenses in the area. Hosea 1:5, a text which probably predates the appearance of Amos, implies that Israel had already lost much of Galilee and was facing combat in the Valley of Jezreel. If Galilee and Transjordan were no longer under Jeroboam's control, then surely the city of Dan was not.

The Israelites and Israelite towns swearing fidelity by the god of Dan would have been those supporting Damascus and the regional coalition with its anti-Assyrian stance. This certainly would have included the Pekah faction. Whether the god of Dan was still Yahweh or was now a Syrian deity cannot be determined. Damascus may have seen no reason to replace a non-Syrian cult favorable to its cause with a deity and cult of their own.

The present vocalization of the Hebrew text of verse 14 refers to "the life of the way (*derek*) of Beer-sheba." One way to see this expression as part of an oath is to understand it as a reference to swearing by the road/pilgrimage route to Beer-sheba, similar to the Islamic oath "by the pilgrimage to Mecca." To attribute life to a road or pilgrimage route seems a bit odd, however. As a result, various repointings and emendations of the text have been proposed (see Barstad, 191-98; *Gordis, 258-59). Suggested readings include *dwd* as a title of Yahweh (*Maag, 56, 139-40), *hdrk* = "your honor" (*Hammershaimb, 129-30), *dôr* = "pantheon" (Neuberg; Ackroyd), and *darek* = "the one who dwells in your midst" (*Gordis, 259). Others associated the word *derek* with the Ugaritic term *drkt* and read "might, dominion, Mighty One" (see Barstad, 193-98). Another alternative is to read *derek* as *dorek* a participle meaning "the one treading, the treader," a term already employed of Yahweh in Amos 4:13. At any rate, there is no need to hypothesize a foreign deity, much less a pantheon. The cult at Beer-sheba was surely Yahwistic; thus the southern dissident group was swearing by Yahweh not by some foreign god or pantheon.

Amos's opinion of this opposition to Jeroboam II was negative. In spite of the prophet's condemnation of the situation in Samaria and his proclamation of the end of the house of Jeroboam, Amos apparently did not support the formation of rival groups and political factions within the land. The pro-Syrian faction led by Pekah was obviously one of the strongest, best organized, and most enduring of these parties. Supported by Syria, this group actually created a rival monarchical state with designs on the whole house of Israel. Pekah eventually gained control over Samaria (2 Kings 15:25) and sought to depose Ahaz, the uncooperative king of Jerusalem (Isa. 7:3-6). The faction that eventually exterminated the house of Jeroboam was led by an otherwise unknown Shallum (2 Kings 15:8-10). The Beer-sheba/Judean faction appears to have been less organized, fundamentally a circle of disgruntled pro-coalition cities (see below on 9:11).

Amos describes the dissidents in verse 13 as fainting or swooning from thirst. That is, they capitulated. In terms of the politics of the day, they gave in to the pressure to join an organized opposition faction. Amos, in 5:3, noted and perhaps endorsed passive non-cooperation with Samaria. The "swearing" noted in verse 14 indicates open and coordinated opposition, not just passive resistance. The prophet's pronouncement on the whole endeavor is expressed in verse 14b in terms closely paralleling an earlier verdict on Samaria in 5:2. The plans are condemned and the fate of the swearing ones declared to be disaster: "they shall fall and not stand upright again." Although these factions shared a desire for liberation from the oppressive policies of the house of Jeroboam, they received no approval, no imprimatur from the prophet Amos.

[9:1-4] The multifaceted descriptions of coming disaster in words attributed to the Deity are momentarily broken by the prophet's reference to a vision of the Deity upon or beside the altar. Whether the brief comment about seeing God could appropriately be called a vision report is uncertain. Not only does its brevity contrast sharply with the vision reports in 7:1-3, 4-6, 7-9, and 8:1-3, but other features also differ radically. (1) The prophet "sees" rather then "being shown." (2) No phenomenon such as the locusts, fire, tin, or summer fruit appears in the depiction. Thus no symbolic component is found to serve as an interpretative key or to constitute a point of contact between the world of the vision and the world of actuality. (3) No verbal exchange takes place between God and the prophet.

Even should the prophet's reference to seeing Yahweh and the altar be considered a vision report, it hardly constitutes the climactic vision in a series of five. The imagery is scarcely developed and merely serves to make clear that it is the sanctuary whose destruction is ordered. The altar would surely be understood as the main altar in the royal sanctuary at Bethel (see 3:14). This altar served as the focal point of royal rituals and sacrifices associated with the high point of the fall festival, on the fifteenth day of the eighth month in the north (see 1 Kings 12:33).

The indirect form of address continues in the words attributed to the Deity. The people are not addressed in the second person in the words attributed to the Deity in 7:1-9, 8:1-9:15, only in the first stich of 8:10 and in 9:7a are the people addressed directly.

The addressee of the singular imperative "smite" is unidentified. One could hardly think of the prophet's being commissioned to carry out the task (but see *Reventlow, 50) nor of some angelic figure which otherwise does not appear in the book. One way to remove the uncertainty is to emend the text to read "he (God) smote" (so *Wolff, 334). The ambiguity, however, was probably intended by the prophet, leaving the audience initially to its own speculation.

The emphasis in verses 1-4 is on the impossibility of escape from divine retribution. In speaking of those who could not escape, the prophet probably did not include the whole population. The reference to the altar and portions of the temple building would indicate that it is the worshipers at the royal festival that are concerned. "Capitals" and "thresholds" would parallel our expression "from top to bottom." The imagery in verse 1 has almost universally been taken to imply a destruction by earthquake. The verbal and nominal forms of *r'sh* "shake" are used to describe both the earthquake itself and its physical effects (see 1:1). The term, however, is also used to describe actions produced by human agency (see Ezek. 26:10; Ouellette, 1972). Mention of the sword could easily be understood as implying destruction by an invading army. Imagery and terminology apropos to an earthquake also occur in 8:8 but are used to describe social agitation. The imagery of smiting and shaking was probably employed more to produce an emotional reaction of fear and horror in the audience than to define explicitly the nature of the calamity.

Two pairs of opposites, signifying totality, are employed in verses 2-3 to indicate the thoroughness with which Yahweh will destroy the worshipers. Sheol and the heavens, and the height of the woodlands and the bottom of the sea represent polar opposite geographical areas. The text is not making theological statements such as asserting that Yahweh rules the entire universe. The meaning is much simpler. There will be no place where the victims can escape from the divine. Obviously, Amos never envisioned people actually fleeing to the underground world of the dead, nor taking flight to the heavens, nor cowering at the bottom of the sea. Rather, he implies that even in captivity (v. 4*a*) the people would not be beyond the reach of Yahweh.

The central thrusts of verses 1-4 are found in verses 1*b* and 4*b*. No one can escape the coming disaster because God has turned against them for evil and not for good. Earlier in 5:14-15, Amos had challenged his audience to seek good not evil, implying that their present course was leading to evil. Now he declares that God is personally determined to see that evil comes upon them.

[9:5-6] These verses, like 4:14 and 5:8-9, appear to be hymnic fragments utilized but not composed by Amos. The imagery and much of the terminology of verse 5 already appears in 8:8. In 9:5, the description of Yahweh as the one who touches the earth and it melts, or heaves, causing the inhabitants to mourn, seems clearly to reflect earthquake terminology. (In 8:8, Amos used the earthquake imagery to describe social movement and agitation.) Comparison to a Nile inundation stresses the elevation and settling back of the land. Verse 6 stresses Yahweh's rule over and control of creation. Verse 6*b* repeats 5:8*b*.

This hymnic material fits admirably in the context. The destructive power of Yahweh's touch and the imagery of a Nile inundation reiterate the themes of social agitation, cosmic disorder, and devastating calamity described in 8:8-9:4. The emphasis on the universal rule of Yahweh simultaneously undergirds the view that Yahweh's victims have no place in the universe where they can hide to escape punishment (9:1*b*-4*a*) and prepares for the section that follows in 9:7.

[9:7-10] In this section, Amos provides his last statement about the disasters to come upon Israel. The rhetorical questions in verse 7, assuming an affirmative response, seek to undercut any claim the people might make of special protection from Yahweh because they were Yahweh's people. The text serves to desacralize Israel and to deny the nation any claim on special privilege. Earlier, Amos had used Israel's special status as God's family as the basis for claiming that Yahweh could and would punish it for its wrongs (3:2). Now he not only claims that Israel is and shall be treated like any other people, but also elevates other people to the status of recipients of divine favor.

Two factors about verse 7 deserve special notice. (1) The text follows a hymnic description of Yahweh as the one who controls and rules over the earth. The claims in the hymnic material in verses 5-6 therefore prepare for the conclusion drawn in verse 7. (2) The rhetorical question in 7*a* is presented not only as divine address but also as direct, confrontational address in the second person. Throughout 7:1-9; 8:1-9:6, Israel is primarily the subject discussed rather than addressed in Yahweh's speech. Only in the opening line of 8:2 does any form of second-person address appear and here only in the form of two pronominal suffixes. But in 9:7*a*, the language is highly personal: "are you not . . . to me, O children of Israel?" This is direct interrogative language demanding a response and not merely stimulating thought. With 9:8*b*, the language shifts back to speak about rather than to Israel.

The opening question correlates the "children of Israel" with the "children of the Cushites." The traditional land of

Cush lay south of Upper and Lower Egypt proper, that is, upstream toward the sources of the Nile. This territory, also known as Nubia (=modern Sudan), was south of the second cataract of the Nile. From the time of classical antiquity, the region was referred to in Greek as Ethiopia. The Bible supplies evidence, however, that there was another land of Cush (see Hab. 3:7). This one lay south of Judah in the northern Sinai. Cushites are mentioned as opponents of Judah during the reigns of Asa (906-878; see 2 Chron. 14:9-15) and Jehoram (852-841; see 2 Chron. 21:16) and a Cushite served in the army of David (2 Sam. 18:21-23, 31-32).

To which of these two peoples Amos referred cannot be determined. Of the Sinai Cushites at the time of Amos, nothing is known. The African Cushites, with their capital at Napata, were expanding down the Nile valley into Egypt proper. Ruled by King Kashta (about 772-753), of the XXVth Dynasty, they had moved northward, probably reached Thebes and laid claim to the Delta (*CAH* 3/1, pp. 569-71). Kashta's successor, Piye (about 753-713), later successfully invaded the Delta (see *AEL* III 66-84). Just prior to the Assyrian campaign to suppress the western coalition in late 734 or early 733, Isaiah envisioned an Ethiopian invasion of Palestine (Isa. 7:18-19). To what extent the Egyptians and Ethiopians were cooperating with and encouraging the regional anti-Assyrian coalition in Syria-Palestine remains unknown. Even the Delta Egyptians, however, had a record of anti-Assyrian policies until after the western campaign of Sargon in 720. Certainly, the sons of the Cushites in Africa would have been known by Amos and his contemporaries.

If Amos here speaks of the Sinai Cushites, then he would have been comparing Israel to some insignificant local group perhaps at the time subservient to another kingdom. If the text refers to the Ethiopians, then Amos is comparing Israel to a remote, little known people. In any case, Amos is denying the Israelites any claim of privilege or special status (see 9:10*a*).

In verse 7*b*, Amos reiterates a theme, the bringing up out of Egypt, already found in 2:10*a*, but this time extends the thought to include Yahweh as the patron of both the Philistines and Aram, at the moment Israel's staunchest enemies (see Isa. 9:12*a*). A widespread motif in ancient cultures was "the migration from another place." Stories of national origins frequently depict the people as living in a land to which they had come (see Weinfeld). Here Amos traces the Philistines to Caphtor, probably Crete (see Strange) and Aram to Kir, an unidentified place (see on 1:5).

Verse 8 combines prophetic declaration and divine proclamation. In the declaration, the prophet affirms that Yahweh's eyes are on the sinful kingdom. It is uncertain whether Amos used "kingdom" *mamlakah* to denote the state as a whole (see 7:13) or only the dynasty of Jeroboam (see 7:9*b*). Probably the reference should be read in an inclusive sense, denoting the kingdom of Jeroboam, that is, the royal house and those subject and loyal to it. Although Amos does not declare so explicitly, the destroyer who would function as the instrument of Yahweh was probably none other than the regional coalition, headed by Aram and Philistia (see v. 7*b*). The assurance, made in the form of divine proclamation, is that the kingdom will be destroyed from the face of the earth.

In verse 8*b*, Amos has Yahweh declare that the destruction of the people will not be complete. A literal translation of this line gives: "Except that destroying I will not destroy the house of Jacob." Translators generally assume, however, that the text should be read: "Except that I will not utterly destroy the house of Jacob." Regardless of the choice of translation, the text declares that the coming destruction would not be total. Since this text holds out hope for the survival of some, scholars have frequently considered it a later addition. For example, *Wolff (p. 348) assigns the text to the disciples of Amos while *Soggin (pp. 144-45) considers the material to have been added by those who returned from exile after 539.

The question of whether 9:8*b* and in fact 9:8*b*-15 can be attributed to the prophet Amos does not turn on whether the same prophet could predict disaster and at the same time proclaim and hold out some hope. To pose the question and the issue of authenticity in these terms turns the matter into a theoretical discussion removed from the text. The more practical issue is whether or not the optimistic material is consistent with the remainder of the prophet's preaching and reflects the rhetorical and historical horizons of the total proclamation. In this regard, the following factors are noteworthy. (1) Throughout the book, the prophet's proclamation of disaster is fundamentally addressed against the ruling political hierarchy and economic aristocracy rather than the population as a whole. An analysis of the harshest pronouncements of judgment and disaster illustrates this fact. In 3:2 and 7:14, punishment and oppression do not imply complete annihilation. In 3:11, 12, 14-15; 4:1-3; 5;2, 4-5, 27; 6:7-11, 7:9; and 9:1-4, the aristocratic ruling class, the royal house, and the sanctuaries, but not the total population, are involved. (2) In 2:13-16; 4:12; 5:16-17; and 8:10-12, the description of post-disaster conditions implies the survival of some. (3) In the prophet's admonitions, hope for survival is held out even if such hope was merely hypothetical (see 5:6, 14-15). (4) The class of oppressed and abused in Israelite society (see 2:6b-7a; 4:1; 5:10-11a; and 8:4) are certainly not condemned by the prophet and would be among the mostly likely to survive if the country were overrun by military conquerors, whose tendency was to loot, slay, and exile the upper and skilled classes (see 6:7). (5) Distinctions seem to be drawn by the prophet in some texts between larger collectives such as "the house of Jacob," "Jacob" (3:13; 7:2, 5; 9:8), "children of Israel" (2:11; 3:1, 12; 4:5; 9:7) and more limited entities such as "Israel" (compare 3:12 and 3:13; see 5:9; 7:11, 16) and "house of Israel" (5:1, 25; 7:10-11). The latter appear to denote the reign and the kingdom presided over by the house of Jeroboam. "Joseph" and "the house of Joseph" (5:6, 15; 6:6) also appear to designate a limited entity, namely Ephraim and Manasseh, but an entity torn between those loyal to Jeroboam II and those supporting Pekah (see Isa. 9:18-21). "Isaac," "house of Isaac," and "Beer-sheba" (5:5; 7:9, 16; 8:14) in turn denote a southern entity. (In all likelihood, the Yahwistic strand of the Pentateuch was produced sometime after Amos to argue and propagandize for the unity of these diverse elements, including the Judean Abraham not mentioned by Amos.)

The distinction which Amos makes in 9:8 is a distinction between the narrower kingdom of Israel/Jeroboam and the more inclusive house of Jacob. The former would be terminated (see 7:9b) but the larger entity Jacob would not be totally destroyed. The fact that the prophet proclaimed that some of the house of Jacob would survive should not be understood in some pietistic fashion, that is, that the prophet believed that some would repent and be saved. The matter is much more realistic. Amos seems to have envisioned a military invasion which would defeat the Israelite forces (2:13-16), bring an end to the ruling house in Samaria and destroy the capital city (3:11-15; 6:8-10; 7:9b), result in destruction and oppression throughout the land (6:14), and lead to exile for many of the people (5:27; 6:7), but which would still not result in the complete extermination of the people.

In verses 9-10, Amos elaborates on the nature of the destruction that will overtake the house of Israel. Verse 9 describes the destruction of the house of Israel when attacked and not, as is universally assumed, a scattering of Israel as exiles among the nations after a sieving process. The verse opens with Yahweh declaring that he is now giving the command (see 6:11), that is, giving the surrounding enemy the order to invade. Yahweh's action in the form of the invading forces of all the surrounding nations shall shake Israel like something shaken in the process of being sifted. (See Isa. 7:2 where the shaking denotes trembling from fear.) The house of Israel will be so thoroughly shaken up (*kebarah* here could refer to either the act of sifting or to the sieve itself) that no two adjoining, bonded stones would land on the ground intact. The term *şeror* (from *şrr* meaning "to tie, bind"), rendered above as "bonded joint," is generally translated "pebble" but this makes no sense in the context. The term occurs in 2 Sam. 17:13 where reference is made to dragging a town into the valley with ropes, and no *seror* would remain. Again to read "pebble" does not make sense. What is meant is equivalent to the expression "no stone upon another." In 6:11, Amos expresses an idea identical to that in 9:9, namely, Yahweh is giving order to attack with the result that the great house and the little house shall be smashed into smithereens.

In verse 10, Amos has Yahweh declare that only the sinners among the people would die by the sword, namely, those declaring that evil would never overtake them. Clearly, this text does not presuppose the complete annihilation of the population but only of a certain component of the population. Who the "sinners" were, Amos does not make clear. The only other occurrences of the term *ht'* are in 5:12 and 9:8. In 5:12, a multitude of sins are attributed to those suppressing debate, taking advantage of the poor and innocent through exaction and other means, and owning fine vineyards and homes (5:10-12), that is, the upperclass and ruling authorities. In 9:8, it is the kingdom itself, the dynasty and its loyal subjects, that is declared sinful. Verse 10, therefore, sees the coming military disaster as purging the people of those elements in society condemned by Amos throughout the book.

[9:11-12] Had the rhetorical unit beginning in 7:1 ended with gloomy words of disaster, like all the other units in the book, then this final unit would have concluded with 9:7-10. In 9:11-15, however, we find material and an outlook radically distinct from what has preceded and topics not previously discussed. The distinction between these texts and the rest of the book was characterized in classical formulation as "roses and lavender instead of blood and iron" (*Wellhausen, 96). As a consequence, the majority of scholars argue that verses 11-15 are a secondary and late addition (for the various opinions, see Nel; Wagner; Weimar; *Soggin, 148-49). Those who see the material as secondary generally date it to a time following the fall of Jerusalem in 586.

The material should be considered authentic to the prophet Amos, however, forming the conclusion to the unit begun in 7:1. As we shall see, the grounds for denying the text to him are not as compelling as those in favor of the text's authenticity. At the same time, certain arguments and interpretations which have been advanced in support of the text's authenticity are themselves not compelling. Assigning the material to a hypothetical Judean phase of the prophet's career (*Gordis, 249-53; *Watts, 48-50), viewing the material as an example of the normal prophetic message anchored in a covenant renewal service (*Reventlow, 90-110), seeing the material as reflecting an ancient Davidic empire ideology (Carlson; Mauchline), understanding the verses as a criticism of the reign of Jeroboam II (Seybold, 17-19, 60-67) or as a call to rebellion against the house of Jeroboam (S. Yeivin, *WHJP* IV/1, pp. 164-65), and interpreting the optimistic passages as indications of a psychological and/or theological tension within the prophet (*Maag, 246-51; *Hammershaimb, 135-39) are not satisfactory as approaches to understanding the text.

In verses 11-12, Amos speaks about the future of Davidic rule. The terminology used here to speak of the reign of the Davidic king in Jerusalem is unique. "Booth/canopy" of David occurs nowhere else in the scriptures (on *sukkah*, see 5:26). Elsewhere Jerusalem is compared to a *sukkah* by Isaiah (1:8) who also spoke of God establishing a *sukkah* in Jerusalem as a shade from the heat and a refuge and shelter from the storm and rain (Isa. 4:6; see also Pss. 27:5; 76:2). The nearest parallel to Amos's expression is Isaiah's reference to the tent of David (16:5). Amos 5:26 refers to the *sukkah* of the king which we suggested probably referred to the canopy under which the king marched in the new year/fall festival. In verse 11, Amos seems to be using the term metaphorically to denote the rule or kingdom of the Davidic house reigning in Jerusalem.

Amos describes the "booth/canopy" of David as "tottering/falling" (see JB). The term *nopelet* is a participle describing a present state. Thus Davidic rule is spoken of as a present reality not as a past phenomenon. For a booth/canopy to be tottering would indicate that it was in trouble but not that it had fallen. An examination of the historical circumstances of Davidic rule at the time of Amos can illustrate why the prophet described its rule as tottering. (1) For decades, the house of David and Jerusalem had played subordinate roles to the house of Jehu and Samaria, functioning in a vassal-like status to the more powerful north (see Chapter 1, section 4). (2) The patriarch of the Judean house, Uzziah/Azariah, lived in Jerusalem scarred by the marks of leprosy, a disease considered a direct curse from God, and because of which he had been forced to abdicate the throne (2 Kings 15:5). (3) The reigning king, Jotham (759-744), was confronted with a rapidly deteriorating kingdom plagued by dissent against the continuing pro-Assyrian stance of Israel/Judah. In the better days of Jeroboam II and Uzziah, the Judean king had regained control of the seaport at Elath (2 Kings 14:22), made war against the Philistines and other southern peoples, built military towers in the wilderness regions, and controlled the Shephelah and the coastal plain north of Philistia (2 Chron. 26:6-10). In Jotham's reign, matters had taken a drastic turn for the worse. After his third year, he lost control over the Meunites (so read for Ammonites in 2 Chron. 27:5; see 26:7). He was forced to prepare for defense of the Judean hill country (2 Chron. 27:4), presumably having lost power over the Shephelah and the plain. Numerous Judean cities were in open rebellion against Jerusalem's authority so that the troubles reached the gate of Jerusalem (see Micah 1; see also the references to Beer-sheba and Isaac in Amos 5:3; 7:9, 16; 8:14). By the time of the Syro-Ephraimitic siege of Jerusalem in late 734, King Ahaz was reigning over a kingdom that included only Jerusalem and perhaps a few military outposts and loyal towns (see Isa. 8:6). From Uzziah to Ahaz, the Davidic house ruled over an ever diminishing realm. Rezin of Damascus and Pekah were harassing Judah probably from the north and west (2 Kings 15:37).

The house of David was in deep trouble; the booth was unsteady.

Amos has Yahweh promise to set upright the booth of David. The first action involved in this was the walling up of breaches. Although the term "breach" *pere$* often refers to gaps or holes in a wall, it could also be used in the sense of breaking away, bursting forth (Gen. 38:29; Judg. 21:15; Hos. 4:2; Micah 2:13). The plural suffix "their" would indicate that what Amos is talking about is the action against the family of David, namely, the insurrection by Judean cities. (Almost universally, translators ignore the fact that three different pronominal suffixes, "their," "his," and "its," occur in verse 11 and simply level them all to "it." The suffixes are basic to a correct understanding of the passage.) Halting and repairing the breakaways from the house of David refer to the ending of insurrection and disaffection from Davidic control by Judean cities, the house of Isaac/Beer-sheba group.

The second part of the promise concerns the restoration of Davidic authority where it had been repudiated. The semantic range of the verb *hrs* includes not only the idea of demolishing or destroying something (see 2 Sam. 11:25; 1 Kings 18:30; Jer. 1:10), but also the idea of deposing or removing from authority or repudiating someone (see Isa. 22:19). The noun *harisah*, occurring only here in Scripture and, in plural form, refers to repudiations or those who repudiate authority; the third masculine singular pronominal suffix refers to the Davidic king. Those who have renounced the authority of the Davidic dynasty, Yahweh will return to Davidic authority.

Thirdly, the *sukkah* shall not only be stabilized and the process of rebellious attrition halted, but also it shall be restored to its former glory as in the days of old. Amos does not clarify what is meant by "as in the days of old." The expression could be translated "as formerly." To assume that he is referring to the days of King David himself is not necessarily warranted. He may be referring to nothing more than the status of Davidic rule prior to the time when severe troubles began, that is, to the earlier days of Uzziah. The restoration would allow the house of David to possess what remained of Edom and the other nations over whom Yahweh's name had been called. Edom was, of course, Judah's nearest enemy (see above, on 1:11-12) and the foreign country over which Davidic kings had most frequently ruled (see 1 Sam.

14:47; 2 Sam. 8:13-14; 1 Kings 22:47; 2 Kings 8:22; 14:7). The other nations are not named (see Isa. 11:14), so it is impossible to know what nations Amos had in mind. The expression "to call the name over" was equivalent to laying claim to (see Galling). Had Amos here been advocating the reconstitution of the ideal empire of David, one would have expected him to say not "all the nations over which Yahweh's name has been called" but rather "over which my servant David ruled."

Since the ascription of this text to Amos is so widely challenged, two comments on this issue are required. (1) The historical context presupposed by the text and its allusions synchronize perfectly with what has been seen elsewhere in Amos and with what can be reconstructed from other Old Testament texts. The text presupposes the troubled existence but not the demise of the house of David. (2) If the text is a late addition, its terminology is not consistent with that known from any other source. Although scholars have sought to associate it with the deuteronomistic presentation of Israel's history (see Kellermann), even *Wolff, who is otherwise prone to see numerous deuteronomistic additions to the book of Amos, argues for "the hand of a redactor not in evidence elsewhere in the book" (p. 353). The uniqueness of the terminology in verse 11 argues for the text's authenticity. References to the booth of David occur nowhere else in Scripture. One would assume that a redactor adding a complete passage rather than merely glossing an existing text would have employed traditional terminology.

If the text is authentic, the issue of why Amos took a positive attitude toward the Davidic dynasty must be addressed. At a minimum, Amos may have considered the Davidic house to represent the only viable political entity among his people. Numerous options existed from which Amos could have chosen. (1) The prophet's harshest condemnations fell on the house of Jeroboam and the government in Samaria. Certainly the prophet could take no favorable attitude toward this dynasty. (2) The rival claimant to the throne in Samaria, Pekah, received no favorable response from Amos. To all appearances, Pekah was a puppet to the king of Damascus and thus a proponent of the regional coalition. (3) The breakaway cities in the south, the house of Isaac, were likewise condemned by Amos. This group seems never to have moved to the point of setting up a rival king to the Davidic ruler in Jerusalem but may have cooperated with pro-coalition powers like Philistia and Edom (see 2 Kings 8:20-23 where the rebellion of the Judean town of Libnah is associated with the revolt of Edom). Lachish was an important center of the renegade movement (Micah 1:13). (4) The faction that supported Shallum's extermination of the house of Jeroboam (2 Kings 15:10) may already have been forming at the time of Amos. Nothing specific of this group is known although it must have been quite formidable and popular to have toppled the family of Jeroboam. Shallum's movement seems to have acted independently of Pekah's although the two probably shared a common position, namely, rejection of a pro-Assyrian policy.

Neither Amos nor any other prophet ever proclaimed the absolute extermination of their people. For Amos, political realism may have led him to base his hope on the house of David. How he evaluated the reign of Jotham is never stated. The statements against Judah in 2:4-5 are so general as to offer no help in this regard. The accusations, however, could be understood as political in nature and perhaps made against the Judeans rather than the house of David. At any rate, no reference is made in the Judean section to the ruler (compare 1:5, 8, 15; 2:3).

Another approach to understanding the prophet's favorable attitude toward the house of David is to see it as reflecting a Judean, pro-Davidic bias (von Rad, 138). Amos after all was probably a Judean and his attitude toward rebel Judean cities was negative. His opening comments in 1:2 stress the association of Yahweh with Jerusalem and Zion. Nonetheless, Amos's words about the Davidic dynasty in 9:11 are rather subdued and restrained when compared to other claims made on behalf of the Davidic house (see Pss. 2:7-9; 72; Isa. 9:6-7; 11:1-9). No reference is made to any special promises to David.

[9:13-15] These verses describe ideal future conditions to prevail beyond the coming disasters when Yahweh reverses the fate of his people (see Bracke). The land shall become so fruitful that the tasks of harvesting cannot be completed before the planting and sowing fall due. The people shall live in tranquility, enjoying the fruits of their labors, without the fear of being uprooted again and exiled from their land.

This text shares many characteristics with other prophetic descriptions of the new age to come (see Isa. 11:6-9;

Hos. 14:4-7). In no way does it deny the coming disaster. The passage shows no special pro-Jerusalem or pro-Davidic claims. The text makes no reference to a return from exile, to divine forgiveness, or to the role of a Messianic figure, as one might expect, had the text originated in late exilic or post-exilic times (see *Maag, 60-61; Seybold, 17-19).

9. THE AMOS NARRATIVE (7:10-17)

P. R. **Ackroyd**, "Amos vii.14," *ET* 68(1956-57)94; **Ackroyd**, "A Judgment Narrative Between Kings and Chronicles? An Approach to Amos 7:9-17," *Canon and Authority: Essays in Old Testament Religion and Theology* (ed. G. W. Coats and B. O. Long; Philadelphia: Fortress Press, 1977)71-87; R. **Bach**, "Erwägungen zu Amos 7, 14," *Die Botschaft und die Boten. Festschrift für Hans Walter Wolff zum 70. Geburtstag* (ed. J. Jeremias and L. Perlitt; Neukirchen-Vluyn: Neukirchener Verlag, 1981)203-16; A. J. **Bjørndalen**, "Erwägungen zur Zukunft des Amazja und Israels nach der Überlieferung Amos 7, 10-17," *Werden und Wirken des Alten Testaments. Festschrift für Claus Westermann zum 70. Geburtstag* (ed. R. Albertz; Göttingen: Vandenhoeck & Ruprecht, 1980)236-51; S. **Cohen**, "Amos *Was* a Navi," *HUCA* 32(1961)175-78; G. R. **Driver**, "Amos vii.14," *ET* 67(1955-56)91-92; **Driver**, "Affirmation by Exclamatory Negation," *JANESCU* 5(1973)108-14; J. **Galil**, "An Ancient Technique for Ripening Sycomore Fruit in East-Mediterranean Countries," *Economic Botany* 22(1968)178-90; A. H. J. **Gunneweg**, "Erwägungen zu Amos 7, 14," *ZTK* 57(1960)1-16; P. **Haupt**, "Was Amos a Sheepman?," *JBL* 35(1916)280-87; Y. **Hoffmann**, "Did Amos Regard Himself as a *nabi*'?," *VT* 27(1977)209-12; O. **Loretz**, "Die Berufung des Propheten Amos (7, 14-15)," *UF* 6(1974)487-88; G. **Pfeifer**, "Die Ausweisung eines lästigen Ausländers, Amos 7, 10-17," *ZAW* 96(1984)112-18; H. N. **Richardson**, "A Critical Note on Amos 7:14," *JBL* 85(1966)89; J. J. M. **Roberts**, "A Note on Amos 7:14 and Its Context," *ResQ* 8(1965)175-78; S. N. **Rosenbaum**, "Northern Amos Revisited: Two Philological Suggestions," *HS* 18(1977)132-48; H. H. **Rowley**, "Was Amos a Nabi?," *Festschrift Otto Eissfeldt zum 60. Geburtstag* (ed. J. Fück; Halle an der Saale: Max Niemeyer, 1947)191-98; H. **Schmid**, "'Nicht Prophet bin ich, noch Prophetensohn? Zur Erklärung von Amos 7:14a," *Judaica* 23(1967)68-74; H. **Schult**, "Amos 7, 15a und die Legitimation des Aussenseiters," *Probleme biblischer Theologie. Gerhard von Rad zum 70. Geburtstag* (ed. H. W. Wolff; Munich: Chr. Kaiser, 1971)462-78; R. **Smend**, "Das Nein des Amos," *EvTh* 23(1963)404-23 = his *Die Mitte des Alten Testaments* (BEvTh 99; Munich: Chr. Kaiser, 1986)85-103; S. **Spiegel**, "Amos vs. Amaziah," *The Jewish Expression* (ed. J. Goldin; New

Haven: Yale University Press, 1976)38-85; G. M. **Tucker**, "Prophetic Authority: A Form-Critical Study of Amos 7:10-17," *Int* 27(1973)423-34; E. **Vogt**, "Waw explicative in Amos vii. 14," *ET* 68(1956-57)301-2; T. J. **Wright**, "Amos and the 'Sycomore Fig,'" *VT* 26(1976)362-68; Z. **Zevit**, "A Misunderstanding at Bethel - Amos VII 12-17," *VT* 25(1975)783-90; **Zevit**, "Expressing Denial in Biblical Hebrew and Mishnaic Hebrew, and in Amos," *VT* 29(1979)505-9.

7:10 *Amaziah, priest of Bethel, sent to Jeroboam king of Israel saying, "Amos has advocated conspiracy against you in the midst of the house of Israel; the country is not able to tolerate all of his words.* **11** *This is what Amos has said, 'Jeroboam shall die by the sword, and Israel shall surely go into exile away from its land.'"*

    12 *And Amaziah said to Amos, "O seer, go, flee to the land of Judah, and there eat bread and there prophesy!* **13** *But do not prophesy again in Bethel because it is the king's sanctuary and a royal temple."*

    14 *And Amos responded and he said to Amaziah, "I am no prophet and I am no son of a prophet, but I am a herdsman and tender of sycomores.* **15** *And Yahweh took me from behind the sheep and Yahweh said to me, 'Go, prophesy to my people Israel!'* **16** *And now hear the word of Yahweh, you who say do not prophesy against Israel, and do not preach against the house of Isaac,* **17** *therefore thus Yahweh has said,*

    'Your wife shall be a prostitute in the city,
      and your sons and daughters shall fall by the sword;
    and your land shall be portioned out with a measuring-
        line,
    and you will die in an unclean land;
    and Israel shall surely go into exile away from its land.'"

    The account of Amos's encounter with the priest Amaziah is the only narrative preserved about the prophet. When in his ministry this episode occurred cannot be determined. Some scholars (*Gordis, 249-53) have argued that after Amos's disclosure of his third vision, he was accosted by Amaziah, forced to leave Bethel, and then returned to Judah where he concluded his preaching with the proclamation of 8:1-

9:15 (and the repetition of 7:1-9; so *Watts, 32-35). More likely, the narrative has been placed in its present context because of thematic and structural rather than chronological considerations. A number of factors suggest that the narrative was editorially inserted into the speech material at this point. (1) Reference to the death of Jeroboam by the sword in the narrative (v. 11a) parallels the statement in the immediately preceding speech material that Yahweh will rise up against the house of Jeroboam with the sword (7:9b). (2) It is more logical to assume that all four (five) visions were proclaimed consecutively in the same speech than that Amos later, in Judah, delivered a speech that coincidentally began with a vision report paralleling in both form and content an earlier vision report preached at Bethel. (3) Had the narrative been attached at the end of the book, it would have formed an anti-climax to the material in 9:11-15. (4) The overall content of the narrative, with Amaziah's comment that Amos should go to Judah and prophesy, makes better sense if the episode followed Amos's favorable comments about Judah in 9:11-12.

[10-11] These opening verses of the narrative serve to set the stage for the subsequent dialogue between Amaziah and Amos. They seem poorly integrated into the narrative as a whole. The reader is left to wonder about the disposition of the communication to the king, about the king's response, and about its effect on the prophet's fate. Were there once other narratives that gave fuller contexts to what appears in 7:10-17 in such truncated form? (see Ackroyd, 1977). The editors who incorporated this narrative seem primarily interested in only the proclamation of Amos, in the certainty that that message had its source in Yahweh, and that subsequent events testified to its authenticity, rather than in the fate of the prophet himself.

One would assume that Amaziah was the chief priest or the priest in charge of security forces at the royal sanctuary and in this capacity conveyed to the king a report about Amos (see Jer. 20:1-2; 29:26). Of the three characters in the story, only Amos is not initially identified by reference to any office. Even in tradition, he is not designated by any title (see on 7:14). Nothing is said about the logistics involved in Amaziah's communication with King Jeroboam II. There is no reason to assume that Amos and Amaziah were in Bethel while the Israelite king was in Samaria, some thirty miles away. If Amos performed his preaching ministry at Bethel just prior to the climactic day of the fall festival, then the king would no doubt have been in Bethel since the monarch played a central role in the festival ritual (see 1 Kings 8:1-6; 12:32-33).

The priest's report charges Amos with sedition. The term *qshr*, in a political context, denotes plotting and acting to overthrow the ruling authorities (1 Kings 15:27; 16:9, 16, 20; 2 Kings 11:14; 12:20; 14:19; 15:10; 17:4). Jehu, the ancestor of Jeroboam II, had secured the throne in Samaria through conspiracy (2 Kings 9:14; 10:9). Successful conspiracies were generally followed by the complete eradication of all males of the ruling line (see 1 Kings 15:27-29; 16:8-11; 2 Kings 10:11).

Amos is the only prophet known to have been accused of conspiracy. Uriah, a prophetic contemporary of Jeremiah was extradited from Egypt and put to death, but the exact charges against him are not known (Jer. 26:20-23). Jeremiah himself was charged with unpatriotic behavior (Jer. 26:7-19, 24), but conspiracy is not explicitly stated as the charge. That a person like Amos could be accused of conspiracy indicates that he addressed a very volatile situation. Had the nation been devoid of civil strife and militarily secure, it is unlikely that Amos's preaching would have rippled the waters in Bethel.

That Amos was charged with conspiracy against the Israelite king has been considered evidence of his northern origin (see Rosenbaum). The argument is based on the assumption that only a citizen of a state could be guilty of conspiracy. This line of reasoning and the evidence are not sufficient to prove Amos was a northerner. Since Judah was subordinate to Israel and thus subject to the house of Jeroboam, a Judean could be charged with conspiracy against the Israelite king. Ahaz and his supporters in Jerusalem were later accused of conspiracy by their fellow Judeans ("this people") for failure to follow King Pekah's policy of anti-Assyrianism after the latter seized the throne in Samaria in 734 (see Isa. 8:12). Amos himself may have been in the employ of either the court or temple in the north (see on 1:1).

That Amos could be charged with or even accused of conspiracy indicates that his message was understood as contributing to and encouraging internal, inner-Israelite opposition to the house of Jeroboam. For him to have proclaimed that Israel was weak and would be defeated by a foreign power might have been discouraging and unpatriotic but hardly conspiratorial. Jeremiah, condemned for proclaiming Jerusalem's fall to the Babylonians, may have been considered a traitor, but that did not lead to a charge of conspiracy (Jer. 38:1-6). Amos's declaration that Yahweh would rise against the house of Jeroboam with the sword must have been interpreted as a call to overthrow and assassinate the reigning family.

The expression "in the midst of the house of Israel" probably means no more than "publicly and in a prominent place." A conspiracy implies the participation of more than one party. Thus, Amos was considered to be giving public expression to what was already a strong sentiment. The statement that the country was not able to tolerate all his words indicates widespread anti-Jeroboam feelings and the opinion that if Amos could get away with this, then the king's cause was lost.

Amaziah's summary of the prophet's preaching, and the basis for the charge of conspiracy are given in verse 11: (1) "Jeroboam shall die by the sword" and (2) "Israel shall surely go into exile away from its land." Neither of these statements reproduces exactly a saying attributed to the prophet. Amos does speak about exile (5:5, 27; 6:7) and about action with the sword (7:9; 9:4, 10) but never in exactly this terminology. If we only had the prophetic narrative about Amos, with its two "quotations" of his preaching in 7:11, 16-17, we would never understand the richness and artistry of his preaching. (This serves as a warning against using the prophetic narratives as the standards by which to determine the form and content of prophetic preaching!)

[12-17] The dialogue between Amaziah and Amos is introduced without any overt connections being made between it and verses 10-12. The reader is left to wonder whether the dialogue takes place while Amaziah's message is still in transit or while the king is pondering a course of action. Is the priest to be understood as acting on his own? If so, is he to be understood as attempting to offer advice to benefit and even save the life of the prophet? Or is one to assume that Amaziah is acting to carry out a royal decision to banish Amos from the region and is therefore issuing commands and directives to the prophet? None of these questions, of course, can be answered. At any rate, Amaziah seems to play a paradigmatic role in the narrative as representative of the doomed northern kingdom.

The designation of Amos as a "seer" *hozeh* is not necessarily to be understood as derogatory. "Seer" and "prophet" are used as practically synonymous terms (2 Sam. 24:11; 2 Kings 17:13; Isa. 29:10). The verb *ḥazah* is used in Amos 1:1. Amaziah's designation of Amos as "seer, visionary" may have been influenced by the prophet's proclamation of visions, although in these the Hebrew term used is *r'h*, a synonym of *ḥzh*.

Amaziah's directives to Amos may be interpreted either as expressions of good will on his behalf toward the prophet or as official orders. If the former, then Amaziah is to be viewed as respecting Amos's role and work and as attempting to get him away from Bethel before the king could act. If the latter, then Amaziah is to be seen as representing official policy toward radically judgmental prophets and troublemakers (see 2:12*b*). Amos's response to the priest might imply that he understood the latter to be the case.

Amaziah's advice or order to Amos is that he flee from Bethel and go to the land of Judah. The term "flee" is generally used in Old Testament texts with reference to taking flight from a locale of residence to a place where one is a non-resident (see Gen. 22:27; 27:43; 31:20; Exod. 2:15; 4:15 and so on; Rosenbaum, 134-35; but compare Num. 24:11). This could imply that Amos was either a native of the north or that his occupation had brought him into northern territory as a resident. On the other hand, flight terminology may have been employed because of the special circumstances involved. Amos was encouraged or ordered to leave immediately. The literal content of the expression "flee for yourself (your own good)" would indicate that he is advised to make haste for his own sake.

The meaning of the expression "there eat bread" (literraly "eat there bread") would appear to be equivalent either to "there earn your living" or "there follow your profession" or even more generally "live there." The Hebrew does not suggest that Amaziah intimated that Amos should go to Judah and "prophesy there to earn your bread" (*Soggin, 126; see also *Wolff, 311). In the comment attributed to Amaziah, prophesying is described as an adjunct to Amos's normal career. By using the verb "to prophesy," the story indicates that although "to see" and "to prophesy" might indicate different activities, they could presumably be performed by the same individual.

In verse 13*a*, Amos is ordered never again to prophesy at Bethel. The reason is offered in 13*b*; the place was a royal sanctuary and a national temple. A royal and national place of worship would have been directly under the control of the monarchy and the location of national rituals and festivals. Anti-dynastic and defamatory critique, as evident in Amos's preaching, was apparently prohibited (see 2:12b). If one considered Amaziah favorably disposed toward Amos, then the order would be a warning for Amos's own safety.

The response of Amos to Amaziah in verses 14-17 consists of three elements: (1) a statement regarding his profession, (2) an explanation of why he has engaged in prophetic activity, and (3) a proclamation of judgment against the priest.

(1) The statement regarding his profession contains two parts. In the first part, he responds with a verbless sentence which has been one of the most discussed texts in Scripture. A literal translation of the text as it is presently pointed gives, "No prophet I and no son of a prophet I." Four main interpretations of this text have been proposed and debated.

(a) One understanding takes the statement as descriptive of a past condition (see Rowley). This provides the following translation: "No prophet was I and no son of a prophet was I." This interpretation assumes that Amos stated he was not a prophet by profession but became one when especially called by God and divinely commissioned to prophesy (see v. 15).

(b) Another reading of this text interprets it as stating a present reality (see *Wolff, 311-14). This adopts the following translation: "No prophet am I and no son of a prophet am I." According to this interpretation, Amos never claimed to be a prophet by vocation.

(c) A third approach to the issue understands the negatives as interrogatives and sees Amos affirming a prophetic vocation for himself by what is termed "affirmation by exclamatory negation" (see Driver; Ackroyd, 1956-57). This provides the following translation: "Am I not a prophet and am I not a prophet's son?"

(d) Another way of reading the text is to postulate that the term lo' is not to be read as the negative particle ("no" or "not"), but actually represents an emphatic particle (l, lu, or la) known from the Ugaritic texts (see Richardson). This provides the following translation: "Surely a prophet am I and a son of a prophet am I" (see Cohen; Zevit).

Attempts to combine two of these interpretations have also been made (see Ackroyd, 1977, 83) resulting in a transla-

tion like, "Surely I am a prophet but no son of a prophet am I."
These make nonsense of the grammatical form of the text.

A translation and interpretation of the text should be
based on the following considerations. (i) Verse 14 contains
two verbless sentences. The same tense should be assumed for
both sentences. (ii) Attempts to solve the issue of interpretation by appeal to non-biblical evidence, such as the use of
Ugaritic material, should be avoided if a satisfactory reading
can be attained otherwise. (iii) The terms "prophet" and "son of
a prophet" are to be understood as parallel terms. The expression "sons of the prophets" which appears primarily in the Elijah
and Elisha stories (1 Kings 20:35; 2 Kings 2:3, 5, 15; 4:1, 38; 6:1;
9:1) does not indicate that "a son of a prophet" was a prophet's
disciple or a member of some guild. "Son of a prophet" is
simply a way of saying "one who belongs to the class of the
prophets," that is, a prophet (see the construction in Pss. 8:4;
144:3). (iv) The passage does not indicate any disdain for the
office and vocation of prophet whether one understands Amos
as affirming or denying the office for himself. (v) The interpretation of verse 14a should take into consideration what is
said about prophets and prophesying elsewhere in the book.
The following are pertinent in this regard. (a) The comments
of both Amaziah and Amos indicate that the activity performed
by Amos constituted prophesying. Amaziah told Amos to go to
Judah and prophesy there (v. 12b) but never to prophesy again
at Bethel (v. 13a). According to Amos, Yahweh commanded
him to go prophesy (v. 15a). (b) In 2:11-12 and 3:7, Amos
shows respect for the office of prophet and nowhere casts
aspersion on the office. (c) In 3:8, Amos indicates that under
certain conditions anyone could and should perform the activity
of prophesying.

In light of the above considerations, verse 14a should be
translated: "And Amos responded and he said to Amaziah, 'I
am no prophet and I am no son of a prophet.'" This represents
a straightforward and literal reading of the text. Amos denies
that he is a prophet but does not deny that he engages in
prophesying (see below on v. 15).

In verse 14b, Amos comments further on his occupation.
Here the verbless sentence is formulated postively. Thus verse
14a indicates what Amos was not vocationally and verse 14b
indicates what he was. Again several theories have been proposed about the meaning and interpretation of the tasks men-

tioned in verse 14*b*. One issue stems from the fact that in 7:14*b* Amos describes his work in terms that differ both from those found in the superscription (1:1) and in 7:15. In 1:1, Amos is said to have been among the *noqedim* ("shepherds"?) from Tekoa. In 7:15, he refers to being taken from behind the sheep. In 7:14*b*, neither sheep nor shepherding is mentioned. Instead reference is made to two other occupations.

First of all, Amos describes himself as a *boqer*. The term *bqr* is used with reference to cattle, not sheep, and apparently means something like "herdsman, cattleman." In this form, the term occurs only here. Second, Amos declares himself to be a *boles* of sycomores. The fig-bearing sycomore (*Ficus sycomorus*) can grow to a height of forty feet or more. It served as a source of both food and lumber (1 Kings 10:27; 1 Chron. 27:28; Isa. 9:10). Unfortunately, the term *bls* appears only here in Scripture. In Arabic and Ethiopic, it occurs as the name of a kind of fig while in Aramaic the term means "to mix." The term has been considered synonymous with the Akkadian and Syriac *plsh* which means "to bore/break through" (see Haupt). A number of possibilities exist for understanding what *boles* sycomores means.

(1) The Targum reads "and I have sycomore trees in the Shephelah." Here ownership of trees is made the point. This reading, however, gives the impression of an interpretation of the text rather than a translation.

(2) Amos may have been involved with the gathering of sycomore figs and/or their leaves for human and animal consumption. Already in the Middle Ages, Salomon ibn Parchon argued that Amos mixed sycomore leaves with barley for cattle feed (see Wright).

(3) Most interpreters assume that *boles* refers to some specialized task associated with sycomores. At least three activities could fall into this category.

(a) Unlike their Central African and Yemenite relatives, East Mediterranean sycomores are not seed-bearing. Thus propagation depends on producing new trees through cuttings. Presumably such cutting and sprouting required special skills.

(b) It was possible to remove the large spreading limbs of the sycomore for use as timber without killing the tree itself. The *Mishnah* distinguishes between virgin, uncut, and cropped sycomores which have had limbs removed for timber (*Shebiith* 4:5; *Baba Metzia* 9:9; *Baba Bathra* 4:9; see *Niddah* 8*b*).

(c) In Egypt and Cyprus and perhaps ancient Israel, sycomore figs were incised or slashed to hasten the ripening process (see Galil). Cutting the fig with a sharp instrument traumatizes the fruit, stimulating the production of ethylene gas, thereby accelerating the ripening process. This practice, but not the rationale, was already noted and described by such ancient writers as Theophrastus (372-287 BCE; *Enquiry into Plants*, IV ii 1) and Pliny (CE 23-79; *Natural History* XIII xiv 57) and is followed in some of the ancient Greek translations (see Wright). Slashing the fruit causes the figs to ripen in a few days and is generally performed prior to the extensive development of the wasps (*Sycophaga sycomari*) that naturally inhabit the figs. This provides a better quality fruit and can increase the number of annual harvests to four or five.

No ancient or modern evidence exists explicitly indicating that sycomore figs were slashed in Palestine. The modern fruit in the region matures and is edible without the slashing procedure. In the *Mishnah*, reference is made to oiling and piercing green normal figs probably to induce ripening (*Sebiith* 2:5; the verb is *nqb* rather than *bls*) and sycomore figs are distinguished according to whether or not they burst open naturally on the tree (*Demai* 1:1). Such evidence might imply that slashing sycomore figs was practiced in the region in antiquity.

In spite of such evidence, we still do not know what function a *boles* sycomores performed. Since sycomores grow in moist, low-level terrain, they probably were not native to Judean Tekoa because of the region's elevation (see on 1:1). They are and were found mostly in the Jordan Valley, coastal plain, and the Shephelah (see 1 Kings 10:27; 1 Chron. 27:28). The *Mishnah* distinguishes upper and lower Galilee by noting that "where sycomores do not grow is upper Galilee; . . .where sycomores grow is lower Galilee" (*Shebiith* 9:2). Whatever task Amos performed with sycomores would thus have been pursued somewhere other than in Tekoa.

In verse 15a, Amos declares that Yahweh took him "from behind the sheep." This statement may be related to his profession or may simply be an expression indicating he was going about his normal business when God intervened and ordered him to prophesy to Israel. In spite of the expression's use in reference to David's elevation to kingship in 2 Sam. 7:8, there are no good reasons to assume that it stresses "both the legitimation of one who is exalted to high office with a convention of lowly origin" (Ackroyd, 1977, 83; also Shult). All that Amos seems to be implying is that his normal routine was broken and he assumed a task which was assigned him by God. He is neither claiming an exalted office nor protesting about lack of qualification for an office. No office, only an activity, is involved. Nothing in this text nor in the vision reports would suggest that they should be associated or the prophet's call related to the vision reports.

Verses 16-17 contain a judgment speech against Amaziah. Verse 16 states the charge against the priest. The text is partially formulated impersonally, referring to Amaziah as "you, the one saying." As we have seen before, an impersonal participial construction is used in lieu of direct second-person address. Amos's quotation of Amaziah's orders to him serve as the grounds for the judgment proclaimed in verse 17. Presumably the narrative has Amos in verse 16*b* summarize the words of Amaziah found in verse 13. Just as Amaziah's summary of the prophet's preaching in verse 11 bears little relationship to the recorded words of Amos, so the prophet's summary of the priest's orders bears little relationship to what is recorded of Amaziah's words. Verse 16*b* and verse 13 share only the single word "prophesy" in common. Clearly, what we have in this biographical narrative is a story told about Amos summarizing what were considered the significant points in his preaching which brought him into conflict with the political and religious authorities in Bethel.

The statement "do not prophesy against Israel" is clear. It refers to stopping what Amos has done throughout his proclamation, namely, condemning Israel and announcing its disastrous future. The statement "do not preach against the house of Isaac" is more problematic. The word "preach" *ntp* is a rather rare term. In the qal stem, it is used with the sense "to drip" (see Judg. 5:4; Ps. 68:9; Job 29:22; Prov. 5:3; Song of Songs 4:11; 5:5, 13: Joel 3:18). In the hiphil stem, it is used with the sense "to preach, to let flow (words)." The eighth-century prophet Micah uses the term more than any other prophet (Micah 2:6, 11; see also Ezek. 20:46; 21:2). The expression "house of Isaac" occurs nowhere else in Scripture. The only other prophetic text that refers to Isaac is Jer. 33:26. The spelling of the name Isaac in Amos 7:9 and 7:16 differs from that generally found in the Old Testament, reading *yshq* instead of the normal *yshq*. This spelling occurs elsewhere only in Jer.

33:26 and Ps. 105:9 (the only appearance of the name in the
Psalter). The spelling may be nothing more than a dialectical
variation. Since late pentateuchal texts in the Old Testament
utilize the more normal form one would assume a late text to
use the more customary spelling. (See *t'b* for *t'b* in 6:8 and *srp*
for *srp* in 6:10). "House of Isaac," like Isaac in 7:9 and Beer-
sheba in 5:5 and 8:14, probably refers to the southern, rebel
cities that had broken with the Davidic house (see on 9:11).
Judean opposition to Davidic rule began during the reign of
Jotham, probably in the 750s, and continued until the Philistine
campaign of Tiglath-pileser III in late 734 or early 733. This
would indicate that this biographical narrative about Amos was
given its shape during this period in circles (probably Davidic)
critical, like Amos, of this Judean insurrection.

The judgment pronounced on Amaziah, formulated in
direct address, involves his wife, children, landed property, and
himself personally. His wife will be forced to support herself as
a prostitute, since she will be deprived of children and husband.
This would have been a horribly degrading punishment since
exceptional sexual standards were required of the wives of
priests and especially of high priests (see Lev. 21:7-9, 13-15).
His children would die by the sword, and his estate would be
parceled out to others (see Micah 2:1-5). The priest himself,
for whom distinguishing between cleanness and uncleanness
was a fundamental task (see Lev. 10:10) and who was
scrupulously to avoid personal uncleanness, is to die in a foreign, unclean land. Amaziah is thus assured that he will be one
of the deportees when Israel is exiled from its land.

General Index

General Index

Author Index

Scripture Index

Scripture Index

Scripture Index

Scripture Index

Scripture Index